JUNG AND THE QUESTION OF SCIENCE

Jung and the Question of Science brings to the foreground a controversial issue at the heart of contemporary Jungian studies. The perennial debate echoes Jung's own ambivalence. While Jung defined his analytical psychology as a science, he was aware that it did not conform to the conventional criteria for a scientific study in general psychology. This ambivalence is carried into twenty-first century analytical psychology, as well as affecting perceptions of Jung in academia. Here, eight scholars and practitioners have pooled their expertise to examine both the history and present-day ramifications of the 'science' issue in the Jungian context. Behind the question of whether it is scientific or not there lie deeper issues: the credibility of Jung's theory, personal identity as a 'Jungian' and conceptions of science, wisdom and truth.

The book comprises a collection of erudite essays, Part I, and linked dialogues in which the authors discuss each other's ideas, Part II. The authors of *Jung and the Question of Science* share the conviction that the question of science is important, but differ in their understanding of its applicability. Drawing upon their different backgrounds, the authors integrate Jung's insights with bodies of knowledge as diverse as neuroscience, literary theory, theology and political science. Clinical practitioners, psychoanalysts, psychologists, scholars and students interested in the Jungian perspective and the philosophy of science will find this book to be insightful and valuable.

Raya A. Jones is a senior lecturer in the Cardiff School of Social Sciences, Cardiff University, UK. Previous books include *Jung, Psychology, Postmodernity* (Routledge, 2007), *Mind and Healing after Jung* (Routledge, 2010), *Cultures and Identities in Transition* (Routledge, 2010) and *Education and Imagination* (Routledge, 2008). She has served on the Executive Committee of the International Association for Jungian Studies.

JUNG AND THE QUESTION OF SCIENCE

Edited by
Raya A. Jones

LONDON AND NEW YORK

First published 2014
by Routledge
27 Church Road, Hove, East Sussex BN3 2FA

Simultaneously published in the USA and Canada
by Routledge
711 Third Avenue, New York, NY 10017

Routledge is an imprint of the Taylor & Francis Group, an informa business

© 2014 Raya A. Jones

The right of the editor to be identified as the author of the editorial material, and of the authors for their individual chapters, has been asserted in accordance with sections 77 and 78 of the Copyright, Designs and Patents Act 1988.

All rights reserved. No part of this book may be reprinted or reproduced or utilised in any form or by any electronic, mechanical, or other means, now known or hereafter invented, including photocopying and recording, or in any information storage or retrieval system, without permission in writing from the publishers.

Trademark notice: Product or corporate names may be trademarks or registered trademarks, and are used only for identification and explanation without intent to infringe.

British Library Cataloguing in Publication Data
A catalogue record for this book is available from the British Library

Library of Congress Cataloging in Publication Data
Jung and the question of science : academic and clinical perspectives /
edited by Raya A. Jones.
　　pages cm
　　1. Jung, C. G. (Carl Gustav), 1875–1961. 2. Jungian psychology.
3. Science and psychology. I. Jones, Raya A.
　　BF109.J8J85 2014
　　150.19'54—dc23
　　2013023245

ISBN: 978–0–415–64411–2 (hbk)
ISBN: 978–0–415–64414–3 (pbk)
ISBN: 978–1–315–85709–1 (ebk)

Typeset in Times New Roman
by Swales & Willis Ltd, Exeter, Devon

Printed and bound in the United States of America by Publishers Graphics, LLC on sustainably sourced paper.

CONTENTS

List of contributors   vii

Introduction   1
RAYA A. JONES

PART I
Essays   7

1 **Romanticism and revolution in Jung's science**   9
JOE CAMBRAY

2 **Science friction: Jung, Goethe and scientific objectivity**   30
MARK SABAN

3 **Vicissitudes of a science-complex**   50
RAYA A. JONES

4 **Speculations on Jung's dream of science**   70
LESLIE GARDNER

5 **Explanation and interpretation**   82
ROBERT A. SEGAL

6 **Analytical psychology, narrative theory and the question of science**   98
TERENCE DAWSON

7 **Knowledge, wisdom, and the science-complex in Orthodox Christianity and Jungian psychology**   118
BYRON J. GAIST

CONTENTS

8 Jung's relationship to science and his concept of psychocultural development — **140**
PETER T. DUNLAP

PART II
Dialogues — **151**

9 Dialogue 1: Placing Jung — **153**
MARK SABAN AND RAYA A. JONES

10 Dialogue 2: Typological determinism and the possibility of transcending subjectivity — **156**
LESLIE GARDNER, TERENCE DAWSON, PETER T. DUNLAP, MARK SABAN AND ROBERT A. SEGAL

11 Dialogue 3: Truth, facts and interpretation — **165**
TERENCE DAWSON, MARK SABAN, PETER T. DUNLAP, ROBERT A. SEGAL AND LESLIE GARDNER

12 Dialogue 4: Wisdom and archetype — **174**
RAYA A. JONES AND BYRON J. GAIST

13 Dialogue 5: Ways forward — **179**
JOE CAMBRAY, PETER T. DUNLAP AND RAYA A. JONES

Name index — 185
Subject index — 189

CONTRIBUTORS

Joe Cambray, PhD, is President of the IAAP and past US Editor of the *Journal of Analytical Psychology*, of which he is now on the Advisory Board. He is past president of the C. G. Jung Institute of Boston and a faculty member of the Center for Psychoanalytic Studies at Harvard University. He has a PhD in Chemistry from the University of California, Berkeley. His recently published books are *Synchronicity: Nature and Psyche in an Interconnected Universe* (Texas A&M University Press, 2009) and *Contemporary Perspectives in Jungian Analysis* (co-edited with Linda Carter, Routledge, 2004). He is in private practice in Boston, MA, and Providence, RI, USA.

Terence Dawson is an associate professor at Nanyang Technological University, Singapore, where he teaches English and European literature. His research interests include the application of Jungian theory to literature and the relation between literature and the other arts. With Polly Young-Eisendrath, he co-edited *The Cambridge Companion to Jung* (1997; 2nd ed. 2008) and he is the author of *The Effective Protagonist in the Nineteenth-Century British Novel: Scott, Brontë, Eliot, Wilde* (2004), as well as numerous articles on English, French and German literature and European film.

Peter T. Dunlap is a psychologist working in private and political practice. As founder of the Center for Political Development, he helps progressive leaders, their organizations, and community groups to develop a public emotional intelligence, which supports their capacity for community engagement. He has published his research with progressive leaders in a book entitled *Awakening Our Faith in the Future: The Advent of Psychological Liberalism* (Routledge, 2008). He has recently written about Jung as a pioneering force of political psychology for *Jung Journal* in an article entitled 'A Transformative Political Psychology Begins with Jung', and is a contributing author to *Tikkun* magazine.

Byron J. Gaist is a registered counselling psychologist and psychotherapist based in Cyprus. His interest in the relation between Christian theology and psychology led him also to an MA in Theology and Religious Studies, and later to a PhD in Psychoanalytic Studies which was published in a revised version by the

CONTRIBUTORS

Orthodox Research Institute as the book, *Creative Suffering and the Wounded Healer: Analytical Psychology and Orthodox Christian Theology* (2010). His main vocation is counselling clients in private practice, but he is also employed at the Cyprus Monitoring Centre for Drugs and Drug Addiction, part of a European-wide network of such monitoring observatories, and he teaches psychology and sociology to undergraduates at the American College, Nicosia.

Leslie Gardner, PhD, has been a member of the Executive Committee of the International Association for Jungian Studies since 2002. Her doctoral thesis, to be published as *Rhetorical Investigations: G. B. Vico and C. G. Jung* (Routledge, 2013), considers how Jung's style reveals his scientific theories. As a literary representative since founding Artellus Ltd in 1986, she has had long involvement with Jungian and Jung-inspired publications, both academic and fiction. She was the co-editor with Luke Hockley of *House: The Wounded Healer on Television* (Routledge, 2011), and a guest editor of a special issue of the *International Journal for Jungian Studies* (2012).

Raya A. Jones, PhD, is a senior lecturer in the Cardiff School of Social Sciences, Cardiff University, UK, where she teaches courses on personality, developmental psychology and applications of psychology in education. She is the author of *Jung, Psychology, Postmodernity* (Routledge, 2007) and *The Child-School Interface: Environment and Behaviour* (Cassell, 1995), editor of *Body, Mind and Healing After Jung: A Space of Questions* (Routledge, 2010), and co-editor of *Jungian and Dialogical Perspectives* (Palgrave Macmillan, 2011), *Cultures and Identities in Transition: Jungian Perspectives* (Routledge, 2010) and *Education and Imagination: Post-Jungian Perspectives* (Routledge, 2008). She has published numerous journal articles. She was a member of the Executive Committee of the International Association for Jungian Studies.

Mark Saban is a senior analyst with the Independent Group of Analytical Psychologists and practises in Oxford and London. Recent publications include the articles 'The disenchantment of C. G. Jung' in the *International Journal of Jungian Studies* and 'Entertaining the stranger' in the *Journal of Analytical Psychology*. He also contributed two chapters to the book *Body, Mind and Healing After Jung: A Space of Questions* (Routledge, 2010). He is a member of the Executive Committee of the International Association of Jungian Studies.

Robert A. Segal is Sixth Century Chair in Religious Studies, University of Aberdeen. Previously, he was Professor of Theories of Religion, Lancaster University, UK. Born, raised and educated in the US, he taught at Reed College, Stanford University, the University of Pittsburgh and Tulane University before relocating to the UK in 1994. Among the books he has written or edited are *The Poimandres as Myth, Joseph Campbell, Explaining and Interpreting Religion, The Gnostic Jung, Jung on Mythology, Hero Myths, The Myth and Ritual Theory, Theorizing about Myth, Myth: A Very Short Introduction*, and the *Blackwell Companion to the Study of Religion*.

INTRODUCTION

Raya A. Jones

'We have, as you know, been more or less running your planet for the last ten million years in order to find this wretched thing called the Ultimate Question,' a mouse tells the man; they already have the Answer (Adams 1979: 147). The sci-fi spoof holds a mirror to our serious pursuits. The humorous inversion of the search for meaning deserves a pause for thought. We often have answers, or at least feel that we know where to look. To paraphrase Jung's adage regarding autonomous complexes, the answers we have *can have us* (cf. Jung 1934: par. 200). Our thinking becomes entrenched in them. Somewhat like the proverbial fish jumping out of the water, asking what might be the ultimate question that is tacitly being answered could provide a glimpse of the sea of answers in which we swim.

What is the 'question of science' and how does it apply to the work of C. G. Jung?

This volume presents several interpretations – eight, to be precise, since there are eight authors. The issue of whether or not analytical psychology is scientific is merely the surface layer of this question. Beneath it lie disciplinary displacements, identity matters, and worldview dissonances.

It may be helpful to distinguish between (a) *analytical psychology* as a contemporary movement in psychotherapy, and (b) the set of principles outlined by Jung (i.e. his analytical psychology), which I try to differentiate from the former by using the term *Jungian psychology*, although the labels are used interchangeably elsewhere. The canonical texts of analytical psychology are, of course, Jung's writings; but many others since Jung have brought about the field's current state of the art. One possibility is that while Jung's work was not scientific, analytical psychology can be. Another possibility is that analytical psychology cannot be scientific because its core assumptions are incommensurable with modern science. Either claim requires a clarification of what is meant by science. While the eight of us contend with that requirement in different ways, we concur that there is a problem. Others, whose voices are not represented here, dispute that there is a problem – either because they hold that analytical psychology is unquestionably scientific (since Jung regarded it as such) or because they maintain that 'science' is irrelevant for Jungian practice. Consequently, the question of science implicates identity politics within the Jungian community, insofar as advocates of particular views on the necessity for scientific verification are positioned in ways that may challenge their identities as Jungians or as scholars.

Jung presented his signature concepts, the collective unconscious and archetypes, as a scientific answer to a riddle posed by 'regularities' he observed. Ostensibly, his immediate question is why do certain motifs regularly recur throughout myths, dreams, etc.; and his answer, put simplistically: there is a collective unconscious generating them. This answer rewrites the question as a causal inquiry, and Jung himself appears to lead in this path: 'Where do these mythological fantasies come from . . .? Indubitably they come from . . . the inherited brain-structure itself' (1918: par. 12). His rhetoric is persuasive, his tone authoritative, but he did not back up his sweeping speculations about the brain with any evidence from neurophysiology, let alone studying the brain himself. Almost a century later, advances in neuroscience support a dismissal of the classical Jungian notion of an inherited brain-structure. Instead, greater support may be found for viewing 'archetypes' as patterns emerging at a higher order of complexity, as Joe Cambray contends in Chapter 1 and Dialogue 5. However, the causal question was secondary and relatively trivial for Jung. His researches and clinical work concern primarily the teleological 'what for' of phenomena such as mythological fantasies. Jung continues in the same essay: 'How does a symbol originate? This question brings us to the most important function of the unconscious: the *symbol-creating function*' (ibid.: par. 25). To say that symbols are 'caused' by a symbol-creating function would be as pointless as saying that someone crossed the road because the body has a 'walking function'; and it's not what Jung is saying about symbols. He consistently locates symbols in the eye of the beholder, and explores their functions for psychological transformations.

Answering whether it is scientific depends on how we answer the question of *which* science Jungian or analytical psychology might be. Is it a natural science, as Jung maintained in keeping with the traditional classification of psychology (which I discuss in Chapter 3)? Is it a social science, since Jungian interests concern matters of social and societal relevance, as Peter Dunlap demonstrates (Chapter 8)? Is it a human science akin to literary theory, as Terence Dawson suggests (Chapter 6), or theology, Byron Gaist's focus (Chapter 7)? Is it something else entirely, transcending conventional disciplinary boundaries, as Mark Saban proposes (Chapter 2)? The array of such options reveals a Rorschach-like peculiarity of Jung's texts. This book's authors share a passion for his work, but we project different expectations onto it, expecting it to address different kinds of intellectual preoccupations, in accordance with our own disciplinary backgrounds. The ease with which we can make persuasive arguments for adopting Jung into different academic contexts may be celebrated as evidence for the wide scope of his work. But this quality has a shadow side, insinuated in the Rorschach metaphor. An inkblot doesn't have any intrinsically correct interpretation. Here the question of science takes a further twist. It implicates not only a wish to ascertain the factual validity of Jungian claims, but also to determine whether Jungian truth-claims refer to facts or to interpretations (see especially Dialogue 3, this volume).

INTRODUCTION

Making a case for psychoanalysis as a specialist science, Sigmund Freud defined *Weltanschauung* (worldview) as 'an intellectual construction which solves all the problems of our existence uniformly on the basis of one overriding hypothesis'; it makes its believer 'feel secure in life, one can know . . . how one can deal most expediently with one's emotions and interests' (1965: 195–6). Religion provides a comprehensive *Weltanschauung*, albeit based in an illusion, according to Freud. In contrast, the *Weltanschauung* of science does not provide final answers. It 'too assumes the *uniformity* of the explanation of the universe; but it does so only as a programme, the fulfilment of which is relegated to the future' (ibid.: 196). Jung held a similar understanding, though he drew a sharper distinction: 'A science can never be *Weltanschauung* but merely a tool with which to make one' (Jung 1927: par. 731). Therefore, 'Analytical psychology is not *Weltanschauung* but a science, and as such it provides the building-material . . . with which *Weltanschauung* can be built up' (ibid.: par. 730).

Upholding the *Weltanschauung* of science does not make one a scientist. Despite Freud's eloquent argument for psychoanalysis as a science, by mid-twentieth century the majority of academic psychologists dismissed him and Jung (tarred with the same brush) as being unscientific in the manner of their pursuit of knowledge. 'Jung' has been thoroughly removed from the scientific gaze. Although there are resistances to Jung also in the humanities (Tacey 1997), scholars currently publishing about Jung or applying Jungian concepts are more likely to be literary critics, historians of ideas, or to specialize in religious studies, film studies, and similar affiliations, than to be psychologists. From the *Weltanschauung* of science, depth psychology is a *Weltanschauung* that (to paraphrase Freud) purports to solve all the mysteries of mind and behaviour on the basis of one overriding (and irrefutable) hypothesis; namely, there is an Unconscious. It could be retorted that its dismissal is entrenched in a *Weltanschauung* that presses upon us the one overriding (and irrefutable) hypothesis that only science can lead to knowledge of reality. Consequently, believing in the power of science might clash with other belief systems. What I have termed 'the question of science' in the Jungian context seems to originate in such a clash.

The issue of the field's scientific status has been a perennial preoccupation in an email-based discussion list run by the International Association for Jungian Studies (IAJS) ever since the forum was launched in 2003. The IAJS (of which all this volume's authors are members) came into being through the initiative of Andrew Samuels in the First International Academic Conference of Analytical Psychology held in Essex, UK, in July 2002. It was formed with the explicit mission of promoting an academic strand of analytical psychology, and was the first Jungian organization to be open to any interested scholar (as opposed to admitting only analysts and, at most, their clients). Consequently, IAJS membership comprises both clinicians and academics; and some who are both. Furthermore, it represents a wide diversity of disciplinary backgrounds. This heterogeneity may account, in part, for why the 'science' question has been not only controversial but also resistant to any consensus. Opinions become polarized, emotions flare, and arguments can slide into ad hominem. For example, when the topic was again hotly debated, one member wrote: 'Jungian psychology, to be scientific, must put itself put at risk [*sic*] – the risk of being wrong or inadequate' (Robert Segal, May 2, 2011). The risk-taking to which he refers is that of testing, the best-known version of which is the principle of falsification articulated by Karl Popper. Segal's earnest-sceptic stance came under fire from members who opined that insisting upon a scientific proof of Jungian hypotheses reflects fears of the unconscious by people who don't engage with their own unconscious by means of the Jungian Method. Those who truly follow Jung need no further proof of his truth-claims. From the viewpoint of a scholar investing in studying or applying Jung's work, their faithful-believer stance undermines the academic credibility of that work.

This book thus brings to the foreground issues that largely remain at the background within the Jungian community. These issues reflect tensions that arguably give the field its character, but are seldom made explicit in the corpus of Jungian studies. One reason might lie in the nature of the query. It problematizes Jungian psychology in ways that 'devout' Jungians might feel are at best unnecessary and at worst unacceptable, a hindrance to studying Jung. Either way, its dismissal stifles a protracted debate in Jungian journals and books. Relevant publications appear sporadically and in virtual isolation, with little or no engagement with each other.

Another reason might reflect the medium. Those who publish in the Jungian context typically present their pieces as soliloquies. Even when essays are collated in an edited volume, authors seldom see the others' works prior to the book's publication, let alone engage with them in the same volume. An innovative feature of the present project is the creation of a space for dialogue. Having written our individual essays (Part I), we discussed issues which others' essays have raised for us, sampled in Part II.

The possibility of a dialogue is contingent on the presence of both similarities and differences of opinion. If we are in total agreement, there is nothing to discuss. If we are in total disagreement, there is no common ground for a discussion. The eight of us have set out with a shared conviction that Jung's work is important, though we differ in why we personally find it important. We concur that the question of science is important, though some of us differ in our understanding of science and its applicability. From the outset, there has been a remarkable consensus regarding the topic's salient dimensions, expressed in three themes that cut across all essays and dialogues, though we differ in how much we emphasize them in our own contributions.

These themes give the collection its overall structure:

1. A *historical* dimension concerns Jung's position about the scientific status of his work, and the ensuing implications for present-day analytical psychology. In a way, the question of science as expressed in the IAJS perennial debate and in the present volume echoes Jung's own ambivalence as to whether his scholarly work conformed to conventional criteria for what is scientific. Most essays mention it, but Joe Cambray (Chapter 1) and Mark Saban (Chapter 2)

explore it most directly and in depth. This dimension extends into issues such as placing 'Jung' in the academia and implications of Jung's own psychological type, as explored especially in Dialogues 1 and 2.

2   A *critical* dimension concerns the nature of science and its implications for Jungian theorizing. All chapters are critical in that sense; but the what-is-science issue features more centrally than do the other themes in the essays by me (Chapter 3), with particular attention to the history of psychology as a science, by Leslie Gardner (Chapter 4), with a consideration of science as rhetoric, and by Robert Segal (Chapter 5), who demonstrates a specific application. Several of us further explore various angles of this issue in Dialogues 3 and 4.

3   A *consolidant* dimension seeks to reconcile Jungian psychology with some other worldview. None of us is a philosopher of science; when engaging with the 'what is science' issue, we ultimately defend some personal vision for what Jungian psychology is about or what analytical psychology ought to be. This is where our differences are the widest. Terence Dawson (Chapter 6) understands Jungian psychology as rooted in narrative theory. Byron Gaist (Chapter 7) compares and contrasts it with Orthodox Christianity, thus implicitly 'calibrating' it with another established body of knowledge. Peter Dunlap (Chapter 8) extends Jungian premises into political psychology, an application different from Jung's medical psychology.

The initial idea for Part II was modelled on the tradition of peer commentaries in academic journals. Some of the entries incorporated into the Dialogues indeed started like formal pieces. However, since we were in constant email contact as a group, authors responded to the commentators, and others joined in with responses to the responses. The discussions soon took novel directions, organically developing into several threads which I selectively edited so as to present issues that bear most directly on what is explored in Part I.

Bakhtin (1984: 293) spoke of the open-ended dialogue as the 'expression of authentic human existence' – an existence made possible through participation in the 'dialogic fabric of human life' – for to 'live means to participate in dialogue: to ask questions, to heed, to respond, to agree, and so forth'. To paraphrase, this book project has sought to capture the dialogic fabric of Jungian studies – an ambition admittedly like trying to give the 'feel' of waves by showing you a still photograph of the sea. Like any snapshot, this collection is a moment frozen in time. We continue to develop and potentially enrich our understanding. Nevertheless, if the book is successful in fulfilling its purpose, it may be assimilated into your own participation in this open-ended dialogue within Jungian studies and beyond.

References

Adams, D. (1979). *The Hitchhiker's Guide to the Galaxy*. London: Pan.
Bakhtin, M. M. (1984). *Problems of Dostoevsky's Poetics*. Minneapolis, MN: University of Minneapolis Press.

Freud, S. (1965). *New Introductory Lectures on Psycho-Analysis*. London: W. W. Norton.
Jung, C. G. The following are from *The Collected Works of C. G. Jung* (CW) London: Routledge and Kegan Paul:
—— (1918). The role of the unconscious. (CW10)
—— (1927). Analytical psychology and *Weltanschauung*. (CW8)
—— (1934). A review of the complex theory. (CW8)
Tacey, D. (1997). Jung in the academy: Devotions and resistances. *Journal of Analytical Psychology*, 42: 269–83.

Part I

ESSAYS

1
ROMANTICISM AND REVOLUTION IN JUNG'S SCIENCE

Joe Cambray

Defining science

At numerous points in his long career, Carl Gustav Jung identified his approach as scientific and referred to his work as 'science'. While some of his publications such as the researches on the word association experiment do readily fall into what is commonly understood by science, other activities especially of an internal, introspective nature are more difficult to classify in this way. However, as a broad elastic category, 'science' is neither a unitary endeavour, definitions proliferate, nor do the activities of its practitioners occur outside historical and cultural frameworks even if one holds an idealistic goal of obtaining truths that transcend these conditions. In the most general terms, science refers to systematized knowledge, though frequently this has focused more narrowly on the physical and natural world, in an effort to maximize objectivity. This effort has in the past led to a distinction between the 'hard sciences' versus those associated with the human, social and cultural realms with their inherent subjectivity being seen pejoratively as 'softer'. Reframing the division in terms of increasing complexity, as the matters under investigation contain more numerous elements with more elaborate interactions, the ability to rigorously (mathematically) describe such systems diminishes, leading to the classical hierarchy of sciences: physics, chemistry, biology, psychology, sociology and anthropology.

By the middle of the twentieth century, the humanities seemed nearly irreconcilably separate from the sciences, with very little dialogue between them possible. C. P. Snow's famous 1959 Rede lecture on 'The Two Cultures' brought attention to this gap and the sad consequences for humanity. However, as recent biographies of scientists are beginning to reveal, the history of science may need significant revision at least in terms of the retrospective polarizations which have traditionally been read into it. As will be discussed later in this chapter, alternative strands of scientific practice and theorizing are being recovered after being abandoned, often because of inabilities to adequately test them with the equipment, methods and theories available at the time they were first articulated. One prominent example is the notion of emergence from complexity theory that required high-speed computation devices to perform simulations that could only be intuited in the past and hence were treated as untestable speculations. However, before turning to the contemporary world, it will be useful to identify some nearly forgotten trends in sciences that had significant influence on Jung, and that are experiencing something of a renaissance presently.

In exploring sources for Jung's *implicit* views on science, I will not be attempting to provide systematic documentation of his direct, conscious incorporation of these views, though when possible I will try to note these. Instead, I am interested in more fully identifying unacknowledged sources, including elements that were in his cultural milieu and likely a part of his general education but not specifically referenced in his own published works. By filling in these missing elements, for example the artistically rendered marine biological portraits of Ernst Haeckel which profoundly influenced some of the imagery of Jung's *Red Book* (Cambray 2011a), I hope to better locate a selection of Jung's use of science within alternative traditions and assess the relevance of these traditions in the post-Jungian world. Because he employed his creative, intuitive genius in ways that absorbed and used these traditions, even if unacknowledged and perhaps unconsciously, Jung can be seen to have anticipated certain contemporary developments in science that I believe are worthy of consideration and perhaps may offer new insights to these emerging areas of science.

The rise of science

Although our Eurocentric scientific traditions have roots in antiquity, the direct origins of modern science are usually associated with the new attitudes and activities about nature and the world arising from the age of discovery (from the early fifteenth into the seventeenth centuries). Long distance maritime travel had opened up vast new regions filled with previous unknown flora, fauna, minerals, and peoples as the Europeans developed ships and navigational tools capable of oceanic voyages.[1] The welter of novel information as well as the need to enhance technologies stimulated the cultures of exploration to organize and systematize the knowledge they were acquiring.

As the pursuit of knowledge gained socio-political importance, the individuals who most helped this advance became cultural heroes. Thus the rise of science is often told in terms of key figures such as in astronomy: Copernicus (1473–1543), Tycho Brahe (1546–1601), Galileo (1564–1642), and Kepler (1571–1630). More generally, those who articulated basic, universal laws of physics are generally heralded as the founders of the Western scientific view of the cosmos. Thus Isaac Newton (1642–1727) as the greatest exponent of the mathematical approach to physics during this inaugural period has tended to be given preeminence in standard history of modern science. Through his conception of universal gravitation and laws of motion, Newton was able to provide an accurate theoretical account for Kepler's strictly observational 'laws' of planetary motion. The subsequent success of Newtonian physics resulted in a reductive, mechanistic worldview that held sway for several centuries, but this achievement was troubled on two major points. First, an understanding of the mechanism of gravity: while Newton's laws gave accurate mathematical description of gravitational forces and the movement of bodies, the means by which this force was transmitted remained enigmatic, as action at a distance without a discernible medium. Second, the model implicitly held space to be empty and absolute, a three dimensional Cartesian framework through which bodies moved. Time was likewise seen in absolute terms, a constant one-way flow from past through the present to the future which could be arbitrarily subdivided into units using mechanical devices such as clocks. The first serious challenges to the Newtonian model came during the nineteenth century, from scientists whose orientation was marked by an interest in Romanticism as we shall see later.

Furthermore, the interests of these early figures were more complex than can be derived from their scientific accomplishments. Newton, for example, wrote far more on alchemy than on mathematical physics (Dobbs 1975 and 1991). Leibniz (1646–1716), the co-discoverer of calculus alongside Newton, and a major precursor/source for Jung's synchronicity hypothesis, was deeply concerned with symbolic thought – for him mathematics was part of a search for a universal language. Frances Yates (1966) placed Leibniz firmly within the hermetic tradition. Similarly, Robert Boyle (1627–1691), considered one of the founders of chemistry, had a lifelong interest in transmutation and alchemy (Principe 1998). Most of the scientists and mathematicians of the period had strong philosophical interests that went well beyond the bounds of what could be quantified but these views were edited out of the subsequent Enlightenment's reductionistic reading of nature. The qualitative, descriptive and holistic elements in their thinking have been downplayed if not expurgated.

In the following century, the pursuit of scientific knowledge increasingly became associated with the state, as the methods and results had practical, economic, military and political uses. One of the more significant of the eighteenth century forms of collecting knowledge was through state sponsored expeditions exemplified by those of Captain James Cook. Cook's three Pacific voyages (1768–71; 1772–75; 1776–79) were acknowledged as a great boon by the scientific community and brought fame to some of the scientists who accompanied Cook, especially the botanist Sir Joseph Banks, and to a lesser degree the German scientists Johann Reinhold Forster and his adolescent son Georg Forster. For this chapter's purposes, the influence of these scientists on the Romantic Movement in literature and science is key.

Banks, an Enlightenment gentleman, was also a skilled writer and captured the public imagination with his account of Cook's first voyage, on which he was a participant. Scientifically his botanical collecting dramatically increased the known number of plant species, by about 25 per cent, but he also made writing about exploration into a form of scientific discourse. According to Tim Fulford and colleagues, Banks subsequently developed a network of explorers and gardeners emanating out of his Soho Square home but encircling the globe. This network allowed him to shape 'the course of botany, natural history and race theory, as well as influencing colonial trade and administration' (Fulford et al. 2004: 45). Banks' influence went far beyond his own intention and his 'projects helped give rise to literary Romanticism (inflecting its political concerns, its symbolism, its very content)' (ibid.). The explorers in Banks' network were a stimulus for poets who internalized and metaphorized the reports, seeing in them moral allegories (Keats and Shelley), and ways to reflect on their own inner development (e.g. Wordsworth's *The Prelude*), which Fulford et al. see 'not in rejection of but in reflexive relation to the exploration of men such as Cook' (ibid.: 21). The Romantics' shift of focus into the inner world is essential to understanding Jung's view of what constitutes science. However, to better understand and appreciate this it will be useful to look to the German Romantic tradition especially in its early days as it was articulated by those doing both science and art albeit in a less differentiated manner.

German Romanticism and science

In response to the French and English domination in science during the seventeenth and eighteenth centuries, which as noted was increasingly aligned with national agendas, German scientists developed a more individual, less state oriented form of science. During the initial rise of science, the Germans, excepting Leibniz, seemed to inhabit a collection of backward provinces having limited contact with the centres of scientific thought in France and England. This may have been partially a result of the decimation of the German population during the Thirty Years War (Berlin 1999: 34–5). In the German lands, there was a 'retreat in depth' and a move into pietism, which Berlin sees as the root of Romanticism (ibid.: 36). In contradistinction to the analytic, reductive methods of the Enlightenment, the German scientists retained a holistic viewpoint congruent with the emerging Romantic Movement.

Closer to Jung's education and cultural affinity, the scientific aspects of German Romanticism have generally not been considered in his works beyond the practitioners' impact as philosophers. The scientific contributions themselves have largely been ignored, or demeaned until recently. With a small but growing scholarly interest in the German Romantics' intertwining of science and art in ways that generate intuitive knowledge about systems of nature, an alternative vision of their approach to the science of wholes is forming. As Andrew Cunningham and Nicholas Jardine note in their introduction to their edited volume *Romanticism and the Sciences*:

> [T]he stereotype of the Romantic sciences as speculative, fantastic, mystical and ill-disciplined, and their alleged defeat by the empirical natural sciences, are polemical constructs rather than the fruits of unbiased historical research.
> (Cunningham & Jardine 1990: 7–8)

The collection of essays they offer provides a useful, broad introduction to the range of accomplishments of the Romantic scientists; I will select a few examples as I proceed.

Goethe (1749–1832)

While the most renowned of the German Romantic scientists is Goethe, his literary influence on Jung overshadows that of his scientific contributions. Like other Romantics Goethe treated the sciences as hermeneutical; an attitude absorbed by Jung. Goethe's theory of colour, which drew upon physiological research and had affinities with the wave theory of light which was being articulated in the early nineteenth century,[2] was a blend of aesthetics and science. His phenomenological stance included a blending of the subjective with objectivity:

> Goethe's great merit, recognized clearly by none of his contemporaries except Hegel, was that he remained faithful to the way things are, while avoiding positivism, and laid the groundwork for a science that preserved objectivity . . . while giving subjective variety, the diversity of human ways of conceiving things, its due.
>
> (Sepper 1990: 196–7)

For him understanding of nature required a method that did not artificially separate science and art:

> Goethe not only rejected this dichotomy of poetry and science, he also tried to show that quite the opposite was true, that the more science divorces itself from the all-embracing contexts of human life and nature the more the scientific imagination became trapped in a particular and sometimes even abstractively fantastic way of conceiving things. . . . He saw both science and poetry, each in its own way, as having the ultimate intention of being faithful to nature, to its actualities and its possibilities.
>
> (Ibid.: 197)

It is this mind-set that I think comes closer to Jung's views of science, which incidentally is also in better alignment with psychoanalytic thinkers such as Jonathan Lear, who in his book on therapeutic action, based on his reading of the work of Hans Loewald, argues for 'a subjective conception of objectivity' (2003: 103).

Alexander von Humboldt (1769–1859)[3]

To return to the theme of scientific exploration through travel to and through unknown realms, there is a particular German Romantic tradition worth explicating, that pioneered by Alexander von Humboldt. Both he and his brother Wilhelm, a renowned linguist and humanist, are memorialized by Humboldt University in Berlin. Alexander, however, was the traveller and scientist. Born in 1769 he developed personal friendships with numerous scientists and philosophers, including Goethe who was twenty years his senior. When Alexander was twenty years old and studying at Göttingen, he met Georg Forster, who by now was a bestselling author with his 1777 travelogue and scientific narrative, *A Voyage Round the World*, based on sailing with James Cook on his second Pacific voyage. Forster brought the young Humboldt along with him on a trip across Europe to London, where they met with Sir Joseph Banks. This trip was life altering for Humboldt and a prelude to his great adventure in Latin America (Helferich 2004: 10–11).

Before turning to his trek in South America, it should be noted that although Humboldt is only mentioned once in Jung's *Collected Works* (Vol. 5: par. 481 n.17) where Jung makes reference to a South American Indian libido symbol (meteors as the 'piss of the stars') that he found in Humboldt's final work *Cosmos*, there is good reason to consider deeper influence. As discussed in chapter one of Bair's (2003) biography of Jung, Alexander von Humboldt is the person responsible for the Jung family living in Switzerland. Briefly, Karl Gustav Jung-Frey a native of Mannheim Germany arrived in Basel via Paris in 1822 to take up a professorship in medicine at the University there, becoming Swiss in the process, due to a letter from Humboldt to the Burgermeister of Basel recommending him for the post (ibid.: 10). More recently, Andreas Jung, C. G. Jung's grandson, has provided a more detailed account of how this occurred: as a young man Karl Jung was involved in German unification politics and was unjustly imprisoned then exiled without trial; he went to Paris where he found Humboldt who 'wanted to make up for what his government did to me in a series of injustices. The unforgotten, gracious man kept his word!' which was to help Karl Jung obtain the professorship (A. Jung 2011: 661). With such a family story directly tied to his namesake, it is not much of a leap to imagine Humboldt's life and works may have held attractions for Jung in unreported ways. One path by which this may have occurred is through Humboldt's scientific travel narrative, itself a clear work of German Romantic science.

Before travelling to Latin America Humboldt had already established himself as a plant geographer with his first significant publication in 1793 *Florae Fribergensis specimen plantas cryptogamicus praesertim subterraneas exhibens* based on his work in the mines around Freiberg. Even at this early date, he argues 'that plants should not be studied in isolation but as an integral part of the environment in which they are found' (Helferich 2004: 343). His holistic-environmental views were later adopted by Ernst Haeckel as when he coined the term ecology. The empiricism Humboldt learned from Forster was deliberately 'combined with enthusiastic recording of emotional responses and subjective impressions' as when studying the morphology of landscape (Nicolson 1990: 171). Humboldt also performed experiments and published on nerve conduction to wide acclaim early in his career; thus he was a well accomplished, respected scientist in Europe before setting off on his travels.

Through a series of complications, Humboldt was in Spain together with the botanist Aimé Bonpland where they were able to obtain permission and royal support for a scientific expedition to Spanish America. In 1799 they left on a voyage that took them to Venezuela and from there inland by canoe to explore the

Orinoco River. Collecting specimens, discovering many new species of plants, insects and animals, they also demonstrated the existence of the Casiquiare Canal a unique, natural link between the Orinoco and Amazon river systems. They made astronomical observations and took data on geomagnetism. However, as Humboldt details in his travel memoirs they also suffered many (mis)adventures, such as experimenting on themselves with electric eels (being severely shocked in the process), of having their pet Mastiff eaten by jaguars, of nearly drowning in capsizes, of becoming violently ill and of enduring seemingly limitless torture of biting insects in the rainforest. At times, there is an inferno-like quality to the narrative, so intense that the reader feels the emotions of the travellers.

After a trip to Cuba to recover their health and to explore that island, the next phase of their travels took them through New Granada (including modern day Colombia and Ecuador) and Peru. In addition to river travel and rainforests, they also trekked through the Andes mountains, with tremendous ascents at the limits of human capacities – they set the world record at the time for altitude, 19,286 feet, unaided by artificial sources of oxygen. This gave them the opportunity to study the diversity of life, especially plant life at differing altitudes and climates as they ascended from rainforest to snow-capped mountain. In an important essay that came from these observations, Humboldt sought to link plant geography, as he termed it, to cultural forms:

> [T]he man who is sensitive to the beauties of nature will . . . find there the explanation of the influence exerted by the appearance of vegetation over Man's taste and imagination. He will take pleasure in examining what is constituted by the 'character' of the vegetation and the variety of sensation it produces in the soul of the person who contemplates it. These considerations are all the more significant because they are closely linked to the means by which the imitative arts and descriptive poetry succeed in acting upon us . . . What a marked contrast between forests in temperate zones and those of the Equator, where the bare slender trunks of the palms soar above the flowered mahogany trees and create majestical portico arches in the sky . . . How does this . . . appearance of nature, rich and pleasant to a greater or lesser degree, affect the customs and above all the sensibility of the people?
>
> (Quoted in Nicolson 1990: 172)

One can recognize in this a precursor to the ideas of James Mark Baldwin articulated at the turn of the last century linking culture and evolution,[4] work that Hogenson (2001) has shown to be important to Jung in his early formulations of archetypal theory. Similarly, historian of science Bowen (1981: 257) notes that for Humboldt '"the apparently impassable gulf between thought and being, the relationship between the knowing mind and perceived object"' is the 'locus of the sciences'; 'science is mind applied to nature'; i.e., science in Humboldt's definition would make central what Jung termed the psychoid.

The travellers then went to Mexico where they stayed, trekking around the countryside for about one year. Before returning to Europe Humboldt made a short trip to the US, including a stay at the White House with President Thomas Jefferson. Jefferson had just sent Lewis and Clark on their famous expedition and Jefferson and Humboldt traded much information. Humboldt was warmly received by political and scientific elite of the fledgling America and made such a positive impression that numerous places in the US have been named after him.

Humboldt's scientific travelogue, the multi-volume *Personal Narratives* (1819–29) was a source of inspiration to numerous scientists including the father of Geology, Charles Lyell and Charles Darwin. For a young Darwin, Humboldt was a hero; he brought volumes of the *Personal Narratives* aboard the *Beagle* (and Captain Fitzroy also had a full set). In a letter to his closest friend the botanist and explorer Sir Joseph Dalton Hooker, Darwin wrote: 'I believe that you are fully right in calling Humboldt the greatest scientific traveller who ever lived' (Darwin 1887, 6 August 1881).[5]

It is difficult to imagine that this material did not also have an impact on C. G. Jung. In particular, I think the nearly solitary journey into the unknown, at great personal risk and expense, for the purpose of seeking knowledge of the interior, has some important parallels with Jung's attitude in the experiences that became moulded into *The Red Book*. From this vantage, *The Red Book* can be viewed as a scientific contribution in line with the travel narrative reports of a Romantic scientist such as Humboldt, the unknown territory moving from the external physical world to the interior, psychological, similar to the way that some of the Romantics moved back and forth between inner and outer worlds. There is however an inversion of the subjective and objective: Jung ultimately seeks the objective quality within inner, subjective experience whereas the Romantic scientists were primarily intent on bringing subjective responses to external objective events or materials.

Humboldt's last great project was his five volume *Cosmos: A Sketch of a Physical Description of the Universe* (1866). A lifetime's passion that began as a young man, when he started to formulate the idea of writing a comprehensive treatise on the physical description of the entire universe, it took his travels, a series of 61 lectures at Berlin University on the whole of the physical sciences and then almost two decades of writing to produce the first several volumes (Helferich 2004: 320–3). As Walls (2011: 216) remarks: 'Historians credit Humboldt's lectures with jump-starting German science, which went on to surpass even the French in brilliance . . . in its power to raise and educate the many' (also see n.11). In its scope *Cosmos* was perhaps the last work of its kind, with one scientist attempting a total description of the world, displaying his essential vision that nature is a single unifying force in which 'Everything is related' (quoted in Helferich op. cit.: 323), or in his own words '*Alles ist Wechselwirkung*' which Müller (1994: 1, n.1, n.2) notes stresses interrelationship or interrelatedness, making Humboldt's perspective the direct background to environmental sciences – and we could add a precursor to Jung's field theory with its highly relational quality (see Cambray 2009: chapter 2)[6] as well as the (inter)relational paradigm in psychoanalysis.

The first several volumes *Cosmos* were immensely popular and influenced generations of scientists. Walls (2011: 216) notes that 'Humboldt himself was rather bewildered by it all. "How has it happened that *Kosmos* is so popular beyond expectation?"' She opines that it was 'as if the age itself were writing through Humboldt, making him its instrument' (ibid.; see also n.14).[7] In the first volume, published in German in 1845, Humboldt focuses on the outer world, an 'objective journey through the external world of the senses' (ibid.: 221). The second volume, also in German, published in 1847, shifts to a focus on 'an inner or "subjective" journey through mind, "the inner, reflected intellectual world"' (ibid.). As Walls observes, for Humboldt this shift to the subjective is not what we would normally understand as a psychological exploration, 'but something more Wordsworthian, the emergence and growth of mind-in-nature, "the reflection of the image impressed by the senses upon the inner man, that is, upon his ideas and feelings." The second volume thus journeys through time – historical time, from the earliest civilizations . . .' (ibid.). In an 1848 letter to Edward Cresy, Darwin proclaimed that *Cosmos* offered 'a grand *coup d'oeil* of the whole universe' (quoted in Richards 2002: 521); all the more remarkable as Darwin can only be referring to the first two volumes as the remaining three were not yet published (volume III did not come out until 1850).

The first section of volume II is entitled 'Incitements to the Study of Nature' referring to 'the image reflected by the external world on the imagination' (Humboldt 1866); it offers an ecologically based archaeology of civilization and mind as formed in response to the natural environment with the life-forms, especially plants, present. The second section of this volume is titled: 'History of the Physical Contemplation of the Universe. Principal Causes of the Gradual Development and Extension of the Idea of the Cosmos as a Natural Whole' (ibid.). In its attempts at a poetics of nature, Richards see Humboldt's explicit intention as arguing that 'the natural historian had the duty to re-create in the reader – through the use of artful language – aesthetic experiences of the sort the naturalist had himself undergone in his immediate encounter with nature' (Richards 2002: 521). In a footnote Richards takes this a step further indicating the objective aspect of Humboldt's endeavour:

> At the beginning of the second volume of *Cosmos* (p. 19), Humboldt contrasts his 'objective,' physical account of nature with his observation about the way nature impresses the sensations and fancy of the naturalist. In reading this, one might assume that Humboldt's aesthetics of nature were entirely 'subjective' . . . If we make a simple distinction between epistemic and ontological claims, on the one hand, and the objective or subjective bases of those claims, on the other . . . then one would have to interpret Humboldt's aesthetics of nature as epistemically objective, since it deals with the universal reactions of different subjects.
>
> (Ibid.: 521 n.14)

Hence, I believe this volume can be seen as a partial precursor not only to Jung's formulation of a collective unconscious but even more closely anticipating some of the work of Jungian analyst James Hillman, with his 'poetic basis of mind' (1975: xi) and his attention to the *anima mundi* (the soul of the world). These lines of filiation have not previously been identified or commented upon as far as I know.[8]

Humboldt's project in creating a vision of *Cosmos* involved marrying scientific measurement and precision to artistic, aesthetic experience. In his words:

> It is by a separation and classification of phenomena, by an intuitive insight into the play of obscure forces, and by animated expressions, in which the perceptible spectacle is reflected with vivid truthfulness, that we may hope to comprehend and describe the *universal all* . . . in a manner worthy of the dignity of the word *Cosmos* in its signification of *universe, order of the world*, and *adornment* of this universal order. May the immeasurable diversity of phenomena which crowd into the picture of nature in no way detract from that harmonious impression of rest and unity which is the ultimate object of every literary or purely artistical composition.
>
> (Humboldt 1866: I, 79)

In the grand vision of *Cosmos*, Humboldt seeks to weave a coherent unity of nature, self, and nation or 'race' (in his study of human differences, Humboldt is one of the first Western scientists to challenge the notion of difference in human groups being due to inherent traits, his views are remarkably democratic for his age and this is part of what won him Boas' admiration). According to Walls (2011: 223) this synthesis 'is a necessary part of the *Bildung*, or growth and integration of the self in the world . . . One could call what he was after *grounded imagination*'.

The cosmological vision Humboldt is seeking through his study of the physical universe in fact bears resemblance to Jung's late life cosmological musing. As I have written about elsewhere, Jung's goal in his Synchronicity monograph to supplement the triad of classical physics (space, time and causality) with a fourth principle, synchronicity, is founded on a cosmogonic insight (Cambray 2012a). In response to the articulation of the "big bang" model of the universe of the astrophysicists of his day, Jung sought to locate a pattern-forming tendency emerging from an originary singularity that he identifies as synchronicity. At that time, there was no complexity theory available. Starting from Jung's intuitions, I suggest his work on synchronicity deserves reconsideration, and some modification in terms of modern theory. Thus the phase transitions proposed in the immediate wake of the big bang which are the ultimate source of all of known physics are now understood in terms of symmetry breaking that leads to increasing complexity (Mainzer 2005: 147–58). Patterns of increasing complexity emerged as the early universe cooled and evolved; much later in cosmic time this same propensity leads to the origins of life and to the psyche. All of these key events occur through phase transitions that are associated with self-organizing systems that yield new, higher level/emergent properties. Therefore, through this late argument Jung at his most far-reaching places the origins of the psyche in the same milieu as belongs to the origins of the physical universe; mind and even the imagination is thereby most fundamentally grounded in nature. In making this link, it should be noted that Jung is hardly a consistent writer, he draws on many sources over the course of his long life, and his views alter as his understandings change. As I have argued elsewhere, his views on topics such as symmetry breaking vacillate (Cambray 2009: 57–67); my interest is pursuing the edges of his thought, which is where influences outside consciousness often enter, rather than his definitive, unconflicted statements.

Johann Wilhelm Ritter (1776–1810) and Hans Christian Ørsted (1777–1851)

Both men were physicists and chemists who worked on electricity and magnetism; and both were friends of Alexander von Humboldt. In his early work on chemical and electric process in animals and plants, it was Ritter to whom Humboldt turned to critique his manuscript (Wetzel 1990: 200–1). Shortly thereafter Ritter went on to found the discipline of electrochemistry and in the process he resolved the apparent conflict between the findings of Volta (on inorganic sources of electricity), and those of Galvani (on bioelectricity) (ibid.: 201–2). This bridge between inorganic and living matter was seen as validation of the Romantic notion of the universe being more like a cosmic organism than an inanimate mechanism. For Ritter it was electricity which 'unifies nature and endows everything with "life"' (ibid.: 205) and leads to speculations about a world-soul, again a holistic vision of nature.

Already at the University of Jena as of 1796 when Schelling and the Schlegel brothers made their first visit to Jena, Ritter quickly became part of a core group of Romantics (ibid.: 200). Applying thinking in opposites, characteristic of Schelling's *Naturphilosophie*, Ritter hypothesized that Herschel's recent discovery of infrared rays, detected by thermometer, should have a counter-pole at the ultraviolet end of the light spectrum and proved this using silver chloride (ibid.: 207–8). While he also performed a number of key experiments in the electrolysis of water, *Naturphilosophie* failed him here for he saw water as an element, unitary in nature and therefore could not fully accept his own experimental results (ibid.: 208–9). Nevertheless, Ritter was a source of scientific inspiration and revelation to the group of Romantics in Jena and his ideas influenced scientific thought as well as German education, including at the time of Jung's own university years.

In 1801 Ørsted made a visit to Jena, developed a friendship with Ritter and together for about three weeks, they worked on galvanism (Snelders 1990: 233). Curiously Ritter prophesied to Ørsted in a letter of 22 May 1803 that there would be a remarkable discovery in the field of electricity at the end of 1819 or in 1820 and indeed in the spring of 1820 Ørsted made his serendipitous discovery of the link between electric current and magnetism (ibid.: 228–31). This discovery was one of the great achievements of Romantic science and led directly to field theory as this result was picked up by Michael Faraday and through him articulated into a form of mathematical laws by James Clerk Maxwell, which subsequently underwent a revolutionary transformation in the hands of Albert Einstein (see Cambray 2009: 39–44). Field theory was eventually to have important consequences for Jung through Einstein, and Pauli, but also in psychology via William James (Cambray 2011b).

Ørsted was critical of Schelling's ideas for the way in which he employed empirical propositions; he was more comfortable with Kant's views on physics. According to Snelders (1990: 238), his discovery of electromagnetism 'was a direct consequence of his metaphysical belief in the unity of all natural forces'. Furthermore, historian of science Brain (2005: online) concludes that 'Ørsted was both a more highly skilled experimentalist and a more rigorous philosopher than Humboldt'. Nevertheless, Brain stresses the importance of the link between art and science that characterized this discerning Romantic scientist: 'Oersted and his Jena friends attempted to reconceptualize experiments in galvanic (electric) phenomena and acoustics as works of art, produced by the human hand, which produced the conditions for an intellectual intuition of the Absolute in the experimentalist' (ibid.).

He was clearly committed to the Romantic agenda, even though he held critical views of some of his contemporaries. His last publication was a collection of articles entitled *The Soul in Nature* in which he states that 'soul and nature are one, seen from two different sides' (Ørsted 1852: 384); echoing forward the passions of Humboldt. As already noted this is a topic that Jung repeatedly explored (see a selection of relevant writings in Sabini 2002), culminating in his ideas about the psychoid archetype.

Ernst Heinrich Philipp August Haeckel (1834–1919)

The last figure in this incomplete, abbreviated survey of scientists associated with the German Romantic tradition whose works influenced Jung is Ernst Haeckel. I have already published several articles on Haeckel's influence on Jung, especially as seen in the artwork of *The Red Book* and in key dreams of his that helped determine his choice of career, and later as an indicator of an experience of the self and of significant individuation (Cambray 2011a, 2011c, 2013). These artistic influences went unacknowledged by Jung, though both he and Freud, each in their own way, explicitly incorporated Haeckel's 'biogenetic law' that 'ontogony recapitulates phylogeny' into their theories, especially of memory and inheritance. While I will not review these incorporations here, I will mention my rather recent revaluing of Haeckel's work in the next section.

Often referred to as the 'German Darwin' Haeckel was a major figure in the development of evolutionary theory in the second half of the nineteenth century and early twentieth century, espousing a mix of Darwin, Goethe and Lamarck.[9]

Earning his doctorate and then holding a professorship at the University of Jena (1862–1909) he was well steeped in the German Romantic tradition. In conjunction with his scientific writings, he was also a renowned artist; his work in marine zoology, among the many fields he contributed to, was marked by his extraordinary artistic rendering of sea-creatures. In this work he was one of the essential experts who consulted to another British voyage of discovery, that of HMS *Challenger* in the mid 1870s. The report Haeckel wrote on radiolaria (plankton) from the sea samples he analysed is still in use! (Richards 2008: 77). In 1879 on a trip to the British Isles to consult about the *Challenger* report, he took time for a final visit of his friend Darwin, whom he had visited several times before; both acknowledged the influence of Humboldt and carried some of his ideas forward into evolutionary theory especially with regard to environmental concerns.

Haeckel's roots in German Romanticism were to have wide-reaching impact on biological theories throughout his life and well beyond. His interests following Humboldt on holistic views of natural systems led him to coin the term ecology. He also created a number of other terms still in common use in biology, for example, *phylum*, *phylogeny*, the kingdom eukaryotic organisms (having a distinct nucleus) without specialized tissues, *Protista*, and from his phylogenetic and embryological studies, *stem cell* (Maehle 2011: 2–3). In keeping with the Romantic tradition Haeckel's "scientific art" was a significant influence on the culture of his times (see Cambray 2011a). It is this same tradition of aesthetic rendering of scientific observations that I suggest can help us better assess Jung's own view of what he was doing as 'science'.

Jung's ambivalent attraction to revolutionary science

Trained in the science of his day in medical school, Jung had an ambivalent relationship to the classical view of science at the turn of the last century as is readily discerned from reading his Zofinga lectures (Cambray 2011a). The transformations in understanding of the world that were underway as he entered professional life attracted him; it was a time when the well-established, authoritative views of reality (both physical and psychological) were crumbling under the weight of observations that could not be integrated into the known. Although Jung was not particularly adroit at math and physics by his own admission, he was fascinated by the new vision of the world in the first three decades of the twentieth century emerging from the remarkable findings in theoretical physics, relativity and quantum mechanics in particular. His involvement with Pauli and to a much lesser extent, Einstein, is evidence of this fascination.

More immediately the foundation for a new psychological science which would include unconscious activity of the mind was a primary interest from the start of Jung's career, one in which he conducted research through the word association test. As has often been mentioned in the literature on 'the discovery of the unconscious', the immediate background for these ideas came from the German

Romantic tradition, though usually the contributions of the philosophers are the acknowledged source. I would like to expand this to include the scientists of this tradition, especially in their efforts to include aesthetic and holistic perspectives in scientific thought.

Jung was clearly conflicted on these matters. While working on *The Red Book* he reported an internal struggle around defining what he was doing, seeing it as neither art nor science; his conscious conclusion was that it was 'nature' (Jung 1961: 186). His mistrust of the aesthetic dimension to his work is captured by his irritable dismissal of the inner voice that was insisting he was doing art: 'I recognized it as the voice of a patient, a talented psychopath who had a strong transference to me' and his fear of his vulnerability to her suggestions (ibid.: 185). This struggle peaked following receipt of a letter from this woman who stressed 'the fantasies arising from my unconscious had artistic value and should be considered art' (ibid.: 195). Jung's subsequent emotional distress provoked a rupture in the mandala he was working on 'part of the periphery had burst open and the symmetry was destroyed' (ibid.). As I have discussed elsewhere such symmetry breaking is essential to emergence, and Jung was both fascinated and repelled by such breaks, making and then backing away from them (Cambray 2009, 2013). In *The Red Book*, the broken mandala can be seen to reflect the inauguration of a transformative process stemming from an activation of the unconscious (Cambray 2013).

It is just at this point that the images from Haeckel's rendering of sea creatures enter *The Red Book* unacknowledged. This seems curiously like an unconscious solution to Jung's struggle: art and science are married in these romantic images from nature. That he makes no reference to Haeckel's (1998 [1904]) *Kunstformen der Natur* seems to reflect an unconsciousness of this direct, specific influence as well as his more general ambivalence about Haeckel's mechanistic and monist views and his *Monistenbund*, despite his embrace of the biogenetic law (see Cambray 2013). My suggestion is that in *The Red Book* Jung is in fact attempting to engage his own psychological nature in a manner consistent with the way the German Romantic scientists sought to engage objective reality with their subjective responses. That Jung felt threatened by the artistic pull of his work, and the mystical grandiosity that came with some of his active imaginations may have led to his compensatory efforts to re-enter the world and ground himself in the realities of science. But his attraction was always to the more revolutionary forms of science; he sought to locate his thought where the paradigm shift was occurring. It is this aspect of Romanticism[10] which Jung both values and avoids, i.e., is conflicted over, that makes its influence on Jungian thought worth examining. However, such reflections would mainly be of historical interest were it not for contemporary revival of these traditions within some branches of science, and the excellent work of the last several decades of historians of science who have helped us appreciate the importance of previous, often forgotten contributions to our scientific worldview.

Romantic roots resurfacing in contemporary science

With increasing sophistication of methods and theories, groups of scientists in the later part of the twentieth century began to tackle non-linear dynamical systems. Such systems undergo changes in which the output is not directly proportional to the input (only true for linear systems); they exhibit complex spatial and temporal evolution. Despite the ubiquity of these systems, especially in the biological world, prior to the advent of high-speed electronic computers modelling of such systems was quite limited. One of the first breakthroughs was chaos theory which stemmed from attempts to model weather patterns. With further developments came complexity theory and the study of complex adaptive systems, which exhibit emergent properties.[11] This interdisciplinary branch of science has proven to be useful at all levels of scale (from the subatomic to the clustering of galaxies, and includes human activities), leading to a renewed interest in holistic perspectives thereby rekindling a major concern of the German Romantic scientists, now with enhanced scientific rigour.

Similarly, the role of emotions, images and imagination in the formation of the mind is gaining interest as articulated by cognitive and neurosciences, as exemplified by the writings of Damasio (1999, 2003, 2010) among many others. In particular the discovery and exploration of the 'default mode network' is opening up new understandings of how trauma disrupts the contributions of these elements of mindfulness and offers new potential therapeutic approaches which are close to some of Jung's methods (Lanius et al. 2010). The International Association for Analytical Psychology (IAAP) is currently involved in supporting research in this area in the laboratories of Professor Lanius (a preliminary report will be made in August 2013). There has also been a parallel revaluing of aesthetics in the formation of mind, e.g., in the work of the visual neurologist Ramachandran (2011) and the recent, burgeoning field of neuroaesthetics. The return of subjectivity, affect and imagination to scientific discourse can naturally be seen as an affirmative return to the scientific tradition discussed in this chapter, again with increased rigour – the hope would now be that the tendency for the pendulum swings between reductionism and holism to diminish and that both poles might be held on to more fully in any ongoing discourse.

For this chapter's purposes, I will offer one final example that draws on the ecological developments spawned by the German Romantic scientists: epigenetics. This derives in part from the much older term 'epigenesis' which refers to a theory whereby 'an individual is developed by successive differentiation of an unstructured egg rather than by a simple enlarging of a preformed entity' (American Heritage Medical Dictionary: online). The history of epigenesis is traceable to Aristotle and recurs throughout Western science and medicine. According to science historian Stefan Willer:

> [In] the 18th century embryology, 'epigenesis' was the key-word for conceptualizing the gradual self-organization of new life by means of

an essential power or potency, provided by the generative matter of both parents – in contrast to theories of preformation with their concepts of pre-structured, pre-existing germs which were not to develop, but only to unfold.

(Willer 2010: 13)

The German Romantics were especially drawn to the self-organizing (emergent) aspects in the theory of epigenesis and as Willer comments, this is 'why *generation* in an epigenetic view could become closely linked to *genius* and furnish a leading model for philosophical and poetical productivity' (ibid.: 17).

During the course of the nineteenth century, epigenesis was linked with vitalism and Lamarck's ideas on inheriting acquired characteristics. Hence with the advent of genetics, especially through the work of August Weismann, there was a general rejection of epigenesis. Weismann held that nothing essential was added after fertilization of an egg, and used the Darwinian focus on 'evolution' in the service of a new version of the preformationist camp, genetics, again separating development from heredity.[12]

The resurgence of a developmental component to evolutionary biology began with the work of C. H. Waddington who coined the term 'epigenetics' in 1940.[13] This viewpoint was significantly reduced from an entire theory of inheritance to a description of the way environmental effects act on and modify an individual's genetic programme of development. What is essential, however, is that the heritable epigenetic modifications do not alter the actual DNA bases or their sequences. The reintroduction of the role of the environment in heredity does return the German Romantic theme of ecology into the discussion of evolutionary biology.

Beginning in the later phase of the human genome project when the limits of genetic information were coming into view, an explosion of scientific and medical interest in epigenetics has occurred. Topics of intense interest have included various disease and ageing processes such as the origins of different cancers (see, e.g., Gilbert & Epel 2009). Elsewhere I noted the inclusion of epigenetics in recent debates in the Jungian literature on the nature of the archetype; and also mentioned neuroscientific studies on memory, which have potential value for contemporary Jungians (Cambray 2011a).

Here I would like to conclude by noting that epigenetic influences on biological transmission of traumatic memory have begun to be identified and examined; reviving in modified form the Romantic notion of 'organic memory'. For example, research on the victims of the Dutch Hunger Winter (November 1944 until May 1945), when the German authorities halted food supplies in the portion of the Netherlands that they occupied at this late stage of the Second World War. This tragic situation gives a clearly delineated time frame for this famine. Epidemiologists have been able to study the impact on pregnant mothers and their new-borns as detailed records survive due to the excellent healthcare system in place at the time. The findings have been quite surprising:

If a mother was well-fed around the time of conception and malnourished only for the last few months of the pregnancy, her baby was likely to be born small. If, on the other hand, the mother suffered malnutrition for the first three months of the pregnancy only . . . but then was well-fed, she was likely to have a baby with normal body weight . . . The babies who were born small stayed small all their lives, with lower obesity rates than the general population [despite availability of ample food] . . . the children whose mothers had been malnourished only early in pregnancy, had higher obesity rates than normal. Recent reports have shown a greater incidence of other health problems as well, including certain tests of mental activity. . . . Even more extraordinarily, some of these effects seem to be present in the children of this group, i.e., in the grandchildren of the women who were malnourished during the first three months of their pregnancy.

(Carey 2012: 2–3)

In this case, researchers have begun to identify epigenetic biochemical markers, decreased DNA methylation, compared with same sex siblings who were not exposed to the famine. The data from this study was the first empirical evidence that 'early-life environmental conditions can cause epigenetic changes in humans that persist throughout life' (Heijmans et al. 2008: 17046).

While such results are a long way from ascertaining a biological dimension operating at the level of Jung's purported collective unconscious, they do demonstrate transmission of transgenerational trauma is possible through epigenetic channels. The residue of the trauma operating across several generations here has been analysed solely from the somatic side, though the researchers acknowledge 'An additional contribution of other stressors, such as cold and emotional stress, cannot be ruled out, however. Our study provides the first evidence that transient environmental conditions early in human gestation can be recorded as persistent changes in epigenetic information' (ibid.: 17047–8).

From the psychological side, some contemporary Jungians are beginning to investigate transgenerational trauma, differentiating various types (see Connolly's 2011 useful general review of Jungian contributions). Eventually integration of the psychological impact of the trauma together with the biochemical residues such as in the Dutch Hunger Winter could help refine knowledge of the psychosomatic interface and elements of a shared unconscious (in a group and across generations), as embodied in shared cultural forms. It would be premature to speculate but these types of findings should cause us to remain open minded about the way information is stored and processed in collectives.

Conclusion

Although Jung did not refer to the scientific work of the German Romantics, preferring to orient to the philosophical aspect of this tradition, I believe he was in fact significantly influenced by various key figures and their scientific approaches. Further, a shift can be ascertained in Jung's writing style over his life. A rather straightforward objective, mainstream scientific style marks his hospital research days, studies on word associations and dementia praecox, culminating in 1912 is his 'Theory of Psychoanalysis' delivered at Fordham University. However, after the experiences that led to *The Red Book* had been digested, by the end of the 1920s, Jung's science became more holistic, aesthetic with an imaginative dimension, beginning with his writings on alchemy and proceeding to his theory of synchronicity. His cosmological leanings in the late phase of his life bear an interesting echo to Humboldt's final work providing another clue to the potential line of filiation I have been pursuing in this chapter.

Notes

1 During the early part of this period, the Chinese also initiated a series of maritime explorations, most notably the seven voyages from 1405 to 1433 under Admiral Zheng He. However, by the end of this period for various social and political reasons the Ming emperor chose to end these voyages (see Dreyer 2006).
2 Goethe was aware of the problem of medium of propagation for light waves and was not wholly comfortable with the idea of the ether (Sepper in Cunningham & Jardine 1990). Ultimately in the twentieth century neither the particle theory of light, which Newton subscribed to, nor the wave theory alone were adequate, but the dual nature of light, as well as matter, articulated by quantum theory was necessary. Jung of course was profoundly drawn to the quantum view of reality through his discussions with Wolfgang Pauli.
3 While there is only space here to touch on Humboldt's work, the interested reader is referred to Rupke's (2008) recent 'metabiography' exploring the literature that developed around him and the ways he has been appropriated by various cultural and political groups.
4 Humboldt is also known to have influenced Franz Boas in his formulation of anthropological views of bio-cultural holism. Boas, however, rejected the universalizing tendencies of evolutionary theory especially as applied to cultures.
5 In his Beagle Diary, Darwin writes: 'I am at present fit only to read Humboldt; he like another Sun illumines everything I behold' (quote by Richards 2002: 514).
6 As I have written elsewhere Jung's view of dreams was profoundly inter-relational, thus in a supervisory letter to James Kirsch he wrote: 'With regards to your patient, it is quite correct that her dreams are occasioned by *you*. . . . In the deepest sense we all dream not *out of ourselves* but out of what lies *between us and the other*' (Jung 1973: 172).
7 The recent remarkable commercial success of Jung's *Red Book*, similarly surprised the Jungian community and there have been speculations that it too may speak to our current age.
8 As Humboldt was not a major voice in the archetype theory of German Romantics compared with Goethe, Oken, Carus, Schelling and others, I will not discuss this here. The reader wishing to delve deeper into this area of theory should consult Richards (2002) and Hogenson (2004).
9 Richards (2008: 20 n.2) notes that in Haeckel papers his biographer Wilhelm Bölsche reports that 'in gymnasium his three favorite books were those of Humboldt, Schleiden, and Darwin'.
10 Berlin (1999: 1–2) refers to Romanticism as 'the greatest single shift in the conscious-

ness of the West that has occurred, and all the other shifts which have occurred in the course of the nineteenth and twentieth centuries appear to me in comparison less important, and at any rate deeply influenced by it'.
11 These are self-organizing features which arise spontaneously in response to environmental, competitive pressures; emergence is the appearance of phenomena at a scale one level above the interacting agents from which it derives – see Cambray (2004) for discussion. In various contemporary theories of consciousness, many scientists and philosophers view mind as an emergent property of the body/brain in interaction with the environment (natural and human).
12 For Weismann's germ plasm theory, inheritance occurs only through germ cells. These cells do not undergo development, while the remainder of body cells can be influenced by experience but they do not influence the germ cells.
13 Waddington (1942: 18) linked genetics with epigenetics, seeing that it is 'the interaction of genes with their environment, which brings the phenotype into being'. Discussing the choice of pathways followed during embryological development, linking genetics with environmental effects, Waddington also formulated the notion of 'epigenetic landscapes', which are self-organizing features of foetal development. Recently Skar (2004) has applied Waddington's notion of 'epigenetic landscapes' to clinical work within a Jungian framework.

References

Bair, D. (2003). *Jung*. Boston: Little, Brown and Co.
Berlin, I. (1999). *The Roots of Romanticism*. Princeton, NJ: Princeton University Press.
Brain, R. M. (2005). Report on The Laboratories of Romantic Science: Hans Christian Oersted's Ethnography of European Experimental Cultures. Available: *Max Planck Institute for the History of Science*: www.mpiwg-berlin.mpg.de/en/research/projects/NWGII_Romanticism/index_html (accessed July 1, 2012).
Bowen, M. (1981). *Empiricism and Geographical Thought: From Francis Bacon to Alexander von Humboldt*. Cambridge: Cambridge University Press.
Cambray, J. (2004). Synchronicity as emergence. In Cambray, J. & Carter, L. (Eds.) *Analytical Psychology: Contemporary Perspectives in Jungian Psychology*. New York: Brunner-Routledge.
—— (2009). *Synchronicity: Nature and Psyche in an Interconnected Universe*. College Station, TX: A & M Press.
—— (2011a). Jung, science, and his legacy. *International Journal of Jungian Studies*, 3: 110–24.
—— (2011b). Moments of complexity and enigmatic action: A Jungian view of the therapeutic field. *Journal of Analytical Psychology*, 56: 296–309.
—— (2011c). L'Influence d'Ernst Haeckel dans le Livre Rouge de Carl Gustav Jung. *Recherches Germaniques, Revue Annuelle Hors Serie*, 8: 41–59.
—— (2012a). Cosmos and culture in the play of synchronicity. In Wirth, S., Meier, I., Hill, J. & Cater, N. (Eds.) *The Playful Psyche Entering Chaos, Coincidence, Creation*. New Orleans: Spring.
—— (2013). *The Red Book*: Entrances and exits. In Kirsch, T. & G. Hogenson, G. (Eds.) *Essays on the Red Book of C.G. Jung*. New York: Routledge.
Carey, N. (2012). *The Epigenetics Revolution*. New York: Columbia University Press.
Connolly, A. (2011). Healing the wounds of our fathers: Intergenerational trauma, memory, symbolization and narrative. *Journal of Analytical Psychology*, 56: 607–26.

Cunningham, A. & Jardine, N. (Eds.) (1990). *Romanticism and the Sciences*. Cambridge: Cambridge University Press.
Damasio, A. (1999). *The Feeling of What Happens*. New York: Harcourt, Inc.
—— (2003). *Looking for Spinoza*. New York: Harcourt.
—— (2010). *Self Comes to Mind*. New York: Pantheon.
Darwin, C. (1887). *The Life and Letters of Charles Darwin, including an Autobiographical Chapter* (Volume III). London: John Murray.
Dobbs, B. J. T. (1975). *The Foundation of Newton's Alchemy: Or, The Hunting of the Greene Lyon*. Cambridge: Cambridge University Press.
—— (1991). *The Janus Faces of Genius: The Role of Alchemy in Newton's Thought*. Cambridge: Cambridge University Press.
Dreyer, E. L. (2006). *Zheng He: China and the Oceans in the Early Ming, 1405–1433*. New York: Longman.
Fulford, T., Lee, D. & Kitson, P. J. (2004). *Literature, Science and Exploration in the Romantic Era: Bodies of Knowledge*. Cambridge: Cambridge University Press.
Gilbert, S. F. & Epel, D. (2009). *Ecological Developmental Biology: Integrating Epigenetics, Medicine, and Evolution*. Sunderland, MA: Sinauer Associates.
Haeckel, E. (1998). *Art Forms in Nature*. Munich: Prestel Verlag. (Original work published in 1904)
Helferich, G. (2004). *Humboldt's Cosmos*. New York: Gotham.
Heijmans, B. T., Tobi, E. W., Stein, A. D., Putter, H., Blauw, G. J., Susser, E. S., Slagboom, P. E. & Lumey, L. H. (2008). Persistent epigenetic differences associated with prenatal exposure to famine in humans. *PNAS*, 105: 17046–17049.
Hillman, J. (1975). *Re-Visioning Psychology*. New York: Harper & Row.
Hogenson, G. B. (2001). The Baldwin effect: A neglected influence on C. G. Jung's evolutionary thinking. *Journal of Analytical Psychology*, 46: 591–611.
—— (2004). Archetypes: Emergence and the psyche's deep structure. In Cambray, J. & Carter, N. (Eds.) *Analytical Psychology: Contemporary Perspectives in Jungian Analysis*. Hove: Brunner-Routledge.
Humboldt, A. von. (1819–29). *Personal Narrative of Travels to the Equinoctial Regions of the New Continent, During the Years 1799–1804*. London: Longman, Hurst, Rees, Orme and Brown.
—— (1866). *Cosmos: A Sketch of a Physical Description of the Universe*. New York: Harper and Brothers.
Jung, A. (2011). The Grandfather. *Journal of Analytical Psychology*, 56: 653–73.
Jung, C. G. (1961). *Memories, Dreams, Reflections*. New York: Pantheon.
—— (1973). *Letters. Vol. I: 1906–1950*. London: Routledge and Kegan Paul.
Lanius, R. A., Vermetten, E., Loewenstein, R. J., Brand, B., Schmahl, C., Bremner, J. D. & Spiegel, D. (2010). Emotion modulation in PTSD: Clinical and neurobiological evidence for a dissociative subtype. *American Journal of Psychiatry*, 167: 640–7.
Lear, J. (2003). *Therapeutic Action: An Earnest Plea for Irony*. London: Karnac.
Maehle, A-H. (2011). Ambiguous cells: the emergence of the stem cell concept in the nineteenth and twentieth centuries. *Notes and Records of the Royal Society*, 65 (4): 359–78.
Mainzer, K. (2005). *Symmetry and Complexity: The Spirit and Beauty of Nonlinear Science*. Hackensack, NJ: World Scientific Publishing.
Müller, G. H. (1994). *Wechselwirkung* in the life and other sciences: A word, new claims and a concept around 1800 . . . and much later. In Poggi, S. & Bossi, M. (Eds.) *Romanticism in Science: Science in Europe, 1790–1840*. Dordrecht: Kluwer Academic.

Nicolson, M. (1990). Alexander von Humboldt and vegetation. In Cunningham, A. & Jardine, N. (Eds.) *Romanticism and the Sciences*. Cambridge: Cambridge University Press.

Ørsted, H. C. (1852). *The Soul in Nature*. London: Henry G. Bohn.

Principe, L. M. (1998). *The Aspiring Adept: Robert Boyle and His Alchemical Quest*. Princeton, NJ: Princeton University Press.

Ramachandran, V. S. (2011). *The Tell-Tale Brain*. New York: W. W. Norton & Co.

Richards, R. J. (2002). *The Romantic Conception of Life: Science and Philosophy in the Age of Goethe*. Chicago: University of Chicago Press.

—— (2008). *The Tragic Sense of Life: Ernst Haeckel and the Struggle over Evolutionary Thought*. Chicago: University of Chicago Press.

Rupke, N. (2008). *Alexander von Humboldt: A Metabiography*. Chicago: University of Chicago Press.

Sabini, M. (Ed.) (2002). *The Earth Has a Soul: C.G. Jung on Nature, Technology & Modern Life*. Berkeley, CA: North Atlantic Books.

Sepper, D. L. (1990). Goethe, colour and the science of seeing. In Cunningham, A. & Jardine, N. (Eds.) *Romanticism and the Sciences*. Cambridge: Cambridge University Press.

Skar, P. (2004). Chaos and self-organization: Emergent patterns at critical life transitions. *Journal of Analytical Psychology*, 49: 243–62.

Snelders, H. A. M. (1990). Oersted's discovery of electromagentism. In Cunningham, A. & Jardine, N. (Eds.) *Romanticism and the Sciences*. Cambridge: Cambridge University Press.

Waddington, C. H. (1940). *Organisers and Genes*. Cambridge: Cambridge University Press.

—— (1942). The phenotype. *Endeavor*, 1: 18–20.

Walls, L. D. (2011). *The Passage to Cosmos: Alexander von Humboldt and the Shaping of America*. Chicago: University of Chicago Press.

Wetzel, W. D. (1990). Johann Wilhelm Ritter: Romantic physics in Germany. In Cunningham, A. & Jardine, N. (Eds.) *Romanticism and the Sciences*. Cambridge: Cambridge University Press.

Willer, S. (2010). Epigenesis. In Barahona, A., Suarez-Diaz, E. & Rheinberger, H-J (Eds.) *The Hereditary Hourglass: Genetics and Epigenetics, 1868–2000*. Berlin: Max Planck Institute for the History of Science.

Yates, F. A. (1966). *The Art of Memory*. Chicago: University of Chicago Press.

2

SCIENCE FRICTION: JUNG, GOETHE AND SCIENTIFIC OBJECTIVITY

Mark Saban

> Not to know of what things one may demand demonstration, and of what one may not, argues simply want of education.
> (Aristotle 1995: 47/*Metaphysics* 1006a)

It is impossible to do justice to the question of Jung's relationship to science if it is approached solely from within Jungian discourse. Until Shamdasani's (2003) groundbreaking *Jung and the Making of Modern Psychology*, there had been little scholarly interest in locating analytical psychology in a wider cultural or historical context.[1] Writings about analytical psychology tended to come from a narrowly Jungian perspective, and were mostly aimed at a narrowly Jungian audience.

With regard to the question of science, this endemic parochialism shows up in the form of two contrasting approaches: one characterized by a persistent tone of embattled intellectual defensiveness (Zurich as bunker), and the other which enthusiastically trumpeted any scientific discovery (whether in ethology, quantum physics, or evolutionary science) which could be shown (however implausibly) to prove that Jung had been right all along. Behind these equally unedifying approaches it is possible to distinguish two distinct positions within the tradition of analytical psychology: the first approach, which we might describe as aggressively archetypalist, recognizes science as only one archetypal or mythic mode amongst many, while the second derives from a defensive need to obtain recognition for Jungian psychology within the official scientific world at all costs (in order that it might eventually take up its rightful place as a true science). Each of these responses derives from, and can be defended by, a partial reading of Jung; and each reading maintains its claim to validity for as long as its alternative is ignored.

It is my contention that a reading of Jung which attempts to overcome this partiality by acknowledging the importance of *both* aspects to Jung's thought not only has the advantage of being truer to Jung's psychology as *a whole psychology*, but also offers the only way to gain a better understanding of what Jung intended to achieve with that psychology. My contention is that while Jung's psychology does indeed seek to be seen as part of the western scientific tradition, it does so by offering a radical re-visioning of certain aspects of the very science within which it operates. In order to understand this, we need to recognize the context of Jung's ideas within the wider history of European thought. Such a recognition is in no way intended to diminish the value of Jung's psychology, but rather to allow its full heuristic potential to be released.

In order then further to investigate Jung's relation to science, we need to take into account various historical factors. For example, when Jung writes about '*Wissenschaft*' he does not necessarily mean by the word precisely what Anglo-American discourse understands by the word 'science'. It is true that Jung received a more or less recognizably 'hard' scientific training when he became a psychiatrist, but it is also true that he was deeply read in, and deeply interested by relatively unfamiliar scientific approaches such as that of Goethe. Indeed, parallels with Goethe's writings on science may be traced in the overall project enshrined in Jung's mature psychology, and these must therefore be taken into account in any serious attempt to understand Jung's complex and conflicted engagement with science.

Since Jung's death, many Jungians have reflected that although Jung may have either sincerely believed himself to be a scientist, or have felt it necessary to emphasize his role as scientist in order to enable his ideas to be taken seriously, in these enlightened times we no longer need to maintain this awkward pose. We can now liberate ourselves from this dilemma, they suggest, by simply declaring Jungian psychology to be art not science, or alternatively by re-visioning it as a hermeneutic enterprise that no longer requires justification on a scientific basis. However superficially tempting it may be to cut the Gordian knot in this way, it is crucial to resist it, on the grounds that Jung's importance as a psychologist resides in his very ability, or even his attempt, to hold the tension between apparently conflicting pressures: in this case, science vs. art. It is Jung's repeated emphasis upon the importance of, first the awareness of such tensions, and subsequently the attempt to hold and transcend them, that characterizes Jung's project in psychology.

In the light of this fact, it is crucial that we do not submit to the understandable temptation to free ourselves of such difficulties by simply redefining Jung's project as unscientific. Jung's refusal to choose between science and its other, or rather, his insistence on choosing both, is then the subject of this chapter.

Jung and science

Reading the *Collected Works* it is easy to feel that Jung's attitude toward science is confusing and even contradictory. On the one hand, Jung frequently describes himself as a scientist: 'My pursuit is science'; 'In my view, it is utterly wrong to criticize my scientific work, which does not claim to be anything except scientific, from any other standpoint than that which alone is appropriate to the scientific method' (1973a: 346, 350). He describes science as necessary for the individuation of the modern individual: 'We receive knowledge of nature only through science, which enlarges consciousness; hence deepened self-knowledge also requires science, that is, psychology' (1973c: 331). Indeed, he goes so far as to claim that, 'anyone who belittles the merits of Western science is undermining the foundations of the Western mind' (1929a: par. 2). Jung clearly considers psychology to be scientific (it is, as he describes it, a 'mediatory science' (1921: par. 72)) and his work is therefore evidently intended to be received as science.

On the other hand, these positive statements are more than outweighed by numerous remarks, scattered through the *Collected Works*, the *Letters* and *Memories, Dreams, Reflections* that seem highly critical of science. Jung's main objection to science relates to the gap between its claims to universality and what Jung considers its necessarily limited reach. For Jung there are more things in heaven and on earth than are dreamed of in the scientific perspective. While Jung acknowledges that the scientific revolution enabled great strides forward in many directions, he is also aware that there were corresponding losses, especially during the positivistic, materialistic phase of scientific development:

> In the nineteenth century, the century of technology and exact science, we strayed very far from the intuition of earlier periods in history. Purely intellectualistic, analytical, atomistic, and mechanistic thinking has, in my opinion, landed us in a cul-de-sac, since analysis also requires synthesis and intuition.
> (Jung 1977: 39)

> The people who rely on natural science and the so-called realistic view of the world, based on it, are unaware of the abstracting and isolating nature of science. True reality can only be approached and surmised spiritually.
> (Ibid.: 224)

As these representative quotations show, Jung's criticism of science is consistent with the overall thrust of his psychology, which seeks to discover those aspects of the personality which are undervalued or ignored (in Jungian language, shadow aspects in the unconscious), in order to allow a rebalancing whereby the psyche may achieve a state closer to wholeness, a process Jung describes as individuation. In the case of science, he diagnoses western culture as suffering from a one-sided overvaluation of analytical intellect while more synthetic approaches supported by psychic functions such as intuition or feeling are undervalued or ignored. What, according to Jung, is necessary for the individuation of western culture is a critical reappraisal of these 'shadow' factors, aiming toward their assimilation.

What Jung, as therapist of the west, would *not* recommend is an enantiodromic movement to the other extreme whereby one value is simply replaced by its opposite: a swing from rationality to irrationality, for example. This would result in a state quite as unbalanced as the state which required correction in the first place. What needs emphasizing is that Jung is not opposed to science as such. What he does oppose is the exclusiveness of science: its claims to offer the only explanation of every aspect of human life:

Science is the tool of the Western mind, and with it one can open more doors than with bare hands. It is part and parcel of our understanding, and it obscures our insight only when it claims that the understanding it conveys is the only kind there is.

(Jung 1929a: par. 2)

The reason for the large number of comments in the *Collected Works* which are critical of science is that science, (along with the scientistic ideology which underpins it), holds a position of hegemony at this point in western history, and therefore the corrective movement toward balance requires an aggressive deconstruction of scientific claims to universality. This is not the same as an attempt to undermine science itself.

In order to make his arguments, Jung characteristically invokes various opposites or binaries. Here is a list of those ideas that are relevant to Jung's discussion of science, arranged into binaries:

Material/Spiritual
Analysis/Synthesis
Abstract/Concrete
Intellect/Intuition or Feeling
Objective/Subjective
Logos/Mythos

In each case, the scientific ethos would generally be identified with the first term in these pairs. Jung suggests that if we want to achieve a comprehensive approach to these questions, the second term in the pair needs, first, to be acknowledged, and then to be given an equal hearing. To the extent that a scientific approach excludes these latter terms by dismissing their equal importance and value, its subsequent claims to universality must fail. There is no space in this chapter to explore the different avenues which these different binaries potentially open up. I shall therefore concentrate upon one particular binary, subjectivity and objectivity, on the grounds that it is central to Jung's 'dream of a science' as Shamdasani so accurately describes it. First, though, it is necessary to return to Jung's place in the wider historical and cultural debate about science.

Psychology as science

For the purposes of this enquiry, it is helpful to refer back to the complex nature of psychology's origins in the nineteenth century. As a newly established scientific discipline, it was carved out of the hitherto independent domains of 'philosophy, theology, biology, anthropology, literature, medicine and neurology, whilst taking over their traditional subject matters' (Shamdasani 2003: 4). Psychologists therefore had to lay claim to a field of enquiry which had hitherto overlapped various other disciplines. Their hope and expectation were that the new science would 'be able to solve questions that had vexed thinkers for centuries, and to replace superstition, folk wisdom and metaphysical speculation with the rule of universal law' (ibid.: 4). It was William James, one of the prime movers in the genesis of psychology, who in 1892 struck a note of realism in the face of such optimism:

> When, then, we talk of 'psychology as a natural science' we must not assume that means a sort of psychology that stands at last on solid ground. It means just the reverse; it means a psychology particularly fragile, and into which the waters of metaphysical criticism leak at every joint . . . [We have] not a single law in the sense in which physics shows us laws, not a single proposition from which any consequence can causally be deduced. We don't even know the terms between which the elementary laws would obtain if we had them. This is no science, it is only the hope of science . . .
>
> (James 1983 [1892]: 468)

By the time that Jung set about constructing his own synthetic science of psychology, nothing in this picture had changed. It seemed as though the only factor common to the numerous different definitions of and versions of psychology, and the sole fact supporting their ambition to become a unitary science, was that they all called themselves by the same name. As Shamdasani points out, this

> operation of unification by naming did play a critical role in twentieth-century psychology – not through providing the ideal of univocal meaning and the possibility of effective translation and communication, but through papering over and covering up the incommensurabilities and cleavages that multiplied.
>
> (Shamdasani 2003: 8)

We should remember then, that when Jung classifies his own psychology as a science, it was not in the face of unified agreement elsewhere about what constituted psychological science. On the contrary, not only did no such agreement exist, but nor does it exist to this day. Arguably, it was Jung's awareness of this disunity that kept alive his 'dream' of a science that might synthetically provide the possibility of wholeness here too.

As psychology, in all its heterogeneity, began to achieve at least some sense of continuity, simply by continuing to exist, it became possible to identify two main tendencies within it. One emerged from Wundt's experimental psychology and has persisted into the present in the form of academic psychology which seeks to present itself as much as possible as natural science.

The other tendency within psychology followed William James in a diametrically opposed direction, and developed within a full awareness of the epistemological problems that accompany the necessarily subjective nature of any psychological work. I shall look more closely at the ways in which Jung situated his psychology in this tradition at a later point. However, it needs to be mentioned that the subjectivist strain of psychology too was prone to a tendency to insist upon its right to describe itself as a natural science. As Porter (1995) pointed out, many of the newer and 'weaker' social and economic sciences, including psychology, have tended to suffer from a sense of inferiority in the company of the established natural sciences. In the absence of the kind of hard evidence which paradigmatic 'proper' sciences like physics can offer, they tend to fall into a defensive overuse of statistical methods. Such an approach is aimed at bolstering an impression of solidity in experimental results, and at offering an impressive illusion of objectivity. Psychology as a whole reacted to its endemic need to compensate for various identity problems (including disunity and confusion about its grounds and borders), with a persistent insecurity about its methodology, epistemology and even ontology. Was psychology to serve as merely a junior handmaid to those older harder sciences on which it was to be more or less successfully modelled, or was it instead to rule as the 'queen of all the sciences', providing the superior perspective from which supra-scientific insight might be gained?

Science as science

Before venturing into the question of Jung's scientific project as a psychology, we need to address a wider question about the nature and grounding of science itself. Reflection on such issues tends to take place in the context of the philosophy of science, the history of science, or of the recently developed discipline of science studies. If we look at the history of this kind of reflection during most of the time that Jung was active as a psychologist, we can see that the dominant approaches were those of materialism and positivism. For positivism, the nature of reality is regarded as independent of consciousness. Because it is 'out there', it can be studied independently of the inquirer, in other words, objectively. Because the truths it discovers are represented as objective, they are also seen as independent of social or historical context. Positivism is reductive in the sense that the general and unchanging laws it postulates can be explored only by carefully screening out irrelevant factors. The aim is to create conditions which are as close to neutral laboratory conditions as possible.

It is clear from Jung's writings that he had little sympathy with this theoretical approach: 'In the intellectual world in which I grew up . . . it was . . . straight materialism, which I never shared, knowing too much about its ridiculous mythology' (Jung 1973b: 501). It is striking how little Jung's notion of science seems to share with this approach. As we shall see, this is because it derives from a quite different approach to thinking about science.

Unlike Freud, whose teachers, Brücke and du Bois-Reymond were self-proclaimed positivists, Jung was profoundly influenced by the scientific theories of Goethe and, (through his biology teacher, Zschokke) those of the teleo-mechanists (such as J. F. Blumenbach, Karl Ernst von Baer, and Rudolph Leuckart), whose theories were comprehensively dismissed by the positivists as 'metaphysical' (Sherry 2010: 23).

Before we take a closer look at this approach and its influence upon Jung, it is worth reminding ourselves that the German word that Jung uses, and which we translate as 'science', is *Wissenschaft*. Notoriously problematic, this word can, like our 'science', be applied to the so-called natural sciences and social sciences but it can also be used in contexts in which the English word 'science' would never be used. As Jung himself puts it in a letter to E. A. Bennet, 'On the continent . . . any kind of adequate logical and systematic approach is called "scientific"; thus historical and comparative methods are scientific. History, mythology, anthropology, ethnology, are "sciences" as are geology, zoology, botany, etc.' (Jung 1973b: 567).

Since Jung's death, the more or less monolithic assumptions about science and its methodology which held sway during his lifetime have come under considerable attack and therefore look substantially less solid than they did then. Critics influenced first by the ideas of philosophers of science such as Popper and Kuhn, and more recently by the ideas of constructivism and deconstruction have drawn attention to the historically contingent nature of western science and some have gone on to attempt to undermine hitherto sacred notions such as the objectivity of science and its claim to identify truths which exist as such for all time and in all cultural conditions. The German philosopher of science, Feyerabend (1975), for example, was particularly critical of 'rationalist' attempts to lay down or discover rules of scientific method, suggesting that in practice 'anything goes'. He also provocatively concluded that 'objectively' there may be nothing to choose between the claims of science and those of so-called pseudo-sciences such as astrology or alternative medicine.

Many scientists and philosophers of science have fought these claims aggressively and the result has been the so-called 'Science wars'. No outright winner has emerged from these battles, but it is important to note that some of Jung's critical attitudes to the scientific hegemony of his day are echoed in the questions at the heart of such disputes.

The main issue I want to concentrate upon in this chapter is that of objectivity in science. Jung's approach to psychology drew particular attention to difficulties in this field, and it is worth looking at his contributions in the context both of possible prior influences (in particular that of Goethe), and of parallel contemporary debates around this subject. This will lead to a discussion of Jung's persistent claim to be an empiricist and the posing of the question, what is the nature of a truly psychological empiricism?

Jung and objectivity

The extreme polarization between the arts and the sciences that occurred in the nineteenth century had a great and long-lasting effect upon issues related to objectivity and the imagination.

During the European enlightenment the dangers of the imagination, in both arts and sciences, were highlighted. However, it was nonetheless assumed that, when properly yoked together with reason, the imagination was a healthy and necessary faculty. The development of romanticism brought with it a swing toward the visionary imagination (original, independent and sometimes in conflict with reason), and with it a cult of subjectivity or 'egomania'. In this way the battle lines began to be drawn up between 'objectivity' and 'subjectivity' (these words first enter dictionaries as a pair in the 1820s and 1830s) and between them opened up an unbridgeable chasm. Goethe, who had somehow succeeded in straddling both art and science, became, in the space of a single generation, an inexplicably paradoxical phenomenon. To the extent that scientists were seen as possessing any imagination, it was defined as of a different kind from that of artists. This latter form of imagination was inevitably associated with scientific error: for example the 'false sciences' of astrology, alchemy, and magic represented for French psychologist Theodore Ribot, 'the golden age of the creative imagination' in the history of science (Daston 2005: 27). The sober objectivity posited in opposition to this dangerous imagination was conceived as 'mechanical' in that it replaced 'judgment with data reduction techniques, observers with self-registering instruments, hand drawn illustrations with photographs' (ibid.: 28). So it is that the sciences came to redefine their overt aim as the exclusion of human intervention from the phenomena as much as possible.[2]

As the conviction hardened that all that mattered in science was the objective fact, so there developed a consequent fear of the potentially distorting effects of the imagination. The effect of this awareness was a shift in the understanding of what constituted a fact. In the early modern era, facts were simply 'historical particulars about an observation or an experiment performed at a specific time and place by named persons' (Daston 2005: 17). However, now there developed new-style facts, which possessed the crucial quality of being detached from inference and conjecture. In effect, the fact lost contact with its etymological root: something *made* (by the scientist), and instead became something 'out there' that could be discovered.

This binary split between arts and sciences, subjectivity and objectivity and imagination and reason was particularly pronounced in nineteenth century western culture, and as a child of that century Jung inherited it in this exaggerated form. However, rather than fall into an out and out identification with either of the two poles, Jung, characteristically, was interested in bringing each into tension with the other, on the grounds that neither art nor science will flourish if both are, in their own different ways, one-sided. Jung considered it to be particularly important to find a way to manage the difficult objectivity/subjectivity binary. Psychology was born when this polarity was at its most extreme. Because, as a science, it is committed to a constant reaching toward scientific truth, it is inextricably and unavoidably bound up with the idea of objectivity. But, as Jung recognized, it is equally bound by subjectivity, in that there can be no Archimedean point outside of the psyche from which it may observe itself.

We may perhaps view Jung's attempt to establish a science on this very fault line as a self-conscious return to an earlier point in the evolution of the scientific *Weltanschauung*, before this split had become so extreme. Perhaps the most eminent and representative figure from such a moment was the artist/scientist Goethe, with whose works Jung was intimately acquainted. As Stephenson (2005: 553–8) describes it, Goethe's scientific work was a conscious attempt to hold a mediatory position between 'the complementary heresies of the mechanistic cosmology of Newtonianism and the organicistic speculations of his Romantic contemporaries':

> All effects ... that we observe in the world of experience are interrelated in the most constant manner ... It is inevitable ... that we should separate them and contrast them with one another; but this necessarily created an endless conflict in the sciences. Stubborn analytical pedantry and indiscriminate mysticism both do equal damage.
> (Goethe, quoted ibid.: 553–8)

Goethe was particularly concerned to maintain the value of sensuous perception within scientific observation, as against a tendency to overvalue analysis and rationalization, a tendency he saw embodied in the figure of Newton.

Goethe's reputation as scientist has waned and waxed in the two centuries since his heyday: after many years of condescension and dismissal, his ideas, and particularly those concerned with morphology, have in recent years achieved something of a revival.[3] One of the fields in which Goethe sought to do original scientific work was that of colour. Here he set himself directly against Newton's hugely influential theories on the colour spectrum, and he was particularly critical of Newton's methodology. It is this methodological aspect of Goethe's work, (rather than the colour theory per se) which will concern us here, because of its particular relevance to Jung's writings on the 'personal equation'.

Goethe seeks to transcend the dichotomy of subjectivity and objectivity, not because of any mystical desire for ultimate unity, but because he is looking for an approach that can most effectively do justice to the phenomena. He criticizes Newton for a lack of objectivity, because, according to Goethe, Newton approaches the phenomena with a set of dogmatic theoretical assumptions which inevitably influence his experimental procedures, and most importantly, obviate his ability to allow nature to reveal herself *on her own terms*. Such an insight anticipates twentieth century ideas about the inevitably theory-laden nature of scientific work:

> An extremely odd demand is often set forth but never met, even by those who make it: i.e., that empirical data should be presented without any theoretical context, leaving the reader, the student, to his own devices in judging it. This demand seems odd because it is useless simply to look at something. Every act of looking turns into observation, every act of observation into reflection, every act of reflection into the making of associations; thus, it is evident that we theorize every time we look carefully at the world.
> (Goethe 1988: 159)

Having established that all science comes with theoretical assumptions, Goethe suggests that the way forward is not to seek quixotically to eradicate human involvement, but rather to take it into account, and by identifying and accepting it as part of the picture, avoid its most egregious distortions. Such an idea is evidently consonant with a post-Kuhnian philosophy of science, whereby any scientist needs to acknowledge the scientific paradigm within which they have been trained, in order to open up the possibility of moving beyond it and developing new ways of seeing.

For Goethe what is required in truly objective scientific work is no less than the 'metamorphosis of the scientist' as Amrine (1998: 37) puts it. Such a transformation can occur when the scientist's perceptions are tested not against logical axioms deduced from an abstract hypothesis, but directly against the phenomena themselves. When this is performed in depth, one learns to think within the natural patterns which reveal themselves:

> Always moving forwards and backwards through the graded series, between the phenomenon and its environment, one watches the structure of the phenomena precipitate gradually out of the dynamic of the interaction between the observer and observed.
>
> (Amrine 1998: 37)

Such movement mimics the energetic polarity which Goethe perceived in nature: it is a way of thinking that oscillates continually between idea and experience, hypothesis and empirical data, synthesis and analysis, yet without rigidly sticking at either pole. As the scientist progressively engages in this dynamic interaction he develops 'a potential for infinite growth through constant adaptation of his sensibilities and judgment to new ways of acquiring knowledge and responding with action' (Goethe 1988: 61). In contrast to such theoretical fluidity, Newton's insistence upon a purely abstract, mathematical approach is seen as inflexible and rigid (*erstarrt* and *unbiegsam*), and therefore far less sensitive to the phenomena, because, as Bernhard Kuhn (2009: 86) remarks, it 'excludes the physiological, aesthetic, and even moral dimensions . . . from the realm of experience'.

This epistemological aspect of Goethe's science must be emphatically differentiated from that associated with conventional approaches to scientific objectivity. Perhaps not surprisingly it is precisely this aspect of his work, and its potential compatibility with post-Kuhnian approaches to science that has attracted interest in recent scholarship.[4]

However, what is particularly important in the present context is the congruence of Goethe's epistemology with that of Jung. Such consonance should not surprise us, given the numerous quotations and accolades to Goethe to be found in the collected works. With the important exception of Bishop's (2007, 2008) works on analytical psychology and Weimar aesthetics (upon which I have relied heavily in writing this chapter), scholars have paid scanty attention to the influence of Goethe upon Jung's scientific ideas.

As Bishop points out, Jung initiated his serious engagement with epistemological issues in the wake of his break with Freud. In 'On Psychological Understanding', Jung (1914) seeks to differentiate his own psychology from that of Freud by drawing a distinction between what he describes as the 'synthetic' and 'analytic' approaches. He indicates the difference by comparing two ways of reading Goethe's *Faust*. Freud's 'analytic-reductive' approach, Jung implies, while able to offer an illuminating explication of various features of *Faust*, is incapable of doing full justice to Goethe's poetic drama, or indeed any similarly complex phenomenon. In order to plumb the depths of meaning which would be required, the required approach is what Jung calls 'prospective understanding' (*ein Verstehen nach vorwärts*), which alone can enable a more 'constructive' or 'synthetic' method.

It is interesting how in this lecture Jung uses the word 'objective' in two contrasting ways. The first is the conventional use, whereby Freud's causal/reductive approach is labelled objective, in contrast to Jung's own subjective attitude. However, elsewhere he uses the term to characterize an approach which is 'real and effective' (*wirklich und wirkend*) when it stands 'in accord with that of other reasonable beings', and which is 'objective' when it 'connects with life' (*der Anschluss an das Leben ist erreicht*) (Jung 1914: par. 416). He comments in a footnote that this 'objective' kind of understanding is *different* from causal understanding.

As Bishop (2007: 72) points out, 'In terms of the emphasis on a dialectic between subject and object (and, indeed, on an intersubjective level), this second kind of "objective" thinking is close to the "objective thinking," (*gegenständliches Denken*) espoused by Goethe.' As Goethe himself described it, when this kind of 'objective' thinking occurs,

> [M]y thinking is not separate from objects; ... the elements of the object, the perceptions [*die Anschauungen*] of the object, flow into my thinking and are fully permeated by it; ... my perception [*mein Anschauen*] itself is a thinking, and my thinking a perception.
> (Goethe 1988: 39)

Such an approach transcends the subjective/objective dichotomy, and, when observed in engagement with an aesthetic phenomenon like *Faust*, it enables us 'to understand [the] work subjectively, in and through ourselves' (Jung 1914: par. 396). Eventually, we arrive at point where 'we have understood ourselves with the help of Faust' (ibid.: par. 393).

This early paper shows Jung outlining the ways in which his psychology differs radically from that of Freud and he does so by beginning to formulate a Goethean 'dialectic' conception of objectivity.[5] This enables us to gain a clearer sense of what Jung means in his later writings when he talks about the necessity for 'objective cognition' in order to achieve the true *coniunctio* (1973c: 297), or suggests that active imagination consists in 'observing objectively' how 'a fragment of fantasy develops' (1929a: par. 20) or recounts how Philemon taught him 'psychic objectivity, the reality of the psyche' (1973c: 183). This context also offers a useful way to understand what Jung means when he refers to that difficult but central concept in analytical psychology, the 'objective psyche'. He intends to neither establish it as an ontological realm in its own right, nor to propose it as merely a projection of 'subjective' contents, but rather to suggest that it is that aspect of psyche which can enable the kind of entwined, engaged, fully reflexive observation that Goethe is attempting in his *gegenständliche Denken*.

Jung's reflections upon the nature of the differences between Freud's, Adler's and his own psychology highlighted the importance of what he called the 'personal equation':

> I am profoundly convinced that the 'personal equation' has a telling effect upon the results of psychological observation. The tragic thing is that psychology has no selfconsistent mathematics at its disposal, but only a calculus of subjective prejudices. Also, it lacks the immense advantage of an Archimedean point such as physics enjoys. The latter observes the physical world from the psychic standpoint and can translate it into psychic terms. The psyche, on the other hand, observes itself and can only translate the psychic back into the psychic. Were physics in this position, it could do nothing except leave the physical process to its own devices; because in that way it would be most plainly itself. There is no medium for psychology to reflect itself in: it can only portray itself in itself, and describe itself.
>
> (Jung 1947: par. 421)

The term 'personal equation' has a particular meaning in the history of science. It originated in the early years of the scientific pursuit of astronomy. It was observed that, because speed of visual response varies between individuals, when it comes to collecting astronomical data such a variation needs to be allowed for experimentally. But while in the case of astronomy a single consistent variable such as this may be relatively easily factored into experimental results, when it comes to a science like psychology, which seeks to engage with the psyche of an individual, and can only do so through the medium of psyche itself, the personal equation becomes far more problematic. As Shamdasani (2003: 34) puts it, 'the personal equation, far from being heralded as denoting a quantifiably ascertainable factor, designated the manner in which investigators manage only to see what they are led to expect by their own preconceptions'. In fact, as we have seen, this was Goethe's original objection to Newton's work on colour, and, as Goethe implied, it is a problem that extends much further than the human sciences. Jung emphasizes the particularly acute difficulty it poses for psychology, and especially for the science of psychoanalysis. Since the problem was acknowledged as ultimately ineradicable, the only solution was to manage the difficulty as well as possible: the psychoanalyst had to obtain 'ruthless self-knowledge' (Jung 1910: par. 156), and for that, a thorough training analysis was required. (It was Jung's insistence upon this aspect of psychoanalytic training that resulted in it becoming *de rigeur*.) Such a concern echoes Goethe's warnings against the danger of those 'inner enemies' that can distort the scientist's research:

> Thus we can never be too careful in our efforts to avoid drawing hasty conclusions from experiments or using them directly as proof to bear out some theory. For here at this pass, this transition from empirical evidence to judgment, cognition to application, all the inner enemies of man lie in wait: imagination, which sweeps him away on its wings before he knows his feet have left the ground; impatience; haste; self-satisfaction; rigidity; formalistic thought; prejudice; ease; frivolity; fickleness – this whole throng and its retinue. Here they lie in ambush and surprise not only the active observer but also the contemplative one who appears safe from all passion.
> (Goethe 1988: 14)

Jung also echoes Goethe in the attention he gives to the theory-laden nature of much 'scientific' psychological writing; he castigates not only Wundt and Fechner, but also Freud for smuggling into their work metaphysical premises in the form of physiological and materialistic assumptions. In order to guard against this, Jung recommends a phenomenological and empirical approach (1935: par. 1738; 1936: par. 111; 1939: par. 742). Further,

> [A]n experimental science makes itself impossible when it delimits its field of work in accordance with theoretical concepts. The psyche does not come to an end where some physiological assumption or other stops. In other words, in each individual case that we observe scientifically, we have to consider the manifestations of the psyche in their totality.
> (Jung 1936: par. 113)

This is a point he emphasizes elsewhere:

> A psychology that wants to be scientific can no longer afford to base itself on so-called philosophical premises such as materialism or rationalism. If it is not to overstep its competence irresponsibly, it can only proceed phenomenologically and abandon preconceived opinions.
> (Jung 1949: par. 1239)

Jung's insistence upon representing himself as an empiricist is bound up with his methodology. This leads him, as we have seen, to make note of and bracket out those metaphysical or theoretical assumptions which have the capacity to obscure the 'objectivity' of vision required when approaching psychic phenomena.

In the case of the dream, for example, Jung (1931: par. 319–20) recommends a rigorously empirical approach: 'When we take up an obscure dream, our first task is not to understand and interpret, but to establish the context with minute care . . . a careful and conscious illumination of the interconnected associations objectively grouped round particular images.' In order to carry out this task, one must avoid theoretical preconceptions. The temptation is to impatiently establish meaning as quickly as possible, 'an irritable reaching after fact and reason' as Keats put it. Such an approach is wrong, says Jung, because it depends upon the 'false belief that the dream is a mere facade concealing the true meaning', whereas, in fact 'the manifest dream-picture is the dream itself and contains the whole meaning of the dream . . . To understand the dream's meaning I must stick as close as possible to the dream images' (ibid.).

This is very reminiscent of Goethe's (1988: 307) approach to science, and particularly what he describes as his 'delicate empiricism [*zarte Empirie*]'. This kind of empiricism depends on what he calls a 'precise sensory imagination [*exacte sinnliche Phantasie*]'. As Amrine puts it,

> Goethe has confidence in the phenomena, confidence that they are transparent to the underlying idea . . . [He recommends that] one stays with the phenomena; thinks within them; accedes with one's intentionality to their patterns, which gradually opens one's thinking to an intuition of their structure.
>
> (Amrine 1998: 37)

Here, then, subject is not set apart from object, interpreting from afar, but rather in the immediate and transitive touch of sympathy. This is a phenomenological move, a move 'to the things themselves' as Husserl put it. It relies upon the profoundly scientific assumption that it is unnecessary and distorting to impose a pre-conceived meaning upon the phenomenon, even when that meaning derives from what we 'know' scientifically, but it also accepts as inevitable fact that we, as observers are as much part of the encounter as is the so-called 'object'. The truth which emerges from such an encounter will therefore be objective in Goethe's sense: *gegenständlich*: it will stand over against us, and we against it. The kind of scientific thinking that enables such an encounter, *gegenständliches Denken*, sometimes translated 'concrete thinking', requires the productive input of the creative imagination, and out of the encounter emerges a new sense of self.

It may be objected that Goethe is an artist, a poet: he is merely applying an aesthetic approach to the natural world. This, however, would be mistaken. Goethe's aim is to offer a way of engaging with the world, inner and outer, which transcends such categories. The familiar opposition between art and science depends, according to Goethe, upon assumptions based upon bad art and bad science. Of course, there are differences between art and science but these are more to do with the different object areas of practice and enquiry than to do with any essential conflict in approach. In both cases, what matters is the truth and immediacy disclosed by the meeting of individual and world. In both cases, claims Goethe, the result will be mutual transformation.

This is also what we find, according to Jung, in the mutuality of psychotherapy: 'Between doctor and patient, therefore, there are imponderable factors which bring about a mutual transformation' (1929b: par. 164). For Jung the therapist cannot sit outside of the therapeutic relationship, immune to its twists and turns, observing and interpreting. Jung compares the process of analysis to what occurs in the test tube:

> For two personalities to meet is like mixing two different chemical substances: if there is any combination at all, both are transformed. In any effective psychological treatment, the doctor is bound to influence the patient; but this influence can only take place if the patient has a reciprocal influence on the doctor. You can exert no influence if you are not susceptible to influence. It is futile for the doctor to shield himself from the influence of the patient and to surround himself with a smokescreen of fatherly and professional authority. By so doing, he only denies himself the use of a highly important organ of information.
> (Jung 1929b: par. 163)

For our purposes, the last sentence is crucial: Because Jung is acting as scientist he continues to seek objective information so that he may best further the therapy. But, he claims, such scientific work can only be progressed when the scientist allows himself to be fully present to what he observes: i.e. when he himself enters the test tube. Jung's phrase 'organ of information' is reminiscent of Goethe's (1988: 39) claim that 'every new object, well contemplated, opens up a new organ of perception within us'. As Amrine (1998: 47) amplifies this highly condensed statement: 'the goal of science is not to end with an abstract theorem but rather with new capacities that are themselves incitement to ever greater activity and ever enhanced perception'. Every piece of scientific work will therefore enable transformation in the scientist's mode of perception, and that change will in turn affect the development of science itself. For Jung a detached and 'contraceptive' approach to psychotherapy will inevitably result in the atrophy of psychological science: a sedimenting of dogmatic theoretical structures which can only occlude the kinds of living engagement upon which the healthy development of psychology depends.

There is a parallel here with alchemy, which is perhaps not altogether surprising since it was important both to Goethe and to Jung. According to Jung, the alchemical opus is a process in which the alchemist works the substances into transformation, and is himself simultaneously transformed. In order for this to happen, the alchemist needs to be both in the vessel, and outside the vessel observing. This reflexive procedure, by which the alchemist keeps one foot in and one foot out of the actual chemistry, is also to be found in Jung's descriptions of 'active imagination'. It is vividly evoked in *Mysterium Coniunctionis* (Jung 1954): First, he gives a practical description of what the active imaginer can expect. As the images begin to flow, he says, we can either sit back and enjoy it as an entertainment out there, or we may start to see that

> The piece that is being played does not want merely to be watched impartially, it wants to compel [the imaginer's] participation. If [the imaginer] understands that his own drama is being performed on this inner stage, he cannot remain indifferent to the plot and its denouement.
>
> (Jung 1954: par. 706)

Later Jung comes back to this theatrical image. He talks about the way in which the observer may experience the reality of the psychic process: 'Although, to a certain extent, he looks on from outside, impartially, he is also an acting and suffering figure in the drama of the psyche' (ibid.: par. 753). So long as you just stare at the pictures, Jung says, nothing transformative happens and nothing will happen. But,

> If you recognize your own involvement, you yourself must enter into the process with your personal reactions, just as if you were one of the fantasy figures, or rather, as if the drama being enacted before your eyes were real. It is a psychic fact that this fantasy is happening, and it is as real as you – as a psychic entity – are real.
>
> (Ibid.: par. 706)

What is then required is a participatory consciousness, which engages with a particular phenomenon (e.g. dream image, affect or bodily sensation), such that at a certain 'pregnant point' archetypal meaning begins to unfold of its own accord.

Jung's concept of the archetype can perhaps be fruitfully revised in the light of Goethe's own thinking about the archetype (*Urphänomenon*). For Goethe, as we have seen, science requires a kind of participatory consciousness, which enters into the inner essence of the phenomenon via that matrix that gives birth to both scientific and artistic creativity. In *Faust* Goethe equates this matrix with the realm of the Mothers. Mephisto tells Faust that this realm is eternally empty, and that within it Faust will see nothing, to which Faust replies, 'In this, thy Nothing, may I find my ALL!' (Goethe 1886: 53). In Goethe's scientific work, this potent field equates to the 'pregnant point' in which the archetype shows itself. As Alan Cotrell describes it,

> That is what it means for a point to be pregnant in Goethe's sense. It is not merely a noncommital figure of speech but, rather, an exact description of what he wishes to say: the 'point' of cognition is spiritually alive. It brings forth much 'from out of itself,' just as the blossoms 'bring themselves forth' from the branch in May and the archetypal plant brings forth the splendor of all the plant kingdom, a veritable 'world-garden' (*Weltgarten*) from the mother-ground of spiritual life.
>
> (Cotrell 1998: 267)

The thinking-in-seeing and seeing-in-thinking of Goethe's 'exact sensory imagination' (*exakte sinnliche Phantasie*) enables a perception of the universal within the particular and so, as Henri Bortoft puts it,

> [I]nstead of a movement of mental abstraction from the particular to the general, there is a perception of the universal shining in the particular . . . [so that] what is merely particular to the senses, and the mode of thought which corresponds to them, is simultaneously universal to an intuitive way of seeing which is associated with a different mode of consciousness
>
> (Bortoft 1996: 79)

For Jung this is the participatory balance of subjectivity and objectivity that creates the possibility for the emergence of this archetypal point: a pregnant moment which will enable the active imagination, or the dream work, or the countertransferential event, to deliver its potential into that empty space or matrix which has been opened up between analyst/patient, scientist/phenomena, conscious/unconscious. From this perspective then the archetype must be seen not so much as an identifiable though unknowable pattern-in-itself, somehow lying behind the appearances, but rather as a potential event which is heavy with meaning, waiting to be released through the kind of careful ego-less *gegenständlich* scientific work that we have been investigating in both Goethe and Jung.

Conclusion

In *Memories, Dreams, Reflections*, Jung (1973c: 85) tells us that he finally decided to become a scientist after two dreams. In one dream, he was digging for prehistoric bones, and in the other he encountered a giant radiolarian hidden in the centre of the forest. These dreams aroused an intense excitement in Jung that was translated into an overwhelming certainty that he should pursue the life of science. There are two important factors to be noted here: First, it was the irrational phenomenon of the dream that was compelling him into the rational world of science. Second, far from being coolly logical, Jung describes his decision as charged with emotion.

Later, when he came to decide upon a specialty within medicine his decision was made when he came upon these words in Krafft-Ebbing's *Lehrbuch der Psychiatrie*: 'It is probably due to the peculiarity of the subject and its incomplete state of development that psychiatric textbooks are stamped with a more or less subjective character,' together with a claim that the psychoses were 'diseases of the personality' (ibid.: 108). Jung describes his reaction: 'My heart suddenly began to pound. I had to stand up and draw a deep breath. My excitement was intense, for it had become clear to me, in a flash of illumination, that for me the only possible goal was psychiatry' (ibid.). Evidently, Krafft-Ebbing's stress upon the subjective nature of psychiatric knowledge was what most excited Jung, but what is perhaps also important is the emphasis upon the 'incomplete state of development' of the science. At any rate, Jung, remembering this turning point at the end of his life, amplifies it with these crucial words:

> Here alone the two currents of my interest could flow together and in a united stream dig their own bed. Here was the empirical field common to biological and spiritual facts, which I had everywhere sought and nowhere found. Here at last was the place where the collision of nature and spirit became a reality.
>
> (Ibid.: 109)

He is referring here to his two personalities, and the conflict between them that had dominated his life until this point. He is not suggesting that a scientific career in psychiatry will offer a peaceful end to their conflict; what excites him is the idea that he has found a place where the friction between them will no longer be felt as a crippling disability but will offer rather the best possible conditions for him to achieve his dynamic potential in a field which necessarily straddles both objective and subjective, logical and affective, inner and outer. In short, it is a 'pregnant point' from which will flow the whole of his scientific life.

But it also tells us something about the nature of his ongoing relationship to the official scientific world. Jung's attitude to science will always retain an element of ambivalence, an ambivalence which is mirrored in the way his work is regarded within that world. But it is important to see that this ambivalence stems from the sheer ambition of his scientific project. Though originally formulated in personalistic form as a means of resolving his inner conflict by bringing together both personalities though without short-changing either of them, this project becomes no less than a major extension of the notion of psychology as science, so that it can contain both objective and subjective, logical and affective, inner and outer, personal and collective. Or perhaps it would be better described as a dream of a science that exists in the friction between these opposites. A science so formulated would of course have burst the bounds of science as we know it, and as it recognizes itself.

Perhaps when we regard Jung's work in this perspective it should not be too surprising that there are parallels between Jung and his 'grandfather' Goethe in the areas we have looked at. Goethe's scientific work took place at a moment of creative fluidity just before positivistic ideas become sedimented into dogma at the heart of western science; Jung was writing in the corresponding end moment, when the whole edifice, under pressures from within and without, was beginning to show serious structural problems. For Jung this was a moment that necessitated re-visioning the very presuppositions of western science, and for that task he found his 'grandfather' Goethe's writings invaluable.

Notes

1 The few but important exceptions to this generalization include Ellenberger (1970) and Homans (1979).
2 On this, see also Daston and Galison (1992).
3 See, e.g., contributions in Rowland (2001).
4 See, e.g., contributions in Seamon and Zajonc (1998), Robbins and Holdrege (2005).

5 For various interesting rethinking of scientific objectivity, see Latour (1987), Pickering (1992), Hacking (1983), Megill (1994), and Daston and Galison (2007).

References

Amrine, F. (1998). The metamorphosis of the scientist. In D. Seamon & A. Zajonc (Eds.) *Goethe's Way of Science: A Phenomenology of Nature*. New York: State University of New York Press.

Aristotle (1995). *The Metaphysics* (Vol. II). (Trans. J. Barnes). Princeton, NJ: Princeton University Press.

Bishop, P. (2007). *Analytical Psychology and German Classical Aesthetics: Goethe, Schiller and Jung Volume 1: The Development of the Personality*. London: Routledge.

—— (2008). *Analytical Psychology and German Classical Aesthetics: Goethe, Schiller, and Jung Volume 2: The Constellation of the Self*. London: Routledge.

Bortoft, H. (1996). *The Wholeness of Nature: Goethe's Way Toward a Science of Conscious Participation in Nature*. New York: Lindisfarne Press.

Cotrell, A. P. (1998). The resurrection of thinking and the redemption of Faust: Goethe's new scientific attitude. In D. Seamon & A. Zajonc (Eds.) *Goethe's Way of Science: A Phenomenology of Nature*. New York: State University of New York Press.

Daston, L. (2005). Fear and loathing of the imagination in science. *Daedalus*, 134 (4): 16–30.

Daston, L., & Galison, P. (1992). The image of objectivity. *Representations*, 40: 81–128.

—— (2007). *Objectivity*. New York: Zone Books.

Ellenberger, H. F. (1970). *The Discovery of the Unconscious: The History and Evolution of Dynamic Psychiatry*. London: Penguin.

Feyerabend, P. (1975). *Against Method: Outline of an Anarchistic Theory of Knowledge*. London: NLB Humanities Press.

Goethe, J. W. v. (1988). *Scientific Studies*. New York: Suhrkamp.

Goethe, J. W. v. (1886). *Faust, A Tragedy*. London: Bell & Baldy.

Hacking, I. (1983). *Representing and Intervening*. Cambridge: Cambridge University Press.

Homans, P. (1979). *Jung in Context*. Chicago: University of Chicago Press.

James, W. (1983). A plea for psychology as a 'natural science'. *Essays in Psychology*. Cambridge, MA: Harvard University Press. (Original work published in 1892)

Jung, C. G. Unless otherwise stated, the following are from *The Collected Works of C. G. Jung* (CW) London: Routledge and Kegan Paul:

—— (1910). Morton Prince, 'The mechanism and interpretation of dreams': A critical review. (CW4)

—— (1914). On psychological understanding. (CW3)

—— (1921). Psychological types. (CW6)

—— (1929a). Commentary on 'The secret of the golden flower.' (CW13)

—— (1929b). General problems of psychotherapy. (CW16)

—— (1931). The practical use of dream-analysis. (CW16)

—— (1935). Foreword to von Koenig-Fachsenfeld: '*Wandlungen des traumproblems von der romantik eis zur gegenwart.*' (CW18)

—— (1936). Concerning the archetypes, with special reference to the anima concept. (CW9i)

—— (1939). Forward to Jung: *Phenomenes occultes*. (CW18)

—— (1947). *On the nature of the psyche*. (CW 8)
—— (1949). *Forward to Adler: Studies in analytical psychology*. (CW 18)
—— (1954). *Mysterium Coniunctionis*. (CW 14)
—— (1973a). *Letters, Vol. 1*. Princeton, NJ: Princeton University Press.
—— (1973b). *Letters, Vol. 2*. Princeton, NJ: Princeton University Press.
—— (1973c). *Memories, Dreams, Reflections* (Rev. ed.). New York: Pantheon Books.
Kuhn, B. H. (2009). *Autobiography and Natural Science in the Age of Romanticism: Rousseau, Goethe, Thoreau*. Farnham: Ashgate.
Latour, B. (1987). *Science in Action: How to Follow Scientists and Engineers Through Society*. Cambridge, MA: Harvard University Press.
Megill, A. (1994). *Rethinking Objectivity*. Durham, NC: Duke University Press.
Pickering, A. (1992). *Science as Practice and Culture*. Chicago: University of Chicago Press.
Porter, T. (1995). *Trust in Numbers: The Pursuit of Objectivity in Science and Public Life*. Princeton, NJ: Princeton University Press.
Robbins, B. D., & Holdrege, C. (Eds.) (2005). Goethe's delicate empiricism. *Janus Head*, 8.1. Available: www.janushead.org/8-1/index.cfm (retrieved 25 June 2012).
Rowland, H. (Ed.) (2001). *Goethe, Chaos, and Complexity*. Amsterdam: Rodopi.
Seamon, D., & Zajonc, A. (Eds.) (1998). *Goethe's Way of Science: A Phenomenology of Nature*. New York: State University of New York Press.
Shamdasani, S. (2003). *Jung and the Making of Modern Psychology: The Dream of a Science*. Cambridge: Cambridge University Press.
Sherry, J. (2010). *Carl Gustav Jung: Avant-garde Conservative*. New York: Palgrave Macmillan.
Stephenson, R. (2005). Binary synthesis: Goethe's aesthetic intuition in literature and science. *Science in Context*, 18: 553–8.

3

VICISSITUDES OF A SCIENCE-COMPLEX

Raya A. Jones

What is a science-complex?

On April 15, 2012, a Google search for 'science complex' yielded about 452,000 results in 0.18 seconds. I confess I didn't look further than two pages. The links referred to university buildings accommodating facilities for multiple sciences. For instance, Pennsylvania State University's Millennium Science Complex is 'home to the converging frontiers of engineering, materials research and the life sciences ... more than just a collection of laboratories and instruments', for it 'represents a new style of research in which experts from many disciplines coordinate their technologies and knowledge in ways that produce exponential advances'. This and similar instances convey a utopian community pooling expertise towards the common good. Psychologists were not mentioned. What universities call a Science Complex gives a concrete form to a deeply entrenched way of thinking about science. What I propose to call a science-complex is the dynamic interplay between the 'metanarrative' of science and 'local' (e.g. disciplinary) or personal narratives, whereby we relate to world and self through a relatedness to sciences.

I take my cue from Parker's (1994: 246) notion of a *discursive complex*, which has two aspects: a social aspect contained in the networks of discourses; and an individual-reflexivity aspect contained in the experiential dimension of language use whereby the discursive complex is 'tuned to the complex subjectivity'. In his idiom, 'complex subjectivity' refers to the way in which one's sense of agency is 'tangled up' in the 'particular dominant cultural forms pertaining to self-knowledge that circulate in society at the present time' (ibid.: 244). Likewise, a science-complex pertains to how the ways in which science is talked about and instituted in one's society interact with self-understanding. The spoken language plays a role. Wierzbicka (2011) comments that the English word 'science' does not have exact equivalents in other European languages. In her view, this conceptual artefact of modern English, which is saturated with British empiricism, creates a pressure on English speakers to regard the natural sciences as 'a paradigm of all knowledge' (ibid.: 31). Observing that Jung often described what he was doing as a *Wissenschaft* (usually translated as 'science'), Carter (2011) notes that the term has broader connotations in German than in English. *Wissenschaft* denotes an organized body of knowledge, which entails the gathering and ordering of material from which a logical thesis is derived. The English concept of science is closer to the German *Naturwissenschaften* (natural sciences). However, the issue I want to underline is – not whether Jung is undeservedly chastised for not doing scientific work when we should regard it as *wissenschaftlich* and belonging in the *Geisteswissenschaften* (lit., sciences of the spirit) – but the criteria which may make the Jungian body of knowledge relevant for us personally. It's about us, not him.

The definition of a science-complex can be elaborated in contradistinction with Jung's (1934: par. 201) definition of a 'feeling-toned complex' as an image of a subjective situation that is strongly accentuated emotionally, incompatible with the habitual attitude of the consciousness, and has a powerful inner coherence, its own wholeness, hence a relatively high degree of autonomy. A science-complex is not an image of a subjective situation. It is not emotionally accentuated since its social aspect is a normative metanarrative. Hence, in its individual-reflexivity aspect, it is compatible with the habitual attitude of consciousness. While it could be said to have its own dynamics, this autonomy reflects what we are 'in' (discursive practices) rather than what is 'in' us (an unconscious). This contrast differentiates my concept from the idea of a 'cultural complex' which draws a strict analogy with the Jungian definition: 'Cultural complexes can be defined as emotionally charged aggregates of ideas and images that tend to cluster around an archetypal core and are shared by individuals within an identified collective' (Singer 2010: 234). It doesn't make sense to me to speak of an archetypal core of a science-complex. It is merely an aggregate of ideas, images, and values clustering around 'science'. When strong affect is involved in defending or contesting the significance of science, we may talk of having a complex-about-science, in the colloquial sense of a hung-up or anxious preoccupation; but that's not a science-complex as the term is used here.

This chapter's premise may be outlined as follows. There are established criteria for what counts as the scientific method of the natural sciences. Since traditionally psychology has been positioned as a natural science, those criteria create certain expectancies regarding how psychological theories ought to be developed. Tensions and schisms within the discipline ensue from disparities between what psychologists may wish to investigate and how they are expected to go about it. The derivation and validation of analytical psychology doesn't meet those strict expectations. Instead, science enters the Jungian corpus in a variety of ways, spanning a range of attitudes from scientism to anti-science, which could be viewed as phenomena of a science-complex.

Is psychology a science?

Auguste Comte didn't think so. He spelled out the absurdity of the mind trying to observe itself, contending that psychologists 'have mistaken their own dreams for science', and relegated psychology to a prescientific stage (Comte 2009 [1830]: 33–4). According to Comte, each branch of knowledge undergoes three successive stages: 'the Theological, or fictitious; the Metaphysical, or abstract; the Scientific, or positive' (ibid.: 25). In the most primitive stage, the mind imagines supernatural beings causing natural phenomena. In the Metaphysical stage, those beings are replaced with 'abstract forces, veritable entities (that is, personified abstractions) inherent in all beings, and capable of producing all phenomena' (ibid.: 26). This characterization readily applies to classical psychoanalysis with its libidinal forces construed as causal mechanisms. It applies to the conception of archetypes as veritable personified abstractions inherent in all humans and producing all mental phenomena.

In Comte's final stage, the Scientific, the mind applies itself to the study of the laws of phenomena, describing their invariable relations of succession and resemblances. Psychology has traditionally aspired towards this positivist ideal. Comte's narrative reverberates in the discipline's historiography, implicitly, in the dissociation of scientific psychology not only from philosophy but also from psychoanalysis. Accordingly, answering 'Yes' to this section's title question means answering 'No' to the question of whether depth psychology is scientific.

Noting Comte's omission of psychology from the hierarchy of sciences, Coon (1992: 143) reflects that 'Psychology has never quite lived this down.' Towards establishing a place for psychology in the hierarchy, Simonton (2004) analysed the presence of several indicators of scientific status (theories-to-laws ratio, consultation rate, obsolescence rate, graph prominence, early impact rate, peer evaluation consensus, citation concentration, lecture disfluency, citation immediacy, anticipation frequency, age at receipt of Nobel Prize, and rated disciplinary hardness), averring that these measures allow us reliably to rank five disciplines in this order: physics, chemistry, biology, psychology, and sociology. His analysis, he claims, places psychology 'much closer to biology than to sociology, forming a pair of life sciences clearly separated from the other sciences' (ibid.: 59). There are other sets of indicators (e.g. Cole 1983). Laypersons – and probably most psychologists – are unlikely to employ such indicators in their judgements of psychology. Surveys cited by Lilienfeld (2011) indicate that sizeable percentages of the American general public regard psychology as lacking in scientific rigour and as less valuable to society than physics, business studies, medicine, and engineering. The situation is compounded by confusions about the different boundaries of psychologists, psychiatrists, psychoanalysts, and psychotherapists. Ironically, Lilienfeld's rebuttal of common misperceptions, published in *American Psychologist*, is unlikely to reach laypersons since they are not likely to read that journal.

Generally, three interwoven themes underpin psychologists' story of scientific psychology: (a) its *history*, which begins with the introduction of (b) an experimental *method* to (c) a *subject matter* that, in turn, is constrained by the method.

History

Psychology arguably has a long history as a natural science (or natural philosophy), given that philosophers following the Aristotelian tradition regarded the science of the mind as belonging to physics, i.e., the science of nature (Hatfield 1995). However, in the twentieth century, psychology became equated with quantitative experimental methodology, and this 'scientific' character was contrasted with the 'metaphysical' character of its earlier namesake (ibid.: 185).

Textbooks written by psychologists typically describe psychology as coming into being by virtue of its split from philosophy when Wundt opened the first laboratory in Leipzig in 1879. Between 1880 and 1920, American psychologists waged a battle against spiritualism and psychic research in their attempt to define boundaries for their new discipline (Coon 1992). William James (1892: 146) started his essay 'A Plea for Psychology as a "Natural Science"' with the contention that although psychology was 'hardly more than what physics was before Galileo . . . a mass of phenomenal description, gossip, and myth', it nonetheless included enough 'real material' to justify optimism about becoming 'worthy of the name of natural science at no very distant day'. At a distance of four decades, Lewin (1935: 22) admitted that the 'conquest over valuative, anthropomorphic classifications of phenomena . . . is not by any means complete', but still optimistically opined that the 'most important general circumstances which paved the way for Galilean concepts in physics are clearly and distinctly to be seen in present-day psychology'. To date, a Galilean revolution has not happened. Yet, as Coon (1992: 143) put it, psychology 'has never recovered from its adolescent physics envy'.

Although psychologists today seldom compare their science to physics, they tend to locate it within the natural sciences. Fuchs and Milar (2003) trace the origins of psychology to physiology (not philosophy) and its branching into psychophysics, and then through behaviourism to cognitive psychology. Any telling of a history is selective, but the particular story serves an agenda. Costall (2006: 635) exposes 'a comprehensive and highly persuasive myth' about the origins of scientific psychology. According to most textbooks, psychology began as the study of mind based on the introspective method (associated with Wundt's laboratory). In reaction to the unreliability of that method, behaviourism redefined psychology as the study of behaviour, based on experimentation. In reaction to the bankruptcy of behaviourism, the cognitive revolution restored the mind as the proper subject of psychology, but now with the benefit of the rigorous experimental and statistical methods developed by the behaviourists – a storyline that has the structure of Hegelian thesis-antithesis-synthesis. Revisiting the early literature, Costall demonstrates that all three stages of this history are largely fictional. Moreover, 'the inaccuracies and outright inventions of "textbook histories" are not just a question of carelessness. These fictional histories help convey the values of the discipline, and a sense of destiny' (ibid.: 635).

The psychoanalytic movement has been written out of that history, partly because it was perceived as unscientific, and partly because its own history was largely separate due to the institutional context of medical psychology. In the academia, the vested interests of influential professors played a key role in the designation of experimental psychology to the natural sciences (Kusch 1995).

Wilhelm Dilthey was central in the administrative organization. According to Scanlon (1989), Dilthey maintained that psychology belonged in the humanities because it concerns inner experience. Dilthey contrasted the 'outer' experience of nature (presented as phenomenal and in isolated data) with the inner experience of psychic life, which is holistically presented as a living active reality. He argued that this difference requires different methods. Others at the time were advocating the description of all experience in a way that scrupulously avoided all subjective language. Dilthey contended that for psychology to imitate a method that was successful in the natural sciences would involve treating an interconnected whole as if it were merely an assemblage of discrete entities, and, moreover, 'neglecting the lived sense of dynamic striving for intrinsically posited goals in favour of a non-teleological, hypothetico-deductive system' (ibid.: 349). For most of the twentieth century, this line of argument lost out in university departments.

Method

For most if not all psychologists, it is primarily how psychology is 'done' that makes it different from other disciplines. To some, not just any methodology, but specifically the hypothetico-deductive method makes it a science. Not all psychologists accept its constraints or strictly adhere to it in practice, but historically this ideal – disparaged by postmodernists as the 'master myth of current psychological science' which allows only one voice and privileges the 'experimental story' (Mair 1988: 133) – has dominated the discipline. The hypothetico-deductive method was proposed by William Whewell in the nineteenth century, though Popper (1958) gave it its best-known exposition. In the 1930s, Popper contested the then-prevalent viewpoint associated with logical positivism, which regarded inductive reasoning as the basis for scientific inquiries. Induction proceeds from an initial explanation of some observations to its confirmation by collecting further empirical examples. This can be seen in the progression from Jung's explanation of the 'regularities' he observed in dreams, delusions, visions, myths, etc., by postulating the collective unconscious to observing more of the same, taken as confirming his theory. Popper pointed to the theories of Marx, Freud, and Adler in this vein (Grant & Harari 2005). Grant and Harari rebut Popper's dismissal of Freudian theory by reminding that Freud revised some aspects of his theory. However, they miss the point. Changing one's mind is not the same as submitting a theory in which one believes to rigorous scrutiny. Deduction proceeds from some initial premise to predicting what else must be true if it is. The tentative theory generates specific predictions, ideally formulated in a way that allows for their falsification.

Critics of Popper have pointed out that scientific discoveries might be contingent on flukes of history, political and economic circumstances that favour particular directions of research, and scientists' own motives (e.g. Feyerabend 1993). On the one side, this line of argument conflates a prescription of how developing a scientific theory ought to progress (Popper) with a description of how theories really come about. On the other, it acknowledges that there is more to 'science' than the method. Lakatos places the methodology within a general structure of research programmes. In his definition, a research programme is a field – i.e., a specialism within a given science – that has a 'conventionally accepted (and thus by provisional decision "irrefutable") "*hard core*"' or metatheory; and a '*positive heuristic*', a guiding principle that dictates the choice of scientific problems, i.e., issues to investigate (Lakatos 1970: 99). If we imagine a research programme centred on Jungian archetypes, the metatheory could be the idea of a collective unconscious. The positive heuristic would dictate problems such as cataloguing archetypes, identifying their manifestations, conditions for occurrence, and so on. A research programme thrives as long as the core continues to generate new problems to investigate (a progressive problem-shift). When researchers mostly churn old issues in new guises (a regressive problem-shift), the programme eventually degenerates. Lakatos postulated also a negative heuristic, which prevents scientists from directing the modus tollens at the hard core. Instead, they formulate auxiliary hypotheses that form a protective belt around the core, and redirect the modus tollens to those. If the archetypes specialism were strictly a research programme, scholars would not only present differing reformulations of Jung's concept (as analysts already do) but also test hypotheses designed to eliminate rival explanations in favour of their own – all the while, not challenging the metatheory, but indeed protecting it by seeking to get its facts correctly.

The hypothetico-deductive method is as near objective as possible to get, given the subjectivity of believing in some hard-core metatheory, but not all topics in psychology lend themselves to this method. This creates a cognitive dissonance and a dilemma. The pressure to demonstrate objectivity sometimes results in circumventing it. A common practice is to have two or more trained people rate observational data in accordance with the researchers' criteria (inter-rater reliability). Kline (1983) pointed out the absurdity of 'blind analysis', in which responses to projective tests (such as the Rorschach) are scored by judges who have no knowledge of the person: high agreement among the scorers doesn't mean that they are correct about what the associations mean uniquely for that person. Jung (1954) brings a different slant on objectivity. Acknowledging that psychology, as a modern science, strives to describe the psyche objectively, he maintains that (analytical) psychology is more objective because it is premised on the inescapability of our subjectivity. The conundrum of the mind observing itself is inherent in psychology, for sure; but Jung makes a bolder claim: 'every science is a function of the psyche, and all knowledge is rooted in it' (ibid.: par. 357). In this rhetorical move, he appears to upturn Comte's hierarchy, placing psychology at the pinnacle. Blanchard (1918) took it a step further: she applied Jung's theory of the psychological types in her case study of Comte, attributing his attitude to psychology to his own personality. Before revelling in this one-upmanship, it's worth noting that if we claim (with Jung) that theorists' attitude-types play a formative role in their intellectual pursuits, we must accept the typology as validated, not a figment of Jung's imagination.

Positivist psychology is concerned with predicting behaviour *a posteriori*. To give an oversimplified illustration, knowing how introverts versus extroverts behave (based on robust research showing consistent individual differences) allows a 'prediction' of someone's personality (based on information about their behaviour) which may correlate with other variables. We don't need to go outside the theory that everyone can be ranked on a continuum between extraversion and introversion. A likely biological basis explains the existence of these differences (Eysenck 1967). In contrast, Jung's typology builds upon an *a priori* hunch that everyone has both extrovert and introvert sides, and individuals differ in terms of which side is their dominant side. This theory is difficult to confirm since observations of behavioural differences such as supporting Eysenck's theory show only people's dominant type. The hidden side remains a conjecture unless it is demonstrated that certain 'regularities' in extroverts' behaviour or attitudes can be understood *only* by assuming that they have an introvert inner side, and vice versa. Back in my student days, a classmate who scored highly on the extraversion scale of the Eysenck Personality Questionnaire complained that it conflicted with her experience of herself as very shy. She was always the first to break the ice with strangers or to liven up a party because (she explained) this was how she coped with those unbearably awkward situations. To go from this anecdote to validating Jung's hunch requires finding out how common are self-experiences such as hers. Such evidence would arguably be a step towards an objective description. A separate question is what would be the point. If we are interested primarily in how people make sense of their experiences, my classmate's self-narrative might be more relevant than any statistics.

The crux of the matter, then, is what psychology is about, in one's view. Noting that 'there is only one science of mathematics, of geology, zoology, botany and so forth', Jung (1931a: par. 659) remarked how curious it was that 'there is not one modern psychology – there are dozens'. We can add 'dozens' of postmodern psychologies to the plurality. The 1980s' Interpretive Turn in the social sciences has been associated with strong criticisms regarding the applicability of the hypothetico-deductive methodology in psychology, but a most telling comment comes from a leading cognitive scientist defending his discipline against two 'adversaries', neuroscience and the postmodernist critique:

> The activity that dominates cognitive psychology today is not empirical exploration but something quite different: namely, the making and testing of hypothetical models. . . . The aim of the research is not to discover any secret of nature; it is to devise models that fit a certain range of laboratory data better than their competitors do.
> (Neisser 1997: 248)

This seems to me hardly an ideal towards which a psychology concerned with human life as lived by human beings should aspire.

Subject matter

Although the discipline's subject matter is encapsulated in the definition of psychology as the science of mind and behaviour, a coherent integrative framework has never emerged. The positivist standpoint engendered unification proposals in response to what was construed as a 'crisis of disunity', whereas the post-positivistic standpoint has recognized pluralism as beneficial, though with the caveat that it might result in fragmentation (Healy 2012: 273). Neither standpoint has offered to include psychoanalysis.

While the nascent psychosocial movement in UK universities pivots on a rediscovery of Freud (see, e.g., Frosh & Baraitser 2008), it dismisses traditional psychological science as inappropriate to the study of subjectivity. A convergent sentiment underpins Jung's (1946: par. 170) claim that analytical psychology 'differs from experimental psychology in that it does not attempt to isolate individual functions . . . and then subject them to experimental conditions', because it is 'far more concerned with the total manifestation of the psyche as a natural phenomenon'. This clearly echoes Dilthey's reasoning about psychology (cf. Scanlon 1989). Given Jung's milieu, however, he understandably sought to place his brand of medical psychology within the natural sciences.

Jung's early theory of the complexes accorded well with the experimental psychology of the day (Shamdasani 2003). It fell out of favour partly due to Jung's move into what was vilified as a 'mystical psychology'. Using that label, Allen (1942: 622) applauded Jung's complexes theory as 'scientific as any made before or since' in psychiatry, but reflected that subsequently Jung 'abandoned his clinical work and most unfortunately started upon the study of religions and myths', leading to the 1912 monograph in which he has 'forsaken science for religion'. Nonetheless, psychiatrists could have retained his pre-1912 theory. Another reason for dismissing it was a changing view regarding mental organization. Rapaport (1951) noted that Jung's notion of autonomous complexes was untenable since the thought-process had come to be understood as integral and indivisible. This felt like progress in the field. Progress is the hallmark of a science. But what may count as progress in understanding human experience? The Four Noble Truths stated by the Buddha 2,500 years ago have not lost their truthfulness.

Since its inception as a science, psychology seems to be in a permanent crisis – so much so, that a history-of-science journal devoted a recent Special Issue to crisis discussions in psychology. Its editors, Sturm and Mülberger (2012: 430) conclude, 'Psychology has no one single persistent problem, perhaps not even a clearly definable set of such problems.' Psychologists have long debated which of the different descriptions of scientific progress provided by Popper, Kuhn, and Lakatos is most applicable to psychology. Yet, crises in psychology do not centre solely or even primarily on problems in the relationship of theory to data (Kuhn's condition for a paradigm shift), nor unanimously concern the lack of unity in the field.

Furthermore, I'd like to add, the rhetoric of 'paradigm shifts' positions psychology as a science *in the singular* – and yet none of these paradigms has entirely wiped out previous ones. They continue to evolve in parallel. An unpalatable alternative would describe a succession of intellectual fads which, like art movements, express different timely sensitivities and different aesthetics. On the gloomy side, it may be wondered whether anything has improved since Comte (2009 [1830]: 33) averred that 'After two thousand years of psychological pursuit, no one proposition is established to the satisfaction of its followers.'

Another way of looking at it is to understand psychology, with Foucauldian scholars, as a culturally and historically situated movement, a *psy-complex*: a 'sprawling speculative and regulative network of theories and practices that constitute psychology . . . all that pertains to the individual, self-monitoring subject and the many practices that subjects employ to survey and improve themselves' (Parker 1994: 246). In this view, psychology transpires as primarily a craft or a 'technology of the self' – a set of techniques which permit individuals to 'effect, by their own means, a certain number of operations' on their own bodies, souls, thoughts, and conduct, and doing it so as to 'transform themselves, modify themselves, and to attain a certain state of perfection, of happiness, of purity, of supernatural power, and so on' (Foucault 1993: 203). The fact that technologies-of-the-self developed within the psy-complex preclude goals such as supernatural powers reflects how a science-complex has us.

How does a science-complex have us?

Our autonomous '*complexes can have us*', averred Jung (1934: par. 200). A science-complex similarly has *us*, our conscious attitude. It has everyone who lives in the modern world, even people who are indifferent or oblivious to debates about science, psychology, or Jung. As Max Weber (1946 [1918]: 155) put it, 'The fate of our times is characterized by rationalization and intellectualization and, above all, by the "disenchantment of the world".'

It is still our fate nearly a century later. I believe that photons exist and pixies don't. A consciousness which 'sees' photons but not pixies is a product of a particular form of life, in Wittgenstein's sense of the phrase. Philosophers have debated what exactly he meant; but at bottom, the phrase means a tacit agreement in how 'we size up and respond to what we encounter' (Baker 1984: 278). Weber reflected that science and technology have not enhanced our knowledge of the conditions under which we live. On the contrary, reliance on technology accentuates our alienation in everyday life:

> Unless he is a physicist, one who rides on the streetcar has no idea how the car happened to get into motion. . . . He is satisfied that he may 'count' on the behavior of the streetcar, and he orients his conduct according to this expectation.
>
> (Weber 1946 [1918]: 139)

I want to emphasize the blind faith in technology that his example implies, and to extend it to faith in technologies of the self. Jung (1931a: par. 658) disagreed with all other psychologies, contending that analytical psychology – because it is a 'psychology *with* the psyche' (i.e. centred on the unconscious) – can never be a modern psychology, since 'all modern "psychologies without the psyche" are psychologies of consciousness, for which an unconscious psychic life simply does not exist'. Yet, the psychology-with-the-psyche does not merely state that an unconscious exists. It also posits that its existence can be demonstrated through observations of its effects on concrete human productions. In this sense, Jung's psychology *is* a modern psychology. Although modern (and postmodern) psychologies differ in terms of their ontologies, epistemologies, and methodologies, all of them size up and respond to phenomena of human experience in a similar manner. They all involve some putatively objective system for analysing those phenomena. It is 'not an agreement in opinions but in form of life' (Wittgenstein 1953: §241).

We could speak also of a Jungian form of life. Stakeholders in 'Jung' include clinical practitioners and their patients, Jung fans generally, and scholars from diverse disciplines, all of whom agree in sizing up Jung as important, although they may disagree in what they take from him. A science-complex has these stakeholders in a variety of ways, most conspicuously in forms of scientism. There are several definitions of scientism; but in the present context, it means an exaggerated trust in the sciences. It enters the Jungian form of life in four discrete ways, described below.

(1) Hermeneutics of amplification

Ricoeur (1970) distinguished a hermeneutics of suspicion from a hermeneutics of faith. Whereas a hermeneutics of suspicion (found in Marx, Nietzsche, and Freud) centres on decoding disguised meanings, the hermeneutics of faith (historically applied in Bible studies) centres on restoring a meaning to texts so as to hear their message correctly. Fredericksen (2010) has commented that Jungians tend to apply a hermeneutics of amplification. As extrapolated here, this is an interpretative stance that seeks not only to hear Jung's message correctly but also to bolster up its meaningfulness by reference to scientific knowledge.

A science-complex invariably has us when we try to map the psyche-as-described-by-Jung onto the 'disenchanted' world that the sciences describe, and the validity of which we do not query. As a form of scientism, amplification-by-science manifests in the use of alleged expertise elsewhere to lend weight to Jungian claims, often in allusions to nonspecific scientific knowledge and statements that are generally valid but unrelated to the specific claims being made. For example, Stevens (1999: 56) informs that 'research in child development over the last 30 years has endorsed that the human infant is no blank slate', and that this makes the existence of innate archetypes possible. He does not cite any developmental research, nor mention the most influential thinkers in child development, Piaget and Vygotsky, both of whom (and therefore the majority of developmental research since the 1960s) have described how the mind develops from virtually a blank slate at birth to the sophisticated reasoning of which our species is capable. While evolutionary psychologists postulate innate cognitive structures dedicated to solving a restricted class of survival problems, there is a fundamental disparity between the neo-Darwinian understanding of mental modularity and the archetypal architecture assumed by Jung (Jones 2003).

Applying a hermeneutic of suspicion, an interpretative stance that unmasks and exposes what lies behind Jungian claims, might seem hostile and therefore incompatible with the Jungian form of life. However, there is also a hermeneutic of doubt, a stance that is 'suspicious' of the claims one wishes to support, and seeks to validate them by systematically putting them to the test. In modern psychology, modelled after the natural sciences, specific theories build upon practices that could be labelled the 'ritual' of the scientific method. In postmodern psychology, remodelled as a social science, a hermeneutics of doubt is often enacted in what Shotter and Lannamann (2001) called the ritual of theory-criticism-and-debate. Either way, there is no final word. There are only empirical findings, logical formulations, theories or critiques that haven't been overturned yet. Participating in the ritual is prerequisite to membership in the intellectual community as someone who contributes to its body of knowledge. It is difficult to spot a similar tradition of applying hermeneutics of doubt within the Jungian community.

Nevertheless, works by Joe Cambray, Jean Knox, George Hogenson, and others – whose reformulations draw upon neuroscience, dynamical systems theory, cognitive psychology, and more – transcend the scientism inherent in the hermeneutics of amplification by engaging with *specific* ideas advanced elsewhere in ways that take analytical psychology forward. For example, Cambray (2006) considers, inter alia, Damasio's research on neural body maps towards articulating his own description of the experience of feelings as an emergent process deriving from phase transitions in the brain's body mapping states.

(2) Readerly dynamics

Phelan (2006) drew a distinction between textual dynamics, referring to how something is being told, and readerly dynamics, to do with the reader's reception of the telling. Focusing on the reader's experience, Barthes (1990 [1973]) distinguished between a readerly text, which imposes a meaning on the reader through its representational content (e.g. the traditional novel), and a writerly text, the meaning of which is constructed by the reader; in effect, the reader becomes the writer. Any dissemination of a research study or a theory is inevitably a readerly text (although Jung's writings often function as a writerly text). The form of scientism highlighted here operates through forcing a reader into blind faith in the scientific acuity of the writer's claims.

This form is conspicuous in the application of quantum physics to explain synchronicity, a 'specialism' that takes its cue from the Jung and Pauli collaboration. Unless we are physicists, the text dazzles us with the weirdness of quantum mechanics and perplexes us with mathematical proofs we cannot penetrate. For example, Martin et al. (2009), two of whom are physicists, propose to treat mental states as quantum states, definable as vectors of a Hilbert space (a mathematical concept), towards studying the analogy between synchronistic events and 'quantum entanglement'. Their theory might have merit, but my difficulty starts at the leap of logic that their analogy entails.

My grasp of the key concept is limited to how physicists *without a Jungian agenda* define it:

> Quantum entanglement occurs when particles such as photons, electrons, molecules . . . interact physically and then become separated; the type of interaction is such that each resulting member of a pair is properly described by the same quantum mechanical description (state), which is indefinite in terms of important factors such as position, momentum, spin, polarization, etc.
>
> (Kumar et al. 2012: 1)

According to Kumar et al.'s summative description, entanglement usually requires a direct interaction between two particles at some point. A recent 'entanglement swapping' experiment in Geneva demonstrated entanglement between quantum systems that never directly interacted. But it involved particles of the same kind (photons), and is presumably replicable. If the demonstration can't be repeated, we'd suspect that the original study was either flawed or a hoax. None of those criteria is applicable to the unrepeatable coincidence of a beetle trying to enter Jung's consultation room at the precise moment that a patient was telling him about a dream in which she was given a scarab (Jung 1952: par. 843). The compulsion to explain psychology through physics is a way in which a science-complex has us.

Amazing coincidences happen, but the connecting principle that best explains the significance of synchronous events is the mind's capacity to see connections between empirical concretes and to give them significance (see Hunt 2012 for an exposition in this vein). Someone I once met woke up one day with a dream of being stung by a bee, and subsequently agonized about its meaning. She wondered whether her unconscious was telling her that she was too harsh ('stingy') with her children. Then she was stung by a bee. If I stopped telling the story at this point, it might become an urban legend about precognition in dreams. You need to know that it happened in a summer camp in the countryside. The dream might have expressed a realistic worry about the bees buzzing around.

(3) Methods without Method

This form is a different case of being 'blinded by science'. Here scientism manifests as methodological rigour without applying the scientific method. This Method is not simply the use of experimental and statistical methods, but entails a protracted sequence of questioning within a research programme. Since Jung's experiments with the Word Associations Test more than a century ago, there have been only sporadic, disconnected instances of applying experimental methods vis-à-vis Jungian hypotheses. Without a tradition of critical reflexivity in the field, those instances tend to be uncritically accepted by Jungians who lack a scientific-psychological background (a readerly-dynamics effect).

The Archetypal Symbol Inventory (ASI) is high on the scale of contributions to analytical psychology by reputable scholars, but it evinces the problem highlighted at this juncture. Rosen et al. (1991) purport to have eliminated cultural specificity in their development of the ASI, which consists of forty picture-word pairs validated as universal on the basis of response accuracy by university students in Texas. The writers conclude that the ASI is 'truly an inventory of archetypal (universal) symbols related to the collective unconscious,' because their experiments have revealed that the 'correct' (their word) meanings of these archetypal symbols are not consciously known, and unconscious associations influence the recall of symbol/word pairs (ibid.: 223). Their bottom-line inference is that 'this supports Jung's theory of the collective unconscious and the idea that it contains ancient memory traces embedded in archetypes' (ibid.). Yet, some of those associations are plainly culturally specific. For instance, the ASI pairs a picture of the sun with the word 'masculine' and a picture of the moon with 'feminine'. If that's the *correct* answer, Israelis would fail hopelessly. In Hebrew (which doesn't have gender-neutral nouns), the two words for sun are feminine; two out of the three words for the moon are masculine. There are other languages in which the gender of the sun and moon reverses the ASI designations.

The problem is partly 'technical', easily addressed, since the procedures used by Rosen et al. can be carried out around the world with indigenous samples. Researchers may test auxiliary hypotheses such as, 'if sun-masculine is a universal association, then there will be no occurrences of sun-feminine anywhere'. An instance such as the Hebrew language suffices to falsify the hypothesis. However, even if the universality of particular associations is reliably confirmed, the finding couldn't support the inference of ancient memory traces. Such inference confuses universality for innateness, and fails to consider the likelihood that universality simply indicates typical experience. For example, cognitive-psychologists' experiments cited by Moss and Wilson (2010) reveal that people tend to associate morality and authority with elevated locations in space; e.g., names appearing towards the top of a screen or page are perceived as more moral; leaders located considerably higher in an organizational chart are seen as more powerful; a stranger appearing high in a vertical space is more readily assumed to believe in God. Such associations are irrational and automatic, unconsciously made. Moss and Wilson reflect that since young children are subordinate to adults, who are taller, they tend to see the moral code as emanating from a source elevated in space. Over time, this embodied experience leads to associations which also permeate cultural practices, beliefs (e.g. the locations of heaven and hell), and language.

To eliminate rival explanations ideally requires experiments of some sort. Proceeding in this manner would conform to the scientific method, but carries the risk of ending up eliminating the theory of innate archetypes. Insofar as Jungian researchers are not prepared to risk refutation, and seek only confirmation – resting their case on induction – the finest deployment of rigorous procedures and statistical testing remains a case of scientism. To be clear, I'm not 'pushing' for Jungians to emulate the natural-scientific model of modern psychology (only that those impelled to do so should get it right). I am more enthused by the confluence of Jung's work with postmodern psychology (Jones 2007), and am sceptical about what a 'scientification' of analytical psychology could achieve.

It is because analytical psychology is *not* about the making and testing of hypothetical models that the scientism of methods-without-Method matters. Biases which remain unchecked in state-of-the-art Jungian scholarship become a dogma transferred onto 'lay' practitioners and their customers, for whom Jung *is* Science, as the following vignette illustrates. According to her website (www.jungsoul.com), artist Michelle Christides dispenses 'an effective telephone coaching for Westerners to integrate global spiritual traditions with Science through the classic Jungian method of dream and other archetypal interpretation'. She provides this 'Jungian Mentoring' on the strength of her two years personal analysis with a (named) analyst in Zurich, who has written a 'letter of approval' for her 'to practice the classic Jungian method', and who herself, the analyst, had been trained by a (named) co-founder of the C. G. Jung Institute. My imagination was fired by a fantasy of arcane knowledge passed on from master to disciple in dojo-like consultation rooms, so different from the *en masse* delivery of academic knowledge in lecture theatres. The website includes a Jungian Archetypes Test, which involves naming your favourite animal, tree, colour, etc., and reflecting upon your answer. There is a Key to Symbolism. For example, 'Describe what you would do in a white room if you could do anything or bring anything into it you want.' The Key informs that what you'd do is your attitude toward marriage. The association was incomprehensible to me. Intrigued, I turned to Google and discovered that White Room is a name for bridal-wear boutiques in the USA, UK, and some other (Christian) countries. Running Google in Hebrew yielded nothing similar in Israel, where I grew up. There must be some symbolism I've never acquired, for it doesn't exist in the milieu of my upbringing.

Presumably, Christides obtained the materials from a source she regarded as reliable. Like Weber's streetcar rider, she and her clients must count on the 'classical Jungian method' to work, and they orient their conduct accordingly. If I weren't so cynical, I'd have believed that Science knows the intimate symbolism of my unconscious without knowing *me*. I might have contemplated the state of my marriage in the light of what I imagined doing in the white room and consequently changed my conduct. Through the commodification of Jung, claims that are received as scientific truths impact upon their consumers in real ways, altering what Foucault called 'care of the self' – a certain way of attending to what takes place in our thought, which involves actions or practices exercised by the self on the self, whereby one takes responsibility for oneself and 'changes, purifies, transforms, and transfigures oneself' (O'Sullivan 2010: 54).

(4) Science as a 'generalized other'

Coined by Mead (1934: 195), the term *generalized other* refers to individuals' notion of what is commonly expected from them, an 'organized and generalized attitude' against which one gauges one's own conduct. Similarly, science serves as a kind of 'other' which provides a reference point for defining the Jungian movement. This could be classed as a form of scientism because only science seems to serve this function, out of the culture spheres (conventionally, after Weber: science, morality, art; Schrag, 1997, adds religion).

Depending on viewpoint, the Jungian body of knowledge is variously construed as commensurable with the sciences, as itself scientific, or as diametrically opposed and preferable to Science. The latter is an attitude of anti-science, which could be viewed as the shadow side of scientism. At worst, anti-science demonizes Science in sweeping condemnations portraying it as the nemesis of authenticity, wholeness, and therefore healing. Some works may make a contribution to analytical psychology in their own right, but are vague or ignorant about the scientific knowledge they regard as inimical to the soul (a reversal of the hermeneutics of amplification). I mention it here in passing mainly to note that the same modern *mythos* – according to which, Science is the embodiment of *logos* and is therefore mythless – operates in both scientism and anti-science.

This mythos pivots on the Enlightenment construal of knowledge as organized in oppositions. Seidman (1994: 13) lists 'science/rhetoric, science/politics, science/literature, and science/narrative', where science represents true knowledge, based on reason and fact, whereas its opposites belong in 'the realm of the imagination, feelings, and values'. These binaries are viewed as mutually exclusive: thinking/feeling, rationality/irrationality, intellect/heart . . . 'The utterances of the heart – unlike those of the discriminating intellect – always relate to the whole', says Jung (1932: par. 1719), asserting that 'What the heart hears are the great, all-embracing things of life, the experiences which we do not arrange ourselves but which happen to us.' Presented with these two options, the Jungian mind-set opts for the heart.

Does Jung need science in the twenty-first century?

I was heartened to discover a paper titled 'Carl Jung in the Twenty-first Century' by Carter (2011). He succinctly and intelligently summarizes the basics. However, it is the same old Jung, reloaded for people who haven't yet heard of him in the 2010s. To demonstrate a present-day relevance, Carter points to an 'ongoing' debate surrounding the anima/animus, and cites works that Hillman and Samuels published in the 1980s. Most of my current students were born in the 1990s. What can Jung offer them? This is not a rhetorical question. The fact that gender issues still matter doesn't automatically mean that notions of anima/animus have anything to contribute.

My students who came of age in the 2000s have not known a world without mobile phones or the internet. There is a burgeoning body of research investigating how the social media may alter the construction of identities. Yet, since such research centres on individualization, it might be deemed as irrelevant to the Jungian focus on individuation (but see Roesler 2008; Farah 2010). The convergent rise of information technology, biotechnology, genetic engineering, nanotechnology, AI, and robotics has generated lively debates concerning a posthuman condition – debates centring on whether a near-future creation of humans with machine parts, genetically enhanced bodies, or machines with human or superhuman intelligence, will dehumanize or enhance humanness (Wilson and Haslam 2009). In contrast, Jungianism is oriented towards the distant ancestral past: 'every civilized human being . . . is still an archaic man at the deeper levels of his psyche' (Jung 1931b: par. 105). Will cyborgs retain the archaic man? Will the posthuman generations still seek individuation? We have no idea. Our descendants won't find out for decades. To place Jung 'in' the twenty-first century might be premature, because anyone old enough to publish about Jung is a twentieth-century person.

'"For me," the elder analyst said, "Jung's greatest contribution to psychology was the discovery of an inner world."' With these words, Stein (2005: 1) opens his incisive paper on individuation as inner work. Whereas the practitioner position pertains to a *process* described by Jung, the 'popular' appeal of Jung often lies in the promise of a scientific account of what the *content* of our dreams, etc., reveal about us. Both stances reflect the nature of analytical psychology as part of an early-twentieth-century movement whereby the human subject became understood as 'characterized by inner diffuseness', and as able to 'organize or structure the inner, personal, and private dimension of his experience of the contemporary world *only through psychology*' (Homans 1995: 5; my italics). Later, the postmodernists redescribed the human subject as characterized by narrativity: 'a storyteller who both finds herself in stories already told and strives for a self-constitution by emplotting herself in stories in the making' (Schrag 1997: 26). This has led to the emergence of post-psychological therapies (McLeod 2006) which posit narrative performativity as antithetical to the psychologism of psychoanalytical practices – including Jungian 'inner work' – and conceptualize the therapeutic process in terms of effecting a change in clients by altering their problem-saturated self-narratives.

Nowadays, however, neuroscience increasingly tells us about our subjective states, sociality and empathy. Jung needs Science in order to survive in the Age of the Brain: 'we Jungians cannot go on basing our theory of archetypes on scientific assumptions which have been falsified . . . It is important that we stop arguing that archetypes are transmitted genetically if we want to be taken seriously' (Roesler 2012: 234). That's not the same as saying that analytical psychology must be a science.

Jung makes sense to me when reading his work as akin to the social sciences (see Hunt 2012 for a similar standpoint). Neither Jung's 'collective unconscious' nor Emile Durkheim's 'collective mind' are falsifiable hypotheses, on the one hand, or purely interpretive, on the other. Each concept serves a function within a systematic description of human life. Such concepts should be judged, not in terms of their veracity but in terms of verisimilitude. That is, instead of asking whether it is true that a collective unconscious exists in the psyche (in the way that it's true that a liver, spleen, etc., exist in the body) we should ask how well this concept conveys some aspect of reality as lived by human beings. Examining Jungian concepts in terms of their verisimilitude implicitly redescribes them as philosophical 'facts'. According to Kusch (1995), a specific argument, idea, concept, or theory, starts as barely more than a wild speculation, gradually gains acceptance, and becomes a philosophical 'fact' when it is widely cited in textbooks and is taken for granted as having a particular meaning.

Extrapolating that trajectory here, few if any of Jung's concepts seem to have achieved the status of such facts. The verisimilitude criterion also repositions Jung's work as a web of concepts that has the 'flavour' of a metanarrative. Metanarratives presuppose an ahistorical, Archimedean standpoint, from which the human mind, society, etc., can be understood (Lyotard 1980). Lyotard defined the postmodern era as characterized by incredulity toward metanarratives. Jung's work has not lost its potency for those persuaded by it, but it is nested within metanarratives that have been subjected to scepticism. For some who find a deeper meaning in Jung, his web of concepts may indeed compensate for the declining power of the 'grand narratives' of modernity.

The postmodern condition identified by Lyotard in the 1970s might be already a thing of the past or at least localized to intellectual enclaves, given the power that metanarratives of neuroscience and religious fundamentalism currently have. Nevertheless, the distinction that he drew between the pragmatics of scientific knowing and narrative knowing is still valid. While Lyotard's distinction pertains to how knowledge develops at the level of society, Bruner (1986) applied a similar distinction to the ways in which human minds make sense of the world. He postulated two modes of thought, a 'paradigmatic' (logico-scientific) and 'narrative', which are both fundamental and irreducible to each other. The paradigmatic mode is concerned with categorization, internal connections or logical relationships, and absolute truths. The narrative mode is concerned with personal and social ramifications of events and relationships, strives to establish and affirm consensual meanings, and consists of organizing and evaluating the vicissitudes of experience.

A switch to the narrative mode in the present context implicates not only a reclassification of the Jungian body of knowledge but also a change in our own stance. The 'problem' with Jung might be a consequence of conflating the two modes. Jung's narrative feels as true to some because it sounds like a scientific theory, and feels as false or phoney to others because it only *sounds* like that. Either way, the judgement constructs the 'Jung versus Science' debate with the connotation of the 'versus' as adversarial, where only one side tells the truth. Alternatively, regarding the 'versus' as comparative, the debate becomes a discussion in which 'Jung' is compared and contrasted with 'science'. Instead of pinning the merit of Jung's legacy on categorical judgements of its scientific status, the evaluation would be contingent on its relevance for particular purposes. That is, instead of asking is it scientific or unscientific, we should ask what is its purpose, for whom and in what context it serves specific purposes, and whether these would be served by the scientific method.

References

Allen, C. (1942). A mystical psychology. *Nature*, 149: 622–3.
Baker, L. R. (1984). On the very idea of a form of life. *Inquiry*, 27: 277–89.
Barthes, R. (1990). *S/Z*. Oxford: Blackwell. (Original work published in 1973)
Blanchard, P. (1918). A psycho-analytic study of Auguste Comte. *American Journal of Psychology*, 29: 159–81.
Bruner, J. S. (1986). *Actual Minds, Possible Worlds*. Cambridge, MA: Harvard University Press.
Cambray, J. (2006). Towards the feeling of emergence. *Journal of Analytical Psychology*, 51: 1–20.
Carter, D. (2011). Carl Jung in the twenty-first century. *Contemporary Review*, 293: 441–52.
Cole, S. (1983). The hierarchy of the sciences? *American Journal of Sociology*, 89: 111–39.
Comte, A. (2009). *The Positive Philosophy of Auguste Comte*, Vol. I. New York: Cosimo. (Original work published in 1830)
Coon, D. J. (1992). Testing the limits of sense and science: American experimental psychologists combat spiritualism, 1880–1920. *American Psychologist*, 47: 143–51.
Costall, A. (2006). 'Introspectionism' and the mythical origins of scientific psychology. *Consciousness and Cognition*, 15: 634–54.
Eysenck, H. J. (1967). *The Biological Basis of Personality*. Springfield, IL: Thomas Publishing.
Farah, R. M. (2010). The body in the postmodern world: A Jungian approach. In Jones, R. A. (Ed.) *Body, Mind and Healing after Jung: A Space of Questions*. London: Routledge.
Feyerabend, P. (1993). *Against Method* (3rd ed.). London: Verso.
Foucault, M. (1993). About the beginning of the Hermeneutics of the Self: Two lectures at Dartmouth. *Political Theory*, 21: 198–227.
Fredericksen, D. (2010). Arguments in favour of a Jungian hermeneutic of suspicion. In Stein, M. & Jones, R. A. (Eds.) *Cultures and Identities in Transition*. London: Routledge.
Frosh, S. & Baraitser, L. (2008). Psychoanalysis and psychosocial studies. *Psychoanalysis, Culture & Society*, 13: 346–65.
Fuchs, A. H. & Milar, K. S. (2003). Psychology as a science. In Freedheim, D. K. & Weiner, I. B. (Eds.) *Handbook of Psychology: Volume 1, History of Psychology*. New York: Wiley.
Grant, D. C. & Harari, E. (2005). Psychoanalysis, science and the seductive theory of Karl Popper. *Australian and New Zealand Journal of Psychiatry*, 39: 446–52.
Hatfield, G. (1995). Remaking the science of mind: Psychology as natural science. In Fox, C., Porter, R. & Wokler, R. (Eds.) *Inventing Human Science*. Berkeley: University of California Press.
Healy, P. (2012). Toward an integrative, pluralistic psychology: On the hermeneutico-dialogical conditions of the possibility for overcoming fragmentation. *New Ideas in Psychology*, 30: 271–80.
Homans, P. (1995). *Jung in Context*. Chicago, IL: The University of Chicago Press.

Hunt, H. T. (2012). A collective unconscious reconsidered: Jung's archetypal imagination in the light of contemporary psychology and social science. *Journal of Analytical Psychology*, 57: 76–98.

James, W. (1892). A plea for psychology as a 'natural science'. *Philosophical Review*, 1: 146–53.

Jones, R. A. (2003). On innatism: A response to Hogenson. *Journal of Analytical Psychology*, 48: 705–18.

—— (2007). *Jung, Psychology, Postmodernity*. London: Routledge.

Jung, C. G. The following are from *The Collected Works of C. G. Jung* (CW) London: Routledge and Kegan Paul:

—— (1931a). Basic postulates of analytical psychology. (CW8)

—— (1931b). Archaic man. (CW10)

—— (1932). On the tale of the otter. (CW18).

—— (1934). A review of the complex theory. (CW8)

—— (1946). Analytical psychology and education. (CW17)

—— (1952). Synchronicity: An acausal connecting principle. (CW8)

—— (1954). On the nature of the psyche. (CW8)

Kline, P. (1983). *Personality Measurement and Theory*. London: Hutchinson.

Kumar, K. N. P., Kiranagi, B. S. & Bagewadi, C. S. (2012). Measurement disturbs explanation of quantum mechanical states – a hidden variable theory. *International Journal of Scientific and Research Publications*, 2: 1–18.

Kusch, M. (1995). *Psychologism*. London: Routledge.

Lakatos, I. (1970). History of science and its rational reconstructions. *PSA: Proceedings of the Biennial Meeting of the Philosophy of Science Association*, 1970: 9–136.

Lewin, K. (1935). *A Dynamic Theory of Personality*. New York: McGraw-Hill.

Lilienfeld, S. O. (2011). Public skepticism of psychology: Why many people perceive the study of human behavior as unscientific. *American Psychologist*, 67: 111–29.

Lyotard, J.-F. (1980). *The Postmodern Condition*. Manchester: Manchester University Press.

Mair, M. (1988). Psychology as storytelling. *International Journal of Personal Construct Psychology*, 1: 125–37.

Martin, F., Carminati, F. & Carminati, G. G. (2009). Synchronicity, quantum information and the psyche. *Journal of Cosmology*, 3: 580–9.

McLeod, J. (2006). Narrative thinking and the emergence of postpsychological therapies. *Narrative Inquiry*, 16: 201–10.

Mead, G. H. (1934) *Mind, Self, and Society*. Chicago, IL: University of Chicago Press.

Moss, S. A. & Wilson, S. (2010). Integrating the most unintuitive empirical observations of 2007 in the domain of personality and social psychology into a unified framework. *New Ideas in Psychology*, 28: 1–27.

Neisser, U. (1997). The future of cognitive science: An ecological analysis. In Johnson, D. M. & Erneling, C. E. (Eds.) *The Future of the Cognitive Revolution*. New York: Oxford University Press.

O'Sullivan, S. (2010). Lacan's ethics and Foucault's 'care of the self': Two diagrams of the production of subjectivity (and of the subject's relation to truth). *Parrhesia*, 10: 51–73.

Parker, I. (1994). Reflexive research and the grounding of analysis: Social psychology and the psy-complex. *Journal of Community & Applied Social Psychology*, 4: 239–52.

Phelan, J. (2006). Rhetorical aesthetics and other issues in the study of literary narrative. *Narrative Inquiry*, 16: 85–93.

Popper, K. R. (1958). *The Logic of Scientific Discovery*. London: Hutchinson.
Rapaport, D. (1951). *Organization and Pathology of Thought*. New York: Columbia University Press.
Ricoeur, P. (1970). *Freud and Philosophy*. New Haven, CT: Yale University Press.
Roesler, C. (2008). The self in cyberspace: Identity formation in postmodern societies and Jung's Self as an objective psyche. *Journal of Analytical Psychology*, 53: 421–36.
—— (2012). Are archetypes transmitted more by culture than biology? Questions arising from conceptualizations of the archetype. *Journal of Analytical Psychology*, 57: 223–46.
Rosen, D. H., Smith, S. M., Huston, H. L. & Gonzalez, G. (1991). Empirical study of association between symbols and their meanings: Evidence of collective unconscious (archetypal) memory. *Journal of Analytical Psychology*, 36: 211–28.
Scanlon, J. (1989). Dilthey on psychology and epistemology. *History of Philosophy Quarterly*, 6: 347–55.
Schrag, C. O. (1997). *The Self after Postmodernity*. New Haven, CT: Yale University Press.
Seidman, S. (1994). Introduction. In Seidman, S. (Ed.) *The Postmodern Turn*. Cambridge: Cambridge University Press.
Shamdasani, S. (2003). *Jung and the Making of Modern Psychology*. Cambridge: Cambridge University Press.
Shotter, J. & Lannamann, J. W. (2001). The situation of social constructionism: Its 'imprisonment' within the ritual of theory-criticism-and-debate. *Theory & Psychology*, 12: 577–609.
Simonton, D. K. (2004). Psychology's status as a scientific discipline: Its empirical placement within an implicit hierarchy of the sciences. *Review of General Psychology*, 8: 59–67.
Singer, T. (2010). The transcendent function and cultural complexes: A working hypothesis. *Journal of Analytical Psychology*, 55: 234–41.
Stein, M. (2005). Individuation: Inner work. *Journal of Jungian Theory and Practice*, 7 (2): 1–13.
Stevens, A. (1999). *On Jung*. Princeton, NJ: Princeton University Press.
Sturm, T. & Mülberger, A. (2012). Crisis discussions in psychology: New historical and philosophical perspectives. *Studies in History and Philosophy of Biological and Biomedical Sciences*, 43: 425–33.
Weber, M. (1946). Science as a vocation. In Gerth, H. H. and Wright Mills, C. (Eds.) *Max Weber: Essays in Sociology*. New York: Oxford University Press. (Original work published in 1918)
Wierzbicka, A. (2011). Defining 'the humanities'. *Culture & Psychology*, 17: 31–46.
Wilson, S. & Haslam, N. (2009). Is the future more or less human? Differing views of humanness in the posthumanism debate. *Journal for the Theory of Social Behaviour*, 39: 247–66.
Wittgenstein, L. (1953). *Philosophical Investigations*. Oxford: Blackwell.

4

SPECULATIONS ON JUNG'S DREAM OF SCIENCE

Leslie Gardner

When I first read Jung's dream reflecting his anxieties about the nature of his work, I struggled to understand why he cared so much about whether analytical psychology was science or art. Pondering his work in *Memories, Dreams, Reflections*, Jung (1989 [1961]: 185–6) recounts this episode: while writing down his fantasies and wondering what it was he was doing, an inner voice, sounding like one of his female patients, imperiously announced, 'It is art.' Why did this categorization trouble him so much? And in what way is it important to designate a body of work as scientific? In my own work with literature, it is assumed that there is deeper truth in the *representation* of a phenomenon rather than in a way that purports to be an empirical, (and therefore, contingent) 'factual' description of it. So it is no bad thing for me if science is deemed an art. (And, indeed, aspects of certain sciences are only viable in their representations – optics, for one.) But Jung resists this designation. His instinct is to disparage his work because it is not a positivist, 'objective' and logical science. I am contending here that not only is his body of work a science, but it is a particular kind of rhetorical science (and, I'd propose, a 'poetical' science, to pick up that aspect of rhetoric in this discussion too).

The urge to know what is happening, and why things happen is a primal drive. Chains of event or phenomena may describe the curve of phenomena but it is only the tantalizing start of an inquiry. Throughout his writings, Jung focused on the anomalies of 'causality' as a motif of science, and used it as an aid in pursuit of defining criteria that could be relied on to designate the scientific enterprise. It is his awareness of the underlying ideological, and affective component of what science is that leads him to identify criteria about science that correlate to artistic endeavour.

Here is Jung on causality:

> [I]t is a rational presupposition of ours that everything has a natural and perceptible cause. We are convinced ... causality, so understood, is one of our most sacred dogmas. There is no legitimate place in our world for invisible, arbitrary and so-called supernatural forces – unless, indeed, we follow the modern physicist in his scrutiny of the minute and secret world of the atom ... but we resent it.
>
> (Jung 1931: par. 115)

'Causality' is explored not only in his essay on synchronicity, but also, as I discuss in this chapter, in his essay on flying saucers (Jung 1958). A full discussion of what it means to him is beyond scope of what I am focusing on here, but he uproots causality from its ground in many different ways and applies it to contiguous data and conceptions fruitfully (and playfully). Fundamentally, the search for cause is perceived by Jung ironically. He seems to say that seeking 'cause' is really about a longing for truth, and that there can only be 'certainty' about things, not *a* 'truth' about it. In effect, then, I'd propose how a sequence of events is 'chained' together is not only a scientific inquiry, and an inquiry about human longing, but is also evidently an inquiry about narrative. It is this analogy that allows me to viably link Jung's science to art.

The core question of why something happens is resolved in literature, and in depictions of reality as well as in the scientific enterprise. It is my contention that Jung understood that this longing seeks resolution in specifically human ways which always include accommodation of affect and irrationality in science and in the arts. In his above comment, he specifically recognizes this interweave of affect, subjectivity and the boundaries of the external as a pre-logical faculty of human cognition.

In this chapter I want to respond to Jung's canny awareness of what comprises the urge to know, and the urge to know with certainty, the truth of things. This is a rhetorical endeavour. I would want to impress this upon him as a way of alleviating his anxiety, and assert to him that it is his re-positioning of what science is that makes of it a 'poetical science' to borrow Vico's notion – a philosopher of the eighteenth century who struggled with 'natural philosophy' as a science in some of the same ways Jung did. Eschewing the metaphysical does not alleviate that longing for certitude, and for meaning.

Statement of the problem

It is Jung's contention that the dynamism of autonomous, archetypal scientific law rests deep in our beings as sense-ridden, sentient and intellectual beings who are both object and subject simultaneously, living symbolic lives, driving ahead of the laws of nature, manipulating them, and yet beset by them too. We long to control them, or to 'own' them. Analytical psychology is authentically a scientific endeavour on the same grounds as any other science when we come to see what science is in Jung's terms. And these terms are practically realizable as the criteria of narrative questioning too, and span the dimension of the human longing to know. His anxieties reside in the institutions of his time, and in his frontiering posture.

Jung's compatriot, Einstein, certainly felt that science was best conceived in the rhetorical realm of 'probabilities', as outlined since Aristotle's time. 'Enthymemic' logic is inferential, and dependent on an understood (but unnamed) third term with all the demurrals – or 'reservations' and 'qualifications' in Toulmin's (1953) argumentative model. It is necessarily a part of any practical or hypothetical endeavour. The justificatory logic Toulmin proposes in his *Philosophy of Science* and elsewhere, suggests that inferences are found by the scientist – the scientist as a persuasive agent – as warrants to support claims based on selected data. As Einstein describes it, in a pejorative sense:

> A proposition is correct if, within a logical system, it is deduced according to the accepted logical rules. A system has truth content according to the certainty and completeness of its possibility of coordination with the totality of experience. A correct proposition borrows its 'truth' from the truth-content of the system to which it belongs.
> (Einstein 1996 [1949]: 12)

It is transparently circular reasoning, and acceptable only on the basis of its being transparent. Any other claim is specious. Throughout Jung's career, we sense the strain to appeal to an authority that is also simultaneously being formulated to find new ground in new definitions. It leads him at the same time to represent scientific data in the form of images of copulating figures, and to 'apologize' for proposing this as the most effective way to do so.

Empirical data justifies scientific propositions not only by how it is accumulated, or by who notices that data and tabulates it, but also by what data and claims meet the criteria the group acknowledges. Further there is an appeal to 'resentment' as he calls it that things must add up in the right way. And the 'right' way is a way that *feels* like certainty.

In the second chapter of the flying saucers essay, Jung talks about the archetypal status of numbers. They even have their own mythology, he points out:

> They are an aspect of the physically real as well as of the psychically imaginary. They do not only count and measure, and are not merely quantitative; they also make qualitative statements and are therefore mysterious something midway between myth and reality . . . Equations, for instance, which were invented as pure mathematical formulae, have subsequently proved to be formulations of the quantitative behaviour of physical things.
> (Jung 1958: par. 777)

He justifies the mandala subsequently for its mathematical effectiveness as a symbol of wholeness. As tools of scientific inquiry, numbers partake of primal drive, of imaginary designation and human invention and yet they are invested with status of external reality. In other words, these psychic representations are invested with materiality, suited to formulating and 'owning' data by resolving that very data into meaningful agreed-on forms of knowledge. As Galileo was able to represent heat as gradients of temperature by using a revolutionary system of numbers, so analysis of data into tabulated incremental number order gives it a significance that we extrapolate in agreed-upon ways. This is the basis of the rhetorical endeavour of science but also equally of the arts.

Narrative representations recounting results of scientific experiment begin with unresolved hypotheses that as readers or as writers of fiction or, for example, of scientific report, we seek to resolve in satisfactory ways. Jung might have taken heart by this formulation. Scientific investigation shifts away from an absolutist inductive process, based on logical and self-evident chains of causality or event. Sifting through existing ideas, and putting them together hypothetically as they seem to fit practically is the process Toulmin (1953: 13) outlines and which along with an attitude of compensation Jung utilizes.

Einstein (1996: 11) critiques conceptual concepts as closed systems, arrived at initially by intuition: 'Although the conceptual systems are logically entirely arbitrary, they are restricted by the aim of permitting the most nearly possible certain (intuitive) and complete coordination with the totality of sense experiences.' In that case, we might look to the language of the humanities, adept at using metaphorical and secondary representations to allude to truth, and, in fact, unafraid of the kind of truth figural reference fashions. Further, as rhetoricians or poets (or scientists) know, deductive methods rely on inferences that must be commonly agreed: and the associations inherent in the language and the time and place of their construal have impact on the science (or on the object invented). It's just that scientists are hard-pressed to agree on the status of inference in their experimental work.

Discoveries of nature are propositional inquiries after all, since we cannot (for example) know how a bee has come to be a creature that collects honey: we propose it is about a chain of biological necessity; and we fix natural principles and experimentation accordingly. And, in scientific experiment, depending on tools used, and methods agreed by a particular school of scientists, so goes the research and outcome. A pyramid of language and practice develops in these cases that contains a hermeneutical circle of inquiry – sophisticated questions depend on earlier decisions that are not analysed each and every time. These are not only basics of scientific endeavour, they also add up to the coordinates of rhetoric: (1) rhetor/scientist, (2) message, (3) audience and, as Overington (1977) suggests, a fourth coordinate: (4) what is the message deployed to accomplish; what is the intention?

I propose to examine the persuasive aspects of Jung's scientific enterprise, and demonstrate that his scientific approach is best analysed as a rhetorical endeavour, and, indeed, science itself is satisfactorily appraised as a rhetorical activity. 'Exigency' is established when a burning question focuses all the elements of an investigation: who is seeking to know, why right now, and who needs persuading. Questions are raised that demand answers. We note here about Jung's discussion that it is an argumentative posturing, inviting us to examine where this scientist's Archimedean point is, to use Jung's phrase (various contexts). A 'discontinuity' is investigated and the ground shifts when, in his science, a new dynamic element is discovered and is weighed in: the innovative notion of a viable sub-personality with autonomous vitality, an archetype emerges. The episode mentioned in this chapter's opening paragraph involved an argumentative female, the 'anima' he calls her; and the call on him to resolve this issue flared up high and persistently (not for the first or last time). The pivot is composite, combining cause, inference, and spins out into logical, rational thought and objectivity. Presented to us in the form of a contention in this case; and elsewhere, when he persistently and emphatically pronounces his work to be a science, Jung involves all aspects of the rhetorical formula. He asks us, his readers, to share this qualm about the nature of his work.

In his memoirs, Jung (1989) insists these early worries were vivid and persistent. Similarly, Einstein (1996: 9) had qualms in his youth when his father 'explained' direction by showing him a compass. This was not satisfactory to the young physicist who wanted to know what drives the compass point one way or the other. 'It is drawn to pointing north because that is where north is' is not the 'motivation' for the compass, it's a description of what happens (ibid.). The direction Einstein seeks will take him in radical new ways, and tools must be invented and methods of inquiry newly formulated to achieve his aims. In fact, his theories about what science is are controversial; and, in fact, he felt science had an unacknowledged mystical element that obstructed new directions of investigation. Einstein reformulated his presumptions in order to find new tools.

Jung (1989) sets out his assumptions: science is 'real' and art is 'fantasy', i.e. it is of a lower-status ontological and epistemological order. In the realm of fantasy, the plausibility of fiction, you might say, is indebted to (or 'warranted' by) its truthfulness, its feel of 'reality' in other words. It adheres to the logic of reality, having consistency, and a quality of unstable subjectivity and yet also it has the feel of 'objectivity' to it . . . that's what 'real' feels like, after all. Jung's strategy in claiming valid scientific exploration of such phenomena as flying saucers can viably accommodate such inquiry. We are reminded of the rift that exists between science and the mystical and that

> The scientist's interest is too easily restricted to the common, the probably, the average, for that is after all the basis of every empirical science. Nevertheless a basis has little meaning unless something can be erected upon it that also leaves room for the exceptional and extraordinary.
> (Jung 1958: par. 701)

But his argumentative approach is twofold. First, he proposes to raise the status of 'fantasy' to make it level with science's place in the world: something he feels more confident about since proclamations of physics in its new dimension were being announced in his time: relativity and quantum mechanics depended on evidence that was *represented*, i.e. mediated, rather than immediately physically available to the eye or ear or touch. (There is also the distinction between 'art' and 'fantasy' to be overcome for Jung, which I will not elaborate here.)

Secondly, he asserts that throughout history and in its fundamental composition, there has been a symbolic dimension of science. He asserts an ideological undercurrent: science's adherence to the religion of 'reality' (cf. Einstein 1996).

Reality is revealed to be a communal undertaking, a rhetorical posture with each unit of theory about natural phenomena emerging as a hypothetical proposition, to be argued out. Here we meet again Einstein's 'hypothetical' method of experimentation – the solution to the question is the one that fits best. It is not derived from law or by induction.

In the flying saucers essay, Jung establishes the anomaly of the autonomous, freakish object that appears physically contemporaneously and in history – as well as in dreams, and in paintings and drawings throughout all time. He establishes exigency by pointing out how pressing the inquiry is for scientists and for sociologists and psychologists.

Overview of the 'Flying Saucers' essay

The essay's text has the appearance of being organized in a scientifically comprehensive way. Jung covers all relevant angles in the investigation after setting up the inquiry (or its exigency); it's a collective repository of psychic energies expunged and projected into space. He calls flying saucers 'rumours' because despite instances where they flashed up on radar screens, somehow no one has ever photographed them up close. Weightlessness and random trajectories baffle scientists who observe them. Appearances in dreams and in art work are explored. Its history back to Egyptians, Greek and Roman times is covered. Then Jung briefly investigates their presence as non-psychological entities (an ironic articulation!).

He establishes a meta-commentary: 'UFOs are real material phenomena of an unknown nature, presumably coming from outer space, which perhaps have long been visible to mankind, but otherwise have no recognizable connection with the earth or its inhabitants' (1958: par. 789). He explores the materiality of the phenomena as part psychic projection and part external phenomenon: as he must do in a discipline like psychology that depends on a subjective agent examining itself, taking itself as its object, as the source of evidence. But there is a new 'hard' science emerging alongside his new science. The new physics deals with invisible data, which is 'made' plausible by its representation. He asks us, is it not really this inextricable knot of confusion of subject (with its sensual and perceptual components) and object that is the locus and also the starting place of the anxiety about the focus of scientific inquiry (particularly his)? Is it because 'science' implies a certitude about necessary results in its activity, perhaps lacking in analytical psychology (as in investigation of a perhaps specious external object like a flying saucer) because of its inability to grasp its own material from outside? He cannot get a distance on the material in a 'clean' and uninflected way. I think Jung means to ask: Can science do that anyway? Can it get a distance on its object?

The important lack of the presence of witnesses or even mediums as in séances is noted too by Jung in his discussion at the opening; most of the encounters with aliens on these ships, or reports from people who were abducted, are not effected by someone with special powers. Jung notes this missing element, but I will not explore it further here. I believe that this touches on issues of 'authority' and mediation important to rhetorical ontology. And for Jung it takes up the theme of mediation to a God that Christians look for.

Open skies are a feature and perhaps nearby military or government buildings too – a consideration which adds to his argument that they are compensating for anxieties the recent war and terrors had stirred up. They are associated to visions, and some people report being carried off in these vehicles. Scientists see them too and they are as curious at their irrational appearance as the farmers are. While these objects have been reported in earlier times, he says, they are more prevalent now; their presence indicates something is seriously disturbing in the present history. Jung comments that they are like gods (for some), or archetypes of collective disturbances, tubular in shape and smooth, weightless and random – the embodiment of autonomous, sensual objects. They are projections he tells us, displaced energies usually due to a void in human imagination and psyche that formerly were absorbed in Christian cultural effects. Where does that psychic energy go now? It seems they are invested in the UFO. There is a 'radar bounce effect' – we project out and an object irrationally appearing in the sky throws energies back at us; the object attracts numinosity, established by viewers in reacting and projecting hopes and longings for meaning. Our psyches constitute this object but not as hallucinations of insanity, but as 'hallucinations' of normal sight, normal perception.

The essay moves on to demonstrate that these objects are in fact universal – and so, in that way, important as he says they are as features of the collective unconscious; and the first way, typically for Jung, is to prove this by reporting on the dreams of his patients in their numbers. (This is the statistical approach on first glance, counting one by one. But he means it in a deeper way, i.e. to refer to a primal collective impulse.) Jung analyses many space travel or space object dreams closely to show us that there are significant elements that emerge from this psychic universality; in doing this he picks up motifs of alienation, or control, or phases of transformation in the dreamers' lives. (These are facets of his scientific inquiry.) Associations to the cultural or technological moment: he notes that the technological status of the contemporary world is intruding and not in a good, reassuring way.

Picking up his association also to dreams and to works of art, especially modern painting (a regular ploy for Jung), in his next chapter, he analyses the pieces of artwork and their demonstrations of themes which are crucial to his psychological system. He interprets the paintings, and mainly his aim is to demonstrate that the themes emerging are associated to loss of meaning, or to quests for meaning. These are empirical data. He does not specifically refer to painters of renown; they are artists he knows, and also only European products. For him an analysis of paintings is similar to analysis of dreams: these are legitimate scientific-psychological questions presented as data conforming to the conclusions he reaches.

To underscore his theme of the universality of these images which appear in human psyches in all time, he discusses the flying object in history. This gives him space to explore scenes as they are described and depicted in ancient literature – he can pick up the Holy Child as a star baby; shooting stars which no longer have otherworldly associations for us as they did in medieval times and were reported accordingly – so we are getting an idea of the potentially radical differences of cultures, yet their similarities in the same moment of an event.

He decides in his continuing narrative (or argument) to move 'outside' the psychological dimension. This leads him then to cover this phenomenon as a non-psychological feature. He delves into how the collective unconscious operates in an external way to the human psyche; he proposes that this can happen in reality as 'fact', and that, since it is an independent and autonomous phenomenon, it is therefore also something to be examined not as a psychological problem. There is a short section then that summarizes the motifs and brings them into global intellectual focus, i.e. 'reasonableness'. We note that this 'reasonableness' is a specific type of casuistry a Western European might propose.

His epilogues describe lengthy books of visionaries who either have travelled on space objects with aliens and return to tell us of spiritual lacks and fulfilments – along the lines of William James, and his own earlier discussions of the quest for meanings in his experiences with mediums; he is free here to talk openly in full belief of the nature of these experiences, and what they might mean for us, having established it earlier in the essay. Throughout, as he points out here again, scientists also see traces on their objective impersonal radar screens (he forgets to mention that these traces are interpreted by humans, of course).

In his discussion, Jung refers to the aspect of wish-fulfilment about the appearance of UFOs: it is part of his theme of the 'as-if' mode of thinking. He often propounds a critique of causality in these terms; what Jung refers to is an inquiry into a type of epistemology that might have the authority positivist science had achieved historically. Can the 'as-if' mode ever have the status of positivist proofs with their aspiration to objective and logical, self-evident certainties in data assessment? He wants to include irrationality and subjectivity as viable and legitimate components of scientific evaluation. But positivist scientists are disinclined to include the personal, or the emotional and irrational – or at least they think they have not included those elements. Here is one source of his disquiet. He tackles this question in the epilogue: does including probability and representations of invisible data mean that if we wish it hard enough, something becomes 'real'? If something is plausible, is that enough to make it 'real'? He reasons, 'Either psychic projections throw back a radar echo, or else the appearance of real objects affords an opportunity for mythological projections' (Jung 1958: par. 782) and goes on, 'even if UFOs are physically real, the corresponding psychic projections are not actually caused but are only occasioned by them' (ibid.: par. 783). The idea is a result of 'a profound psychic need which does not simply disappear when the expression of it ceases to be valid. What happens to the energy that once kept the idea alive and dominant in the psyche?' he asks (ibid.: par. 784). He comes to the conclusion, I'd say, that the energy is transferred to the appearance of UFOs – a scientifically astute conclusion about the human psyche.

Science or art?

The claim that science is fundamentally a rhetorical endeavour is not a new one. In thinking of analytical psychology specifically, however, there is a rhetorical approach that relies on warrants and justifications that suits consideration of psychology as a scientific enterprise. The 'enthymeme' which is the rhetorical syllogism, as mentioned, relies on a third (unnamed) term that is tacitly acknowledged by the rhetor and audience. The reference is to a collective assumption, manipulated, perhaps, by the rhetor. Philosophers refer to this as the 'defective' syllogism not realizing that syllogisms too depend on tacit agreement about assumptions and that they are not at all necessarily self-evident and logical conclusions. It is also not new to make note of science's basis in 'probabilities', and in its underlying persuasive nature. But the emphasis Toulmin (1953) brings to the rhetoric of science as partaking in inferential, justificational logic is controversial. And I think it is useful to bring it more closely in focus thinking of the kind of 'poetical science' or 'artful' science Jung is engaged in.

To agree on what measurements are significant, scientists infer that graphic descriptions of how light travels are meaningful because the outcomes are justified in their practical workings out. Inferences are warrants supporting claims based on (selected) data. Sharing assumptions about premises pertinent to a discipline creates a community referring to commonly agreed-upon authorities. For me, this sounds convincingly like formulations of a collective unconscious – with all its irrationalities, and emotive constitution.

Psychological testing and analysis, in this instance, aims to validate its 'authority' – and throughout Jung's work we sense the strain to appeal to an authority that he is simultaneously formulating in new definitions. Empirical data is given justification as proof of a scientific proposition not only by how it is accumulated, or by who notices that data and tabulates it, but also what data and claims meet the criteria the group acknowledges. When we consider Jung's dissatisfaction with his word association test since he was not able to collect data to make any meaningful conclusion, we sense his drive to find other means of proof and other modes of testing.

In further discussion about psychoanalysis, Toulmin (1948) emphasizes the independent criteria that a psychologist can grasp – stripped of involved observation as a trained analyst might do: the 'motivation' of the subject for certain action, which can be perceived without all the emotional trappings clouding the analyst's assessments. It can be isolated and analysed. He proposed that it was here that a scientist of human psychology might talk about a 'logic' that is consistent and measurable. It is useful here to bring in a commentator on narrative 'logic' to show similarities to scientific investigation.

In his essay on Conrad's *Nostromo*, Edward Said (1985) conceives of narrative as a series of queries that are very close to the mode of scientific questioning I am setting out here. Based on his reading of Vico's key concepts of 'poetic logic' and 'poetic physics', Said explores the nature of the stream of thought involved in reading narrative. Testability and falsifiability are qualities we deploy in evaluating narrative – what is it about the burning discontinuities that generate our drive to read a novel to its end, to solve the puzzles of personalities and their consistencies in the narrative? As Jung says in the flying saucers essay, at the very inception of scientific inquiry, an investigation begins that accommodates what always begins as noting anomalies in the physical world. These anomalies require or compel investigation – the basic impulse of science, to solve puzzles: he points out at the beginning of his essay, 'reports of flying saucers create a clamorous demand for explanation' (Jung 1958: par. 611). The rhetorical or poetical faculty of science is its capacity to notice those anomalies – those 'puzzles' of science – and to frame them in a way that simultaneously initiates fruitful inquiry. The direction of the inquiry depends on critical tools; this is the 'inventional' mode of inquiry noted also by Toulmin.

And these are the drives of science; the data comes together in ways that we can analyse as narrative in representation scientifically or artistically. I would contend that these rhetorical endeavours have more in common than they are different; and this is what I'd say Jung is grappling with.

Said's (1985) criteria match Toulmin's (1953) tests of refutability: testing elements hypothetically and arriving at conclusions that may leave the original proposition in place is what science is doing (Toulmin). Said specifically focuses on the novel as a literary form. He discusses the far-reaching implications of assumptions about narrative sequence, created by an author; or applied here, a fantasist – doing 'art', as Jung's anima labelled his scientific inquiries regarding his own fantasies. The criteria resemble significantly the criteria of refutability or testability as outlined by Toulmin. Testing elements that are hypothetical and coming up with results that leave the original proposition in place is the basis of what a science should do (to put it simply, paraphrasing Toulmin). Said suggests three precepts applicable to the 'truth' of a narrative. First: the basic narrative formula is generated by doubts in the authority of the characters to act consistently and in a comprehensible manner. In other words, this is about the application of the rules of reality to fantasy. Secondly, the truth – 'whatever that may be' (Said 1985: 90) – can only be approached indirectly, 'by means of a mediation that, paradoxically, because of its falseness makes the truth truer' (ibid.: 92). The process of arriving at the 'truer truth' is arrived at by elimination; alternatives are ruled out. Like hypothetical scientific propositions, truth-resembling fiction becomes habitual practice. Choices are made to establish the identity of truth with the factoid, and these choices amount to referral to an authority which establishes 'certainty' not 'truth'. The sequence of authority is attained by preserving choices – a communal process in science – so that certainty is established by 'retrospective reconstruction' – an assemblage of warranted conclusions (to use Toulmin's terminology). And, thirdly, to follow Said, an irrational fear of the chaos of inferential alternatives, a kind of void antedating private authority, generates theories to explain – in narrative terms – character choices. Said points out Vico's philological references to 'authority' as a choice, a matter of certitude owned by a single voice or a group of voices.

Contrasting these analyses of science proofs and of narrative proofs we engage in instinctively demonstrates the common set of drives we apply to wanting to know – a desire to know that spans science and narrative and makes them equally imperative inquiries. It is not that it makes science art, and art science – it's that the inquiry is a common drive using similar methods of analysis. On this basis, science is reformulated as a 'poetical science'.

Amplifications

We might think of this discussion of UFOs as a case study of a quasi-sociological or scientific phenomenon but I am also proposing it is a commentary on the nature of a scientific inquiry even as it is a scientific analysis. Jung flips scientific data over to show its underside as an emotive attachment to the dogma of objective, scientific causality. Might this inquiry be a kind of deconstruction of empiricism? Are facts evolved to explain unlikely interventions in reality? In other words, is it a critique of a certain type of empirical epistemology that mistakes plausibility for truth ('facticity')?

I have proposed that Jung explores a psychic process in the 'Flying Saucers' essay that accommodates (and makes transparent) a kind of longing or desire to be reassured by matters and fact that are certainties; and he wants us to reflect on what this might mean about the relation of longing to the independent reality of external objects. Does the intensity of believing in the reality of UFOs – from farmers in a lonely field, to scientists at NASA – have anything to do with whether they are 'real'? Jung does not allow us to dismiss this question. It is his commentary on the nature of science.

His essay with its mix of science fiction and references to speculative scientific reports hypothesizes about anomalous events. But speculation permeates reality; and so science must also accommodate irrationality by resorting to 'art' to make it 'real' – not only in its expressions but also in its composition. To parse out a scientific fact is to seek out its context and its position among other facts that are social, interpersonal and related to other disciplines including other sciences. It is also to understand 'objective' data as inflected by the seeker, the context of that data (how it's being used), and its verifiability. 'Objective' data is not possible for the scientist or humankind to achieve. We may seek out uninflected truth but if we are not aware of the obligation that it has to maintain the feel of the real – and that it feels 'certain' – it will also not be the truth.

Jung recognizes, it seems to me, that excessive experiences (as we might say seeing flying saucers is), or anomalies, are required to shore up reality as we perceive it. Anomalies are the trigger for research and inquiry and in that way (among other ways) they are the subject of scientific investigation.

Jung is proposing there is an excess of longing for reassurance, in this case, 'superfluous wishing' that functions in the human psyche. It is required to maintain reality. In fact, by revealing the underpinnings of irrationality and intuition in science, a contrary boundary, the criteria of scientific inquiry is clarified. This notion may appear to be related to Lacan's *object petit a* (e.g. 1994; and throughout much of Lacan's writings since the 1950s). However, the excess energy in Jung's conception revivifies an object manifested in relation to a particular *need*; it is not a symbolic object arising arbitrarily, a kind of vessel or fetish of incommensurate meaning standing outside normative experience as I think Lacan has it. Science is critiqued and turned inside out in Jung's commentary. It is indeed, at core, 'science fiction' as he speculates in 'Flying Saucers'. But this is the nature of human realities, including science with its basis in intuition and data assessments oriented by the communal intentions and trajectory of scientists in a discipline.

References

Einstein, A. (1996). *Autobiographical Notes*. La Salle, Illinois: Open Court. (Original work published in 1949)

Jung, C. G. Unless otherwise stated, the following are from *The Collected Works of C. G. Jung* (CW) London: Routledge and Kegan Paul:

—— (1931). Archaic man. (CW10)

—— (1958). Flying saucers: A modern myth of things seen in the sky. (CW10)

—— (1989). *Memories, Dreams, Reflections*. New York: Vintage. (Original work published in 1961)

Lacan, J. (1994). *Four Fundamental Concepts of Psychoanalysis*. London: Penguin.

Overington, M. A., (1977). The scientific community as audience: Toward a theoretical analysis of science. *Philosophy and Rhetoric*, 10: 143–64.

Said, E. (1985) *Beginnings*. London: Granta.

Toulmin, S. (1948). The logic of psychoanalysis. *Analysis*, 9: 23–9.

—— (1953). *The Philosophy of Science*. Cambridge: Cambridge University Press.

5

EXPLANATION AND INTERPRETATION

Robert A. Segal

Is a Jungian analysis scientific?

For me, Jungian analyses of persons and things are exasperating in four ways. First, the analyses tend to assume Jungian tenets rather than to argue for them. Second, the analyses tend to apply only Jungian theory and to ignore any other theory. Third, the analyses tend to be so malleable that applicability is guaranteed. Fourth, the analyses tend to be *ex post facto* rather than predictive. Indisputably, my objections hold for many other theories as well and certainly in the fields that I know best: mythology and religion. And it is on the application of Jungian theory not to patients but to texts that I will be focusing, though I think that my objections hold for the analysis of persons as well.

Internal criteria

Put another way, my objections are both internal and external. Internally, Jungian analyses are unscientific because they are rarely tested. There is therefore scant chance that they will be wrong, in which case there is no evidence that they are right.

Testing can take several forms. In the loosest sense, testing means applicability. In the example that I will be using in this chapter, the ancient Greek myth of Adonis, applicability would mean the translatability of the myth into Jungian terms. It would mean fit. By no means do all theories of myth fit or fit to the same degree. In my first book, *The Poimandres as Myth* (1986), I applied the theories of Jung and Mircea Eliade to the Greek Hermetic myth called the Poimandres. I argued that Jung's theory fits the myth more fully than Eliade's does. Applicability does, then, offer testing of a kind.

My objection is that, ordinarily, Jungian applications are offered in isolation rather than in competition with other possible ones, as I tried to do in using Eliade's theory as well as Jung's. But whether or not limited to just Jungian theory, applications often enlist concepts so broad that success is almost certain. An archetype can be found for any character or thing in any myth, and any archetype can evince itself in an endless number of ways – an issue that I failed to consider in my book.

In a stronger sense of the term, testing means prediction. Take two theories, Freudian and Jungian, that both purport to analyse the place of a character in a myth or, say, a novel. Assume that the theories fit equally well the place of a character – for example, the protagonist's boss. The Freudian analysis: the character, read symbolically, is the father of the protagonist. The Jungian analysis: the character, also read symbolically, is the father archetype of the protagonist.

Is any prediction possible? Perhaps one can ask how, for a Freudian or a Jungian, the character, once encountered, would be expected to behave. But this kind of 'prediction' does not count since the novel is already finished. True prediction requires new data, such as analysing an unfinished novel. So one might have done with the serialization of Dickens' novels. While I stated that I find exasperating the tendency of Jungian analyses to be *ex post facto* rather than predictive, I grant that that objection holds more readily for analysing living persons, whose lives are unfinished, than for analysing finished novels or finished myths.

External criteria

Even if a Freudian or a Jungian analysis of a novel or a myth could be tested for both applicability and predictability, the test would assume the theory. I am most exasperated by the tendency of Jungian analyses to invoke the theory rather than to defend it. Externally, the question is what is the evidence for the theory underlying the analysis. What is the evidence for an Oedipus complex or for a father archetype? Without good evidence, no analysis 'holds water'.

In the terms that I will be using, an interpretation must be supported by an explanation. Admittedly, the terms 'explanation' and 'interpretation' are used in varying and confusing ways. In *Explaining and Interpreting Religion* (Segal 1992), I distinguish these ways. In the present chapter I will not review the options. I will use the terms in one of these possible ways, and will do so to make a single point: that a Jungian analysis of myth or of religion or of anything else is only as persuasive as the theory being applied.

Here an 'interpretation' of a myth answers the question what is the meaning of the myth. An explanation answers the questions why was the myth created and why did it last. Those three questions – of meaning, origin, and function – are the key theoretical questions. By 'explanation' I mean the account – of the mind, the world, culture, or society – that is presupposed by the interpretation. Freud and Jung offer explanations of the mind that get applied in the interpretation of myth.

While interpretation and explanation are more often than not deemed incompatible, in this chapter they are deemed not only compatible but also, and even more so, interlocking. An interpretation of Adonis as a puer archetype depends on the existence of the archetype. The interpretation does not stand by itself and makes sense of the myth only if the existence of archetypes is presupposed. To apply a theory without evidence for the theory is to start *in medias res*, which may be acceptable in the *Iliad* but is not acceptable in an analysis of the *Iliad*.

Reciprocally, the applicability of Jungian theory to the myth of Adonis offers support for the theory. After all, not all theories may prove applicable, and some may prove more applicable than others. But the support for a theory offered by applicability is limited. The theory must rest on more than applicability.

In this chapter I focus on a single issue: how would one justify a Jungian analysis of a text, for which the myth of Adonis will be my example? I am most interested in many of the topics on which other contributors to this volume concentrate – for example, how Jung conceived of science, to what extent he considered his psychology or the psychologies of Freud and Adler scientific, and whether science for him purports to combine subjectivity with objectivity. But here I will limit myself to the question whether Jungian psychology is scientific.

I take my bearings from philosophers of science, as do a few other contributors. Undeniably, philosophers differ sharply among themselves, but all at least agree that there is a distinction between why scientists come to offer the theories they do and how they defend those theories. The difference is that between discovery and justification (see also Jones, Chapter 3). What makes science *science* is justification, not discovery. Why Jung came up with his brand of psychology is a historical or biographical question. How he, or anyone else, justifies his psychology is a scientific question. I am not unfamiliar with attempts, more by sociologists than by psychologists, to make justification itself historical. But these attempts fall outside the philosophical mainstream. Historical and biographical discussions of why Jung invented his brand of psychology and characterized it the way he did are not germane to my chapter, which is about how to determine whether the employment of Jungian psychology in analysing myth is justified.

The myth of Adonis

Because theories in science often compete with other theories, I compare a Jungian approach to the myth of Adonis with that of J. G. Frazer. I take my comparison from a chapter in my book *Theorizing about Myth* (Segal 1999). There I compare three applications to the myth of Adonis: those of Frazer, the Scottish myth-ritualist and author of the classic of classics, *The Golden Bough* (first edition 1890; abridged edition 1922); Jung, who writes about Adonis only in passing but who writes more fully about the archetypes that are key to the myth, the archetypes of the *puer aeternus* and the Great Mother; and Marcel Detienne, the French structuralist, whose book *The Gardens of Adonis* (1977) analyses the myth of Adonis. I concluded that Jung's analysis is more persuasive than either Frazer's or Detienne's. But I am no longer so sure. To make my present chapter manageable, I will limit the comparison to Frazer and Jung.

The myth of Adonis, the main sources for which are Apollodorus and Ovid, describes the miraculous birth of a preternaturally beautiful human out of a tree, the fighting over him by Aphrodite and Persephone, his annual division of the year into a third with Persephone in Hades and two thirds on earth with Aphrodite, and his eventual death while hunting.[1]

Frazer's Adonis

Of all the interpretations of the myth of Adonis, Frazer's remains the most popular. Frazer writes about Adonis in all three editions of *The Golden Bough* (1890, 1900, 1911–15)[2] and also in his abridged edition (1922), which virtually repeats the chapters from the second and third editions and from which the quotations below are taken. From the second edition on, Frazer works out three prescientific stages of culture, and he places Adonis in all three stages: those of magic, religion, and magic and religion combined. (Frazer's stages are only seemingly akin to those of Auguste Comte, whom Jones discusses in Chapter 3.) Though to differing degrees, in all three stages Adonis, for Frazer, is a mere personification of vegetation rather than a personality. Vegetation does not symbolize Adonis; Adonis symbolizes vegetation.

Frazer locates the potted gardens of Adonis in his first, magical stage. Since in this stage humans believe that impersonal forces rather than personalities cause events in the physical world, Adonis here cannot be a personality. Without personality there is no myth, so that this first stage is pre-mythic as well as pre-religious. Greeks would be planting seeds in earth-filled pots not to persuade a divine personality to grant growth but, by the magical Law of Imitation, to force the impersonal earth itself to grow: 'For ignorant people suppose that by mimicking the effect which they desire to produce they actually help to produce it' (Frazer 1922: 396). Mimicking the growth of crops would ensure their actual growth. Magic, like religion and in turn like magic and religion combined, originates and functions to secure food. If our forebears had had science, they would have used it instead of magic or religion.

In Frazer's second, religious stage, Adonis is an outright personality. He is the god of vegetation. In fact, Frazer distinguishes religion from magic on precisely the grounds that now divine personalities rather than impersonal forces cause events in the physical world. As the god of vegetation, Adonis could, most straightforwardly, be asked for crops. Or the request could be reinforced by ritualistic and ethical obedience. Just as there is now religion, so there is now myth: the biography of Adonis. Information from that biography would help worshippers figure out how best to get Adonis to grant crops. Frazer himself says that rites of mourning were performed for Adonis – not, as in the next stage, to undo his death but to seek his forgiveness for it (see Frazer 1922: 393–4). For Adonis has died not, as in the third stage, because he has descended to the underworld but because in cutting, stamping, and grinding the corn – the specific part of vegetation he symbolizes – humans have killed him. Yet Adonis is somehow still sufficiently alive to be capable of punishing humans, something that the rituals of forgiveness are intended to avert. Since, however, Adonis dies because vegetation itself does, the god is here really only a metaphor for the element that he supposedly controls. As vegetation goes, so goes Adonis.

In Frazer's third prescientific stage, which combines the first with the second, Adonis' death means his descent to the underworld for his stay with Persephone. If in stage two as vegetation goes, so goes Adonis, now as Adonis goes, so seemingly goes vegetation. Frazer assumes that whether or not Adonis wills his descent, he is too weak to ascend by himself. By acting out his rebirth, humans facilitate it. On the one hand the enactment employs the magical Law of Imitation. On the other hand it does not, as in the first stage, compel but only bolsters Adonis, who, despite his present state of death, is somehow still hearty enough to revive himself, just not fully. He needs a catalyst, which the enactment provides. In this stage gods still control the physical world, but their effect on it is automatic rather than deliberate. To enact the rebirth of Adonis is to spur his rebirth and thereby the rebirth of vegetation (see Frazer 1922: 377).

Yet even if Adonis chooses to descend to the underworld, he is not choosing infertility, which is just the automatic consequence of his sojourn below. Similarly, even if he chooses to return, he is not thereby choosing fertility, which likewise simply follows automatically from his resurfacing. Adonis proves to be not the cause of the fate of vegetation but only a metaphor for that fate, so that in fact in stage three as well as in stage two as vegetation goes, so goes Adonis. For Frazer, the myth that Adonis spent a portion of the year in the underworld 'is explained most simply and naturally by supposing that he represented vegetation, especially the corn', which lies buried half the year and re-emerges the other half (Frazer 1922: 392).

In a much larger sense Frazer, in all three of his prescientific stages, reduces Adonis to the mere personification of vegetation. For even where Frazer does deem Adonis an independent personality, the only aspect of his life he considers is that which parallels the natural course of vegetation: Adonis' death and rebirth. Yet Adonis' life, from his birth to his 'permanent' death, is anything but natural (see Segal 1999: 101). His final death terminates, not perpetuates, the change of seasons. He is killed and in some versions is even murdered – by either a spurned lover, Artemis, or a bested rival, Ares. To be sure, Frazer need not take the myth literally and therefore supernaturally. But he must *translate* the supernatural terms into natural ones. Instead, he ignores them. It is not hard to see why. Only if Adonis is reborn forever can his life symbolize the course of vegetation (see Segal 1999: 101).

Jung's Adonis

Unlike Frazer, Jung himself mentions Adonis only in passing,[3] but he does mention him as an instance of the archetype of the eternal child, or *puer aeternus*.[4] That archetype too Jung discusses only in passing, though he does devote many pages to an allied archetype, the Great Mother.[5] Marie-Louise von Franz, one of Jung's closest disciples, wrote a book on the puer archetype (1981), but she deals largely with cases other than that of Adonis.

From a Jungian point of view the myth of Adonis originates and functions not merely to present the archetype of the puer but also to assess it. The myth serves as a warning to those who identify themselves with the archetype. To live as a puer, the way Adonis does, is to live as a psychological infant and, ultimately, as a foetus. The life of a puer in myth invariably ends in premature death, which psychologically means the death of the ego and a return to the womb-like unconscious.

As an archetype, the puer constitutes a side of one's personality, which, as a side, must be accepted. A puer personality just goes too far: he makes the puer the whole of his personality. Unable to resist its spell, he surrenders himself to it, thereby abandoning his ego and reverting to sheer unconsciousness.

The reason a puer personality cannot resist the puer archetype is that he remains under the spell of the archetype of the Great Mother, who initially is identical with the unconscious as a whole. Unable to free himself from her, he never forges a strong, independent ego, without which he cannot in turn resist any smothering female he meets. His surrender to the puer archetype means his surrender to the Great Mother, to whom he yearns only to return. A puer 'only lives on and through the mother and can strike no roots, so that he finds himself in a state of permanent incest'. Jung even calls him a mere 'dream of the mother', who eventually draws him back into herself (Jung 1956: par. 392).

Biologically, a puer can range in age from late adolescence to middle or even old age. Psychologically, however, he is an infant. Where for Freud a person in the grip of an Oedipus complex is psychologically fixated at three to five years of age, for Jung a puer is fixated at birth. Where an Oedipus complex presupposes an independent ego 'egotistically' seeking to possess the mother for itself, a puer involves a tenuous ego seeking to surrender itself to the mother. A puer seeks not domination but absorption – and thereby reversion to the state prior even to birth.

Because an archetype expresses itself only through symbols, never directly, the aspects of the mother archetype that a child knows are only those filtered through his actual mother or mother substitute. A mother who refuses to let her child go limits him to only the smothering, negative side of the mother archetype. A mother who, however reluctantly, finally lets her child go opens him to the nurturing, positive side of the archetype.

Approached properly, the puer archetype provides an ego that has managed to sever itself from the unconscious with a re-entry into it. Taken rightly, the puer dimension of a person evinces itself in moments of playfulness, imagination, and spontaneity – moments that complement the rationality and sobriety of the ego. Taken to excess, the puer personality amounts to nothing but these moments. Taken rightly, the puer is childlike. Taken to excess, it is childish.

Although the puer personality arises in infancy, it manifests itself most dramatically at adolescence. A puer personality is even called an eternal adolescent. A puer is impulsive, dreamy, irresponsible, and self-centred. He makes great plans but never acts on them. If he works at all, he works only sporadically and only when interested. A puer avoids commitments and refuses to be tied down. He craves excitement and seeks risks. Scornful of the mundane, everyday world, he waxes spiritual and otherworldly. Sexually, he is promiscuous. The difference between a puer personality and a normal adolescent is that a puer remains an adolescent for life. In fact, it is normally at adolescence that the son finally breaks away from the mother. Rites of passage serve precisely to force a break. Still, the puer personality is infantile. It arises in infancy, not adolescence, and at adolescence merely expresses its infantilism in adolescent form.

A puer may be either conscious or unconscious of his character. To be sure, even a conscious puer experiences alluring females as epiphanies of the Great Mother, but at least he recognizes that other males experience women differently – as possible mates. He simply takes for granted that mystical union alone is right for him. He is both aware and proud of his unconventionality. Examples of conscious pueri are Casanova and Aleister Crowley.

An unconscious puer, by contrast, assumes that everyone else is like him. He assumes that all other males seek oneness with women, for no other relationship exists. He considers himself wholly conventional. A literary example of an unconscious puer is Goethe's character Werther, who dismisses the values of both aristocratic and bourgeois society as artificial and who blames society for coming between him and an otherwise responsive Lotte, with whom, moreover, he seeks not intercourse but maternal absorption. A more spectacular, contemporary example is Elvis Presley, a quintessential mamma's boy who lived his last twenty years as a recluse in a womb-like, infantile world in which all of his wishes were immediately satisfied yet who deemed himself entirely normal, in fact 'all-American'.

A puer can thus be either an actual person or a symbol. Some famous historical pueri eventually become symbols themselves. While a historical puer is biologically an adult, a symbolic one may never grow up. These symbolic pueri exemplify exactly the eternally young life that actual puer personalities strive to emulate. Classical examples are Peter Pan and the Little Prince. Just as a puer may be conscious or unconscious, so he may outwardly be adjusted or maladjusted. Outwardly, he may be settled in a marriage and a job, but he still finds no satisfaction in them. Or he may be unsettled even outwardly, as in the cases of Don Juan and the eternal student.

The opposite of the puer archetype is that of the hero.[6] A hero succeeds where a puer fails. Strictly, there are two stages of heroism. In the first half of life an ego is heroic in managing to liberate itself from the unconscious and establish itself in society. A hero manages to secure a fulfilling relationship and a job. A puer fails to do either. In the second half of life a now independent ego is heroic in managing to break with society and return to the unconscious without thereby falling back into it. Because a puer never establishes an independent ego, he never faces the possible loss of it. Where a real hero is like Daedalus, a puer is like Icarus. Because a puer is a failed hero in the first half of life, he is necessarily a failed hero in the second half as well. Indeed, for him there is no second half.

Adonis is a quintessential puer because he never marries, never works, and dies young. He never grows up. His puer personality spans the period from infancy to adolescence. He must first break out of a tree in order to be born. His mother, transformed into the tree, is reluctant to let him out. Like any other mother, she may be overjoyed at his conception; but unlike normal mothers, she wants to hoard him. In Ovid's version, Adonis himself has to find an exit.

Adonis' mother has herself proved unable to break out of her father, the only male who has ever aroused her. Even if her incestuous desire results from a curse, the curse is punishment for her indifference to other men, for which a prior attachment to her father is likely the latent cause. In any event, her desire is not really for intercourse with her actual father but for absorption in the father archetype. For she too has never severed herself from the unconscious and therefore has never grown up. Not coincidentally, she is incapable of raising Adonis, whom others, whatever their motives, must raise instead. She is a puella.

No sooner does Adonis emerge from the tree than, in Apollodorus' version, Aphrodite thrusts him back – not, to be sure, into the tree but into a chest. She thereby undoes the birth that had proved so arduous. She tells no one, for she wants Adonis all to herself. When Persephone, to whom Aphrodite has entrusted the chest without revealing its contents, opens it, she likewise falls in love with Adonis and refuses to return him. Each goddess, just like his mother, wants to possess him exclusively. Though Zeus' decision leaves Adonis free for a third of the year, Adonis readily cedes his third to Aphrodite. Never, then, is he outside the custody of these archetypal mother figures.

In his analysis of the myth of Adonis, Detienne makes him a seducer. A Jungian analysis would make him the seduced. He may scurry from goddess to goddess, but only because he is attached to each. He does not come and go on his own. He cannot imagine an independent life. Adonis is unable to resist the goddesses not because they arouse him sexually but because he does not even recognize them as goddesses. He sees them not as irresistibly beautiful females but as his mother, with whom he wants not intercourse but absorption. Between him and the goddesses there exists the primordial state of mystical oneness that the philosopher Lucien Lévy-Bruhl, whom Jung often cites, calls *participation mystique*. Psychologically, Adonis is at exactly that stage of humanity which Lévy-Bruhl and, following him, Jung deem 'primitive'.[7]

Adonis is the most extreme kind of puer – an unconscious as well as outward one. Since he never marries, never has children, never works, and dies young, he is conspicuously an outward puer. Since he has no idea of the difference between his life and anyone else's, he is clearly an unconscious puer as well. He lives in a fog.

Seemingly, a Jungian interpretation of the myth faces the same contradiction as Frazer's: that Adonis annually breaks free of the mother yet eventually dies permanently. Like Frazer, a Jungian might dismiss Adonis' final death as an aberration and stress his perennial liberation from the mother. In that case, Adonis would be a hero rather than a puer. Jung himself identifies Adonis with Frazer's annually reborn corn god: 'The corn-god of antiquity was Adonis, whose death and resurrection were celebrated annually. He was the son-lover of the mother, for the corn is the son and fructifier of the earth's womb' (Jung 1956: par. 530 n.79).

Yet a Jungian interpretation need not ignore Adonis' final demise, which is reconcilable with his recurrent revival. For the annual cycle of death and rebirth can symbolize not Adonis' annual liberation from the mother but the opposite: his annual return to the mother, even if that return ends in release. Where a normal child needs to be born only once to liberate himself from the mother, Adonis, as a puer, continually returns to the mother and so must be born again and again. His final death is simply his permanent rather than temporary return to her. It is the culmination of his past returns rather than a break with them. Previously, he had been strong enough to resist the mother temporarily. Now he can no longer do so.[8]

Is a Jungian analysis of the myth of Adonis scientific?

Interpretation

The first step in assessing the scientific status of a Jungian analysis of the myth of Adonis is to match it up with other analyses, as I have done with Frazer's analysis, and would be expected to do with other ones. As I stated at the outset, I find exasperating the tendency of Jungian applications to operate in isolation – as if the sole criterion were whether a Jungian approach works.

I have argued that a Jungian analysis of the myth of Adonis works better than Frazer's does. Frazer must turn Adonis, a human being, into a god – the god of vegetation. Adonis can perhaps be said to die insofar he spends a portion of every year in the land of the dead. But gods who die are usually reborn. They do not stay dead. By contrast, Adonis, while dying and being reborn for untold years, is eventually killed while on earth and stays dead forever. If he still returns to Hades, now he does so permanently. Yet as much of a jump the transformation of Adonis from human to god is, even more of a jump is the transformation of Adonis from personality to vegetation itself. All the characteristics that make a personality, human or divine, a personality thereby get dropped. That Adonis, like vegetation, dies and is reborn is what remains.

The Jungian analysis that I have offered may depart as fully as Frazer's does from the literal meaning of the myth. But it is far more detailed. It delineates the character of Adonis much more closely than Frazer's does. Like Frazer's, it types Adonis: as a puer rather than as a god of vegetation, which really means as vegetation itself. Adonis for Jung is not merely, as for Frazer, someone or something that dies and is continually reborn. Adonis is a personality, or more precisely one side of a personality – and of a human personality, not a divine one. Adonis symbolizes not a god but a human being.

Explanation

The second step in assessing the scientific status of a Jungian analysis of the myth of Adonis is tying the interpretation to an explanation. Again, as I stated at the outset, I find exasperating also the tendency of Jungian analyses to assume Jungian tenets rather than to argue for them. The applicability of the theory once the theory is assumed cannot justify the theory, which must be supported in its own right. Support is required even if there are no rival interpretations. Arguing that the myth of Adonis is illuminated *when* Adonis is taken as a case of a puer personality requires acceptance of the puer archetype and of Jung's whole notion of a collective unconscious.

Like all other theories of myth, Frazer's and Jung's are theories of far bigger domains than myth, which is merely one case in point. Frazer's theory is a theory of culture, of which religion is a part and myth in turn a part of religion. Other parts include magic and science. Frazer's theory is, even more basically, a theory of human nature. All of culture is for him a series of elaborate ways of getting food on the table. Frazer's theory – of myth, religion, culture, and human nature – has been fervently debated. But Frazer does bring to the table more than a classicist's mastery of a specific myth. He brings a twelve- and really thirteen-volume tome, *The Golden Bough* in its third edition. He enlists information from almost the whole world. Of course, his theory can still be wholly wrong, as many critics have asserted. But his analysis of the myth of Adonis rests on more than the ability to interpret a story.

The same is true of Jung, whose theory of myth is even more fully a theory of human nature. Jung does not, like Frazer, automatically subsume myth, which for him can be secular, under religion. The equivalent for Jung to Frazer's erudition is the findings of modern psychiatry and of depth psychology. Jung's theory, like Frazer's, may be wholly wrong, but a Jungian analysis of the myth of Adonis likewise rests on more than the ability to interpret a story.

Where no one disputes the existence of a need to eat, not quite everyone accepts the existence of an unconscious, let alone of a Jungian variety. Jung's theory of myth presupposes the existence of a collective unconscious. Myth for him operates unconsciously rather than, like myth for Frazer, consciously. Myth originates and functions to fulfil the need to encounter one's unconscious and to evaluate the state of it. Only to the extent that Jung's conception of the unconscious is established is a Jungian analysis of the myth of Adonis plausible.

Frazer's theory of myth does not commit one to more than physicalism. For him, myth arises from observation, hypothesis, and generalization: from observing, for example, the falling of rain and hypothesizing a human-like rain god and in turn human-like gods generally to account for physical events. But gods can be physical, and the relationship of the mind to the body – of thinking to eating – is readily compatible with physicalism. Frazer does hold to an old-fashioned view of science, which for him parallels myth and, even more, magic. But whatever his views of not only science but also, if any, metaphysics, they are not germane to his theory of myth.

By contrast, Jung's theory of myth presupposes dualism and, for those Jungians who cannot abide the identification of the soul with the mind, the existence of the soul as well as of the immaterial mind and the body. Physicalism is by far the dominant position in science and in philosophy of science. Dualism, let alone substance dualism, is a position held by few, if any, scientists and philosophers of science. And even if one grants substance dualism, what is the evidence for the specific dualist claims made by Jung: that the human mind contains not just an immaterial unconscious but also an unconscious composed of inherited archetypes? How many scientists and philosophers of science take seriously Jung's claims? Even if, once again, a Jungian *interpretation* of the myth of Adonis is more persuasive than Frazer's is, Frazer's *explanation* of myth is more persuasive than Jung's is. It is more scientific.

Kinds of inference

To apply a theory of myth is to apply a generalization about myth. There are three main questions about myth: what is the origin, what is the function, and what is the subject matter? Not all theories, to be sure, claim to answer all three questions. Some answer only one question or only two questions. But both Frazer's and Jung's theories answer all three questions.

A theory gives a generalized answer to whichever question it considers. It purports to answer the question not merely for any one myth or a group of myths but for all myths. The answer given is the same for every myth. Theories do not deny the differences among myths but instead seek the similarities. They claim not that all myths are identical but that all myths are similar enough to have the same origin, function, or subject matter.

There are three kinds of scientific generalizations: deductive, inductive, and abductive. To take just the Jungian application: all three generalizations would attribute the life of Adonis to his being a puer personality, just as for Frazer all three generalizations would attribute the life of Adonis to his symbolizing the course of vegetation.

Deductive inference

Deductively, the generalization would be as follows:

> A puer personality is one who never grows up, never marries, and dies young.
> Adonis is a puer personality.
> Therefore Adonis never grows up, never marries, and dies young.

Does this inference account for the life of Adonis? No. For while Adonis clearly fits the generalization, the generalization is a definition rather than an account. By definition a puer personality never grows up, never marries, and dies young. That Adonis qualifies as a puer type thus does not account for his personality but merely categorizes it.

Suppose the generalization were changed from a definition to an account:

> A puer personality is a psychological misfit who will never grow up, will never marry, and will die young.

Adonis is a puer personality.
Therefore Adonis will never grow up, will never marry, and will die young.

Now the behaviour of Adonis is the effect of his personality type rather than either the definition of his personality type, as for the behaviourist Gilbert Ryle, or the expression of his personality type, as for Wittgensteinians like Peter Winch.

But this deductive inference from puer personality to Adonis assumes certainty, which goes too far. A puer type is likely but not certain to fail to marry or to die young, as the cases of Casanova and Crowley, who did not die young, and of Crowley and Elvis, both of whom married, illustrate. The major premise is therefore false, even if, let us assume, the minor one is true. Because a puer personality is merely likely to fail to grow up, marry, or live long, the inference must become inductive.

Inductive inference

What makes an inference inductive is, first, that Adonis' not growing up, marrying, or living long is merely statistical. Most other pueri do not do so, in which case Adonis is not likely to do so either. But what makes the inference inductive, even more, is that it is merely a tabulation of all cases to date rather than a universal claim. Even if all other known pueri never grew up, married, or lived long, the generalization would still be less than universal since the lives of all possible, especially all future, pueri would be unknown. The claim would be akin to the claim that all sheep are white – a claim that would also be a tabulation of all known, not of all possible, cases. Therefore the claim that Adonis is unlikely to grow up, marry, and live long would remain merely probabilistic.

That one already knows the outcome of the life of Adonis does not make the inference unscientific. Any explanation starts with the effect and works backwards to the cause. That the outcome of the life of Adonis is merely probabilistic does not make the inference unscientific either. Many scientific generalizations are only probabilistic. What does make the account less than fully scientific is that it is not predictive. It does not predict new facts.

Inductively, the generalization would be as follows:

A puer personality is one who does not grow up, marry, or live long (with high probability).
Adonis is a puer personality.
Therefore Adonis will not grow up, marry, or live long (with high probability).

This argument holds only if the two premises are true: that a puer personality is likely to behave in the ways specified and that Adonis is a puer personality. The difficulty is distinguishing the definition of the type from the behaviour associated with the type – the same problem as in a deductive inference. The definition is like that in a psychiatric manual or a medical diagnosis: the equivalent of the symptoms – the behaviour – is part of the definition. If not failing to marry and dying young, then certainly never growing up is almost identical with *qualifying* as a puer.

But there are ways out of this difficulty. One way is to define the puer type in the way that a psychiatric or medical condition is actually defined: as more than behaviour. After all, a symptom is not equivalent to the ailment, which is the cause of the symptom. A symptom may be necessary to having an ailment but is not sufficient. And some ailments are asymptomatic. The first premise would therefore not be:

> A puer personality is one who does not grow up, marry, or live long (with high probability).

It would be:

> A puer personality is one who suffers from domination by the puer archetype and therefore does not grow up, marry, or live long.

The other way out of the difficulty is to characterize more variedly the behaviour associated with the puer type. Elvis might have married, but he was hardly a faithful husband. Crowley's marriage lasted a year, and Crowley was, as he charmingly called himself, 'pansexual'. That both he and Elvis married hardly made their domestic life settled. A puer can, then, be predicted to have an unsettled domestic life, but with the specific form that life takes as going beyond the definition of the type.

The danger in this second option is that the manifestation of the behaviour of a puer can be so open-ended that success is certain. As I stated at the outset, Jungian analyses tend to be so malleable that applicability is guaranteed. Put bluntly, it is hard not to find evidence of behaviour befitting a puer. Still, some specification can surely be provided.

A mere *interpretation* of the life of Adonis would assume the existence of a puer personality and would apply it to the case of Adonis. A convincing interpretation would be able to match up the characteristics of a puer personality with the characteristics of Adonis. The life of Adonis would be consistent with the data on cases of the puer known to date. An *explanation* of the life of Adonis would seek to prove the existence of the puer personality itself. It would seek to prove true the major premise: that there is such a thing as a puer type. The inference, deductive or inductive, that Adonis will not grow up, marry, or live long is valid insofar as the conclusion follows from the premises, whether with certainty or with likelihood. An explanation would seek to prove true the major premise, though also the minor one. The minor premise assumes an accurate description of the myth of Adonis. That the myth of Adonis, like any other myth, has multiple versions is a separate issue.

Abductive inference

Abductively, the generalization would be the following:

> The myth of Adonis is about someone who never grows up, does not marry, and dies young.
> Attributing Adonis' behaviour to his having a puer personality makes the best sense of his behaviour.
> Therefore Adonis is a puer personality.

To see how abduction differs from induction, take another example: that of the French Revolution. Suppose the inductive argument is that hunger was the cause of the French Revolution. The generalization would be that if people are sufficiently hungry and have no expectation of the arrival of food, they will likely revolt. The evidence for this argument would rest on data showing the frequency with which hungry people revolt and on data showing the prevalence of hunger among the French urban poor.

The difference between attributing the French Revolution to hunger and attributing Adonis' behaviour to a puer personality is that the existence of hunger and of its common effect on behaviour is hardly debatable, where the existence of the puer personality and of its effect on behaviour is rather less obvious. Still, the form of argument is the same – namely, induction. The data support the theory: given the data, we are justified, which means with probability rather than with certainty, in attributing the Revolution to hunger and attributing Adonis' behaviour to his puer personality.

In abduction, the relationship between theory and data is reversed. The theory explains the data: given the theory, we can make sense of the data. Abduction appeals not to other events – other revolutions – but to just the French Revolution. Of course, here too we know that hunger makes sense of the French case because of evidence from other cases, evidence that relies on induction. But in abduction, there is no hedging: hunger, goes the assertion, caused the Revolution. It is acknowledged that hunger cannot, at least at present, explain all other cases, but those cases can be examined anew. The cases unexplained by hunger do not undermine the claim that hunger caused the Revolution. Otherwise one would almost never have an acceptable account, which is to say one that was even statistical rather than certain. Of Adonis, the assertion is that he acted as he did – not growing up, marrying, or living long – because he was a puer personality.

Unlike induction, abduction usually assumes a choice of theories. So assume that if we attribute the French Revolution to hunger, and to hunger without any prospect of alleviation, we can better account for the event than if we attribute it to, say, press 'agitation'. (Let's forgo considering a combination of these explanations.) We can show how frequently those French who revolted had complained of hunger and acted to feed themselves as soon as they secured, say, arms from the Bastille. Past cases of hunger as the cause of revolution are still being used, as in induction. Hunger is assumed to account best for the French Revolution because it accounts best for other revolutions. But in abduction the statistics are used to support the account, which itself is more than statistical.

Conclusion

I have used the myth of Adonis as simply an example of the way one would evaluate the scientific status of a Jungian analysis of any myth, any religion, any artifact, or even any person. I have argued that a Jungian analysis is best evaluated in competition with other analyses. I have argued that the starting point is what I have called an interpretation: making sense of the entity at hand. But I have argued that a Jungian analysis cannot stop at interpretation. It must proceed to what I have called an explanation: justifying the theory – of myth, religion, culture, or personality – applied to the interpretation. Sometimes one analysis will prove superior to another on both interpretive and explanatory counts. Other times, as here, one analysis will prove superior to another as an interpretation but not as an explanation.

In my example I have argued that as an interpretation of the myth of Adonis, a Jungian analysis is superior to Frazer's. But I have also argued that as an explanation of myth and ultimately of human nature itself, Frazer's theory is superior to Jung's. Because Frazer's interpretation rests on a sturdier explanation, it is, for me, superior overall to Jung's. Put summarily, it is more scientific.

Even though I have used only the theory of Jung and not also that of Frazer in the final part of this chapter, I have argued that whenever the subject is something over which there are at least two competing theories, the kind of generalization most suitable is abductive rather than deductive or inductive. It gives us what is actually the familiar phrase for abduction: inference to the best explanation.

Notes

1 See Apollodorus, *Library*, 1.116, 3.182, 183–5; Ovid, *Metamorphoses*, 10.708–39. On both the myth and the cult of Adonis, see Boedeker (1974: 64–7), Burkert (1979: 105–11; 1985: 176–7).
2 See Frazer (1890, I: 278–96; 1913, I: chapters 1–4, 9–10; 1922: chapters 29–33).
3 On Adonis, see Jung (1956: par. 321, 330 n.32, 392, 530 n.79; 1952: par. 715).
4 On the archetype of the *puer aeternus*, see Jung (1956: par. 392, 526; 1954: par. 193; 1976, I: 82). See also Neumann (1970 [1954]: 88–101). Neumann himself uses the term 'son-lover' for puer.
5 On the archetype of the Great Mother, see Jung (1954; 1956). See also Neumann (1970 [1954]; 1972).
6 On the hero archetype, see Jung (1937: 437–41; 1940; 1956). See also Neumann (1970 [1954]: 131–256; 1972: 203–8). On the hero as the opposite of the puer, see Whitmont (1969: 182–3).
7 On 'primitive, or 'archaic', man, see Jung (1931).
8 To be sure, this negative interpretation of the puer archetype and therefore of Adonis represents only the classical Jungian view. The post-Jungian, archetypal view of James Hillman (1979) and his followers interprets the puer archetype positively and would

therefore applaud rather than castigate Adonis for his identification with that archetype. Where for Jung and von Franz the life of a puer ends tragically, if not pathetically, in premature death, for Hillman it ends triumphantly, in a refusal to compromise with the everyday world. The behaviour that for Jung and von Franz is childish would for Hillman be childlike.

Acknowledgements

For indispensable help in sorting me out philosophically, I want to thank three philosophers at the University of Aberdeen: Gerry Hough, Luca Moretti, and Franz Berto.

References

Boedeker, D. D. (1974). *Aphrodite's Entry into Greek Epic*. Leiden: Brill.
Burkert, W. (1979). *Structure and History in Greek Mythology and Ritual*. Berkeley: University of California Press.
——. (1985). *Greek Religion*. Cambridge, MA: Harvard University Press.
Detienne, M. (1977). *The Gardens of Adonis*. Princeton, NJ: Princeton University Press.
Frazer, J. G. (1890). *The Golden Bough* (1st edition). London: Macmillan.
——. (1900). *The Golden Bough* (2nd edition). London: Macmillan.
——. (1911–15). *The Golden Bough* (3rd edition). London: Macmillan.
——. (1922). *The Golden Bough* (abridged edition). London: Macmillan.
Hillman, J. (Ed.) (1979). *Puer Papers*. Dallas, TX: Spring Publications.
Jung, C. G. The following are from *The Collected Works of C. G. Jung* (CW) Princeton, NJ: Princeton University Press:
——. (1931). Archaic man. (CW10)
——. (1937). Religious ideas in alchemy. (CW12)
——. (1940). The psychology of the child archetype. (CW9i)
——. (1952). Answer to Job. (CW11)
——. (1954). Psychological aspects of the mother archetype. (CW9i)
——. (1956). Symbols of transformation. (CW5)
Jung, C. G. (1976). *Letters*. Princeton, NJ: Princeton University Press.
Neumann, E. (1970). *The Origins and History of Consciousness*. Princeton, NJ: Princeton University Press. (Original work published in 1954)
——. (1972). *The Great Mother* (2nd edition). Princeton, NJ: Princeton University Press.
Segal, R. A. (1986). *The Poimandres as Myth*. Amsterdam: Mouton de Gruyter.
——. (1992). *Explaining and Interpreting Religion*. New York: Lang.
——. (1999). *Theorizing about Myth*. Amherst: University of Massachusetts Press.
Von Franz, M.-L. (1981). *Puer Aeternus* (2nd edition). Santa Monica, CA: Sigo.
Whitmont, E. (1969). *The Symbolic Quest*. New York: Putnam.

6

ANALYTICAL PSYCHOLOGY, NARRATIVE THEORY AND THE QUESTION OF SCIENCE

Terence Dawson

In November 1896, during the second year of his medical studies, Carl Jung gave a talk to the Zofingia Students Association entitled 'The Border Zones of Exact Science'. It was on the need to explore all experiences that defy rational and materialist explanation. He berated scientists who try to give immaterial phenomena a materialist explanation, as well as those who sweep the problem posed by the immaterial under the carpet. Jung wanted to see established 'a solid point of departure for further critical excursuses in the realm of metaphysics' that would 'allow the immaterial to retain its immaterial properties' (1896: par. 16, 66). His talk identifies the main thread of all his later work. Jung's dominant concerns changed little in the course of his long and productive life. His career divides naturally into three phases marked not by any major shift in his guiding interest but by the methodologies that he adopted to explore it, as follows.

1. *The Psychiatric Years.* In 1900, even before completing his dissertation, Jung was offered a post in a psychiatric hospital in Zurich, the Burghölzli. During the following nine years, he treated patients from every social class and with wide-ranging problems. This experience with deeply disturbed and psychotic patients taught him to respect 'the reality of the psyche' (Jung 1952a: par. 1507) and provided the clinical foundation for his later work. During these years, his methodology conformed to the rigorous standards expected in psychiatric research. His data was collected mostly from patients, and most of it was quantifiable. His word association test is typical. He measured the patient's responses to trigger words as accurately as was possible, developed a theory to account for divergences in a patient's responses, and presented findings that could be tested by others. Jung argued that the key to psychiatric troubles lay in unconscious feeling-toned complexes (e.g. Jung & Riklin 1904). His word association test won acclaim. Five years after graduating, he was not only appointed Bleuler's assistant, but was also offered a prestigious part-time faculty position at the University of Zürich's medical school. A very promising career in both clinical and academic psychiatry lay before

him. But he had already come to the first turning point in his career: in 1903, Jung became interested in the success of psychoanalysis in treating hysteria. He sent Freud a copy of the first volume of his *Diagnostic Association Studies*, which reprinted a recently published article (Jung 1906).

2. *The Psychoanalytic Years.* In October 1906, Freud sent Jung his most recent collection of papers. This led to their first meeting on the 3rd of March 1907. Soon, Freud came to regard Jung as his 'crown prince' (Freud & Jung 1974: 218). Jung was never convinced by Freud's insistence on the centrality of sexuality, and avowed his misgivings candidly (ibid.: 7, 10–11, 25). What drew him to psychoanalysis was the possibility that the imagery encountered in his patients' dreams and fantasies could provide a key to their alienation from reality. His psychoanalytic years were dominated by the challenge to demonstrate that non-invasive psychoanalytic methods could be employed to treat at least some forms of dementia praecox (schizophrenia). Jung (1907) drew parallels between hysteria and dementia. His director, Bleuler, who regarded schizophrenia as incurable, expressed worries about the time Jung devoted to schizophrenic patients. In October 1908, he asked for Jung's resignation. Both men agreed to postpone this until the spring, when Jung became a full-time psychoanalyst (Bair 2003: 149–59). Dreams, waking fantasies, and instinctive associations were now Jung's primary data. He regarded the dream as an experiential 'fact'. This is why, for the remainder of his life, he thought of himself as an empiricist. As he wrote in 1935: 'I am first and foremost an empiricist' (Jung 1973: 195). And yet neither a dream nor a waking-fantasy can be observed, let alone measured by anyone other than the dreamer. Jung was investigating *a question appropriate to psychiatry* (i.e. science), but no longer approaching it with a methodology recognized in psychiatric research. The second turning point came while he was trying to pursue his ideas about psychoanalysis and dementia praecox.

3. *Analytical Psychology.* In 1906, an article by Miss Frank Miller, 'Some Instances of Subconscious Creative Imagination', appeared in French translation, in the *Archives de psychologie*, with an introduction by Flournoy (Bair 2003: 718 n.65). Jung's (1912) *Psychology of the Unconscious* offers an entirely fresh interpretation of Miss Miller's fantasies. It laid the foundations for Jung's own distinctive brand of psychoanalysis, best-known today as analytical psychology. Jung always thought of his work as scientific. He repeatedly insisted: 'I have a scientific training' (1973: 327); 'As a scientist . . .' (ibid.: 346); 'My scientific duty . . .' (ibid.: 124); 'My scientific methodology . . .' (ibid.: 360); and 'Analytical psychology is not a *Weltanschauung* but a science' (1927: par. 730). But in *Psychology of the Unconscious*, Jung analyses a text (Miss Miller's) by reference to other texts. This is not a methodology recognized in psychiatry. In spite of Jung's ardent protests to the contrary, it is not science. It is a *textual* theory based on wide-ranging reading – i.e. academic scholarship. Jung developed most of his distinct ideas about unconscious processes not from analysing his patients but from his own analysis of ideas and images that he encountered in academic texts.

Because Jung was a qualified psychiatrist who worked most his long life as an analyst, it is usually assumed that Jungian theory is first and foremost a *clinical* theory, and that any reference to Jung's work in other disciplines (literature, religion, etc.) constitutes an 'application' of his clinical theory (see Papadopoulos 2006). My contention is that Jungian psychology is *primarily* a narrative and cultural theory that Jung subsequently 'applied' in his private practice. This chapter aims to contextualize, substantiate, and explore this contention and its implications for analytical psychology.

From psychiatry to cultural theory

It is generally accepted that Jung helped Freud to win international recognition. It is equally accepted that Jung borrowed his clinical method from psychoanalysis, adapting it to suit himself. Rather than sit behind a patient lying on a couch, Jung preferred to sit opposite his patient so they could converse face to face. What is not so widely recognized is that it was Freud who first encouraged Jung to explore the relation between dreams, myth and culture. In other words, Freud nudged Jung into discovering the key to his own distinct theory of unconscious processes.

Freud was quick to see how psychoanalysis could be applied to literature and other cultural products. In 1907, he founded *Papers on Applied Psychology* in order to give psychoanalysis a 'more general appeal' and to show how it could inform *other* fields of enquiry (Freud & Jung 1974: 29, 578). These *Papers* were to revolutionize how we think about the origin and nature of the artistic impulse. Never before had a specific theory about psychological processes been applied either so rigorously or so extensively to cultural products. Others can be mentioned, such as Otto Rank's (1989 [1907]) monograph, the first to consider the urge to create from a psychoanalytic perspective and also to suggest that this urge can be healthy and positive. The application of psychoanalysis to novels, fairytales, legends, myths, Renaissance painting, opera, Shakespeare's best-known tragedy, and the creative process, hugely expanded interest in Freud's work. Freud's *Papers* raised psychoanalysis from a highly controversial method of treating hysteria into a psychological, literary and cultural theory that was to have an enormous impact on the twentieth century.

Throughout his psychoanalytic years, Jung's professional thoughts were absorbed by the challenge to demonstrate that schizophrenia could be cured using psychoanalytic methods. He praised Freud for his *Gradiva* (Freud & Jung 1974: 49) and also some of his followers' ideas, including Rank and later Silberer, but he showed no interest in following their lead. His own contribution to Freud's *Papers*, 'The Content of the Psychoses' (Jung 1908), is atypical of the series: it does not seek to apply psychoanalysis to any kind of cultural product. At the time, his energy was being dissipated by other concerns: developing a private practice, building and settling into his new house, overseeing his growing family, and his close and stormy relation with Sabina Spielrein (Bair 2003). Then came his dismissal from the Burghölzli. Astonishingly, he expressed few regrets about it. Having married the daughter of a wealthy businessman, he may have had less need of an income than most young men. Nevertheless, given his driving interest, his attitude begs an explanation. By resigning, he lost access to his primary data source. A likely explanation for his lack of concern is that he was so confident of producing a work that would put Freud's *Interpretation of Dreams* in the shade that he simply didn't give the matter due attention.

In the summer of 1909, Jung was stalled. Throughout their relationship, Freud had been encouraging him to become more interested in myth and religion (Freud & Jung 1974). Ironically, it was Freud and his followers who convinced him that deeply ingrained cultural practices might provide the key to autonomous unconscious images that he had been looking for. It was not until returning from the Clark conference in October 1909 that he finally settled. He resumed areas of study that he had explored in his teens and as a student, but had left dormant for almost a decade (Jung 1963: 68ff.). Picking up on leads provided by Abraham and Rank, he investigated analogies between the motifs he noted in his patients' dreams and the structures of ancient myths and other ancient cultural practices. He finally realized that evidence that the mind generates autonomous images is most likely to be found in religious writings and mythology.

Jung immersed himself in a wide range of studies of symbolism, ancient religions, philosophy, literature and myth. To borrow Freud's words, his purpose was to 'take possession of the promised land of psychiatry' (Freud & Jung 1974: 197). But as he slowly set about formulating his ideas, something very different happened: *the study of religion and mythology slowly took possession of him*. It was not long before he was writing enthusiastically to Freud: 'Archaeology or rather mythology has got me in its grip'; the 'oldest and most natural' myths are an expression of the 'core complex of the neuroses'; 'I am pursuing my mythological dreams with almost autoerotic pleasure'; and 'We shall not solve the ultimate secrets of neurosis and psychosis without mythology and cultural history [*Kulturgeschichte*]' (ibid.: 251–2, 263, 308, 279). In August 1910, he got so over-excited that he told Freud that it wasn't he who had 'discovered psychoanalysis' but 'Plato, Thomas Aquinas and Kant, with Kuno Fischer and Wundt thrown in' (ibid.: 346). Freud laughed this off (ibid.: 347). Even so, Jung's years of intense study affected him deeply: his enthusiasm has all the hallmarks of what Jung would later call 'possession' (e.g. 1943: par. 111). He used to spend hours of his day with psychiatric patients. Now he spent them alone, in his library, reading material that held him in a kind of spell. The year 1909 marks the beginning of a new period of introversion in his life.

Freud, Abraham, Rank, and Silberer had established that the motifs of mythology were uncannily similar to those found in some kinds of fantasies. However original each of them was in his own way, their forays into myth only tentatively extended the nature of existent psychoanalytic theory. In marked contrast, when Jung began to study early religious and cultural practices, he articulated a view which he had long intuited: that culture is too varied to be satisfactorily explained by classical Freudian theory.

TERENCE DAWSON

Myth criticism and narrative theory

The study of ancient cultures and their myths was fashionable in the late nineteenth century: e.g. Eliot (1871), Tylor (1871), and Frazer (1890). What Casaubon, Tylor and Frazer have in common is their methodology. They were scholars: they worked almost exclusively from texts. *Psychology of the Unconscious* (Jung 1912) grew from the same methods. It was written while Frazer (1906–15) was expanding the third edition of *The Golden Bough*, Harrison (1912) was busy with *Themis*, and Cornford (1912) was finishing *From Religion to Philosophy*, soon followed by Murray's (1913) and Cornford's (1914) works, both of which employ anthropology, religion and myth to analyse literary texts. The term 'myth criticism' is given to a kind of literary criticism that seeks to explain the resonance of a literary text in terms of an underlying cultural experience usually related to either religion, ritual or myth (Guerin et al. 1992). It is characterized by an interest in the various ways in which the writer's imagination transforms source material into the literary work. A classic example is *The Road to Xanadu: A Study in the Ways of the Imagination*, in which Lowes (1927) traces the images at the heart of 'The Rime of the Ancient Mariner' and 'Kubla Khan' to ideas sparked in Coleridge's imagination by his extensive reading. The purpose of myth criticism is to reconstruct a creative process involving a 'transformation' of images and ideas into a literary text. This is very similar to what Jung was doing in *Psychology of the Unconscious*. The major difference is that whereas Lowes explored psychological concerns as a literary critic, Jung did so as a psychiatrist.

All of Jung's major writings represent a variant of myth criticism. Their bibliographies contain few references to recent works in psychiatry and psychoanalysis, and these are outnumbered by references to religious and alchemical works, studies of myth, folklore, early societies, and literary texts. Almost all the evidence for his major ideas comes from various kinds of texts. A large part of *Psychological Types* (Jung 1921) is based on his interpretation of either philosophical or literary works. His writings on the East and on Christianity (e.g. Jung 1937, 1939), and his extensive studies of Western alchemy (see *The Collected Works* volumes 12, 13, and 14) are entirely derived from his interpretation of texts. 'Answer to Job' (Jung 1952b) is based on the biblical text. Even when Jung analyses an isolated image, he is always contextualizing it within a narrative. As he writes: 'I handle the dream as if it were a text which I do not understand properly' (1935: par. 172). Remarkably few of his mature publications are based on case studies; and those that are regard a series of dreams as a *narrative* (e.g. Jung 1934, 1989a [1925], 1984 [1928–30], 1997 [1930–34], 2008 [1936–40]). According to Henderson, by 1934, Jung's 'seminars no longer contained case material' (quoted in Bair 2003: 395). This is illustrated by his lengthy exploration of Nietzsche's *Also Sprach Zarathustra* (Jung 1989b [1934–39]). Although formulated by a practising analyst, Jungian psychology is grounded in a theory about *narrative* and its methodology belongs to an *academic* tradition.

For this reason, it is worth looking at the way in which Jung approaches literary narratives. Two issues stand out. The first is his distinction between the process of artistic creation and aesthetics. In contrast to Freud, Jung was extraordinarily slow to realize that psychoanalysis could be applied to cultural products. It was more than ten years after his break with Freud before he made his first attempt to apply his emergent ideas to literature. 'On the Relation of Analytical Psychology to Poetry' originated as a lecture in 1922. He begins by stressing the distinction between aesthetics, or the study of literature *per se*, and what interests him, *the process of artistic creation*:

> Only that aspect of art which consists in the process of artistic creation can be a subject for psychological study, but not that which constitutes its essential nature. The question of what art is in itself can never be answered by the psychologist, but must be approached from the side of aesthetics.
>
> (Jung 1922: par. 97)

The phrase that Hull translates as 'Poetry' (*zum dichterischen Kunstwerk*) might be better rendered as 'Poetic Art' (as Baynes translated it in 1923) or even 'literary work', for this is what is at issue. Had Jung been speaking about carpentry, the distinction he makes might have been clear. The process by which a carpenter manufactures a table is demonstrably distinct from the merits, whether functional or aesthetic, of the finished product. But Jung was referring to *writing*, and even if one had a writer's every draft, these would provide evidence only of certain choices made by the writer at a given moment. Any claim about the process of artistic creation rests on an act of interpretation.

The second issue is his distinction between bad and good science. Jung always insisted that he was a scientist – a *good* scientist. Poor science is represented by Freud, who regarded the unconscious as a code composed of signs that anyone with a minimal introduction to psychoanalysis could decipher. In Jung's view, such a method of interpretation produces not only reductive readings, but also readings whose findings bring the work of art 'into the sphere of general human psychology' (1922: par. 102). That is, Freud treats the elements he isolates for commentary as '*signs* or *symptoms* of the subliminal processes' that apply to collective experience (ibid.: par. 105). His method cannot isolate what is *specific* to an individual. In contrast, Jung insists that an image encountered in a dream is not a sign, but a *symbol*. Both terms, of course, refer to images: the issue is the nature of the resonance that the image harbours for the individual. For example, a cross on a church steeple is a sign. It means the same to all people: the building beneath this cross is a place where Christians gather for worship. But if we enter the church, we will find another cross on the altar. This is a symbol: a reminder of the mystery of Christ's sacrifice. A devout Christian and a devout Hindu being shown around the church would respond differently to it. The Christian might not be able to explain its full implications to his Hindu friend. The full implications of a symbol lie beyond the power of words to explain, not least because it means something slightly (but often significantly) different to each individual. Jung did not believe that a dream could be reduced to a single meaning, least of all to one that could be articulated in a few words. Jung claims that better *science* is produced by reading the elements in a dream as *symbols*, i.e. 'as an expression of an intuitive idea that cannot yet be formulated in any other or better way' (1922: par. 105; 1921: par. 816). Jung's good science consists in his ability to read the symbol correctly.

Signs indicate; symbols resonate. Freud's arguments are easy to follow, because if one regards an image as a sign, it has only one meaning. Jung's arguments are not always easy to follow, largely because he thought that an unconscious image harbours a 'complex' of meanings. The image will not and cannot tell either the patient or the analyst exactly what the problem is; it can provide only the 'best possible' representation of an intrinsically polyvalent meaning. This is an academic theory about the nature and psychological implications of imagery.

Narrative theory explores not only how narratives generate meaning, but also how readers make sense of narratives. It does not aspire to uncovering truth or any kind of fact. It seeks further to understand the nature and implications of narrative. Every analysis or interpretation of a text – literary or otherwise – reflects a specific point of view. Jungian insistence on the symbol is one such point of view; analytical psychology, one such methodology.

The reality of the psyche

The phrase 'reality of the psyche' is associated with Jung's later writings (e.g. 1952a: par. 1507), but it was a lesson he learned from his psychiatric years: that every inner experience is intensely *real* to the subject. By 'reality of the psyche', he meant that one's fantasies and dreams are just as real and just as significant for the individual who experiences them as are the events of the outer world:

> Even if a neurosis had no cause at all other than imagination, it would, nonetheless, be a very real thing. If a man imagined that I was his arch-enemy and killed me, I should be dead on account of mere imagination. Imaginary conditions do exist and they may be just as real and just as harmful or dangerous as physical conditions.
>
> (Jung 1937: par. 17)

From the outset of his interest in medicine, Jung was convinced that such 'imaginary conditions' are not irrelevant epiphenomena of no significant bearing on patients' mental health. He held that dreams and waking fantasies reflect the issues uppermost in the person's mind at the time. They offer not only the best possible indication of what has caused the impasse in the patient's life, but also how to ameliorate and perhaps cure the condition.

Psychiatrists like Bleuler thought otherwise. How was Jung to demonstrate the validity of his view? How could he demonstrate that one could treat even deeply psychotic patients by understanding the nature and implications of their dreams and waking fantasies, both of which are immaterial and unstable subjective experiences?

Although Jung (1912) does not quote many works of idealist philosophy, his theories belong within the tradition of German idealist philosophy, as many have recognized (e.g. Frey-Rohn 1984; Bishop 1995, 2000; Huskinson 2004; McGrath 2012). The separate concerns of materialism and idealism may be compared through the following example. To tear the meat off the carcass of an animal they had killed, early men probably used sticks, rough stones, and their hands. Then, in Northern Tanzania, *Homo habilis* started to use a hard stone as a tool to chip at another hard stone until one of its edges was even sharper than their immediate needs required. They made the earliest surviving high-quality multi-purpose 'chopping tool' (MacGregor 2010: 9). It represents an enormous step forward in human evolution.

Materialists, interested in things and causal relations, would argue that *Homo habilis* simply saw two material things (two hard stones) and acted on the obvious implications. They assume that an ability to make connections is an attribute of the brain. Neuroscientists may demonstrate that a connection akin to an electric spark occurs within a specific part of the brain at the moment of each new perception. Some post-Jungian analysts similarly seek corroboration for Jungian archetypes in neuroscience (see, e.g., Knox 2003, Wilkinson 2006). Such claims belong to a scientific dialogue. They are concerned with the demonstrable, the quantifiable and the predictable. The achievements of material science, whether in space exploration or neuroscience, are everywhere evident. Nevertheless, it has limitations. The three most obvious are:

1 The materialist cannot explain why a stimulus akin to a spark in a specific part of the brain should trigger a *specific* thought, e.g. about hardness and a sharp edge.
2 Materialism takes insufficient account of the *subject* of experience, the 'I'. As pithily expressed by Schopenhauer: 'materialism is the philosophy of the subject who forgets to take account of himself' (Janaway 2002: 53).
3 Although not central to my argument here, it must also be pointed out that materialism is *a* -moral, as the global challenges facing us today vividly illustrate. These consequences of rapid developments make ethical guidelines increasingly urgent – and these, in turn, are more readily associated with idealism.

Few idealists question that we live within an objective reality. They are interested in the way that subjective factors – i.e. our immaterial inner images and corresponding thoughts – influence what we know and can know of objective reality. Idealists are interested in what happens *within the subjective factor* that enables an individual to see things and connect them in a *specific* fashion. They want to know *how* we recognize what we see; how a *specific* thought comes into being. For the idealist, it is not obvious why something resembling an electric spark should lead to the specific mental connection that enabled early man to make the first chopping tool. To realize that to sharpen one edge of a hard stone, one has to knock it carefully with an even harder stone, *Homo habilis* must have made a series of specific mental connections between the two stones. A sequence of ideas – very probably in images – must have arisen in his mind, which he then tested until he arrived at a satisfactory chopping tool. This process may have taken several generations before producing the tool that is currently displayed in the British Museum. Idealists insist that all we can know of reality stems from our own perceptions. They are interested in how the individual mind not only experiences but also creates the reality it experiences. They argue that even our habitual actions would be impossible unless suggested by an *idea*. For the idealist, every breakthrough – whether in technology, philosophy, the arts or any other field – occurs first in the immaterial world of ideas, inner images, and thoughts. The idealist is no less interested in causes than the materialist is, but he is most concerned with the ever-evolving *process* of connections that lead from idea and/or image to thought.

Because he thought it possible to treat psychosis by psychological (i.e. psychoanalytical), as opposed to psychiatric methods, Jung turned his back on psychiatry. Nonetheless, he approached questions like a scientist. He noted a problem with Freud's theory, and sought a better explanation. His instincts were those of a scientist. Psychiatry treats the brain; philosophy deals with mind. For Jung, the psyche is neither brain nor mind. He avoided the word 'mind' not because it might have suggested something essentially rational, but because he wanted a word that included the intuitive, the corporeal, even the irrational. He knew well that such issues are processed by the brain. But he understood this entity more broadly than is usually implied by 'mind'. By *psyche*, he meant two things:

1 The hypothetical place from which all the *images* we encounter in our dreams and waking fantasies originate, for as he writes, 'The psyche consists essentially of images' (Jung 1926: par. 618). By image, he meant everything from a vague intuition to a vivid visual representation.
2 The hypothetical place from which all kinds of *consciousness* originate – not just intellectual consciousness, but also consciousness related to sensory, intuitive, emotional and physical experience. He thought of psychology as the discipline that deals with the relation between images and consciousness – as a science not of the mind alone but of the whole person, the entirety of his or her *being*.

All of Jung's work is concerned with the relation between image, consciousness and individual identity.

Methodology

Jung's theories have been challenged from so many different quarters that his essential concern is often forgotten. When Freud visited the Burghölzli in September 1908 and saw for himself the kind of psychotic patients that Jung was treating he turned away, disturbed and confused that Jung should wish to spend 'hours and days with [a] phenomenally ugly female' like Babette S., for like Bleuler, Freud considered such cases to be hopeless. Jung was 'dumbfounded' by his reaction (Bair 2003: 148–9, 697). Freud had no interest in psychosis: he preferred to work with his middle-class Viennese hysterics. In January 1909, he wrote to Jung, no doubt partly tongue-in-cheek, but also revealingly: 'Just give up wanting to cure; learn and make money' (Freud & Jung 1974: 203). Jung remained stubbornly insistent that he would find a way to *treat* psychotic patients by the non-invasive methods of psychoanalysis.

Freud was convinced his libido theory provided a *sufficient* explanation for a patient's loss of reality. Jung (1912) came to think otherwise. His suggestion was that one had to go deeper if one wanted to explore the 'rhizome' from which all autonomous fantasy originates (Jung 1952c: xxiv–xxv). Although Jung quotes from works representing a broad range of academic disciplines, he shows little interest in their overarching arguments. He read these works neither to confirm nor to refute their main concerns. He was looking only for what interested him – evidence that inner images harbour very real implications for the subject who experiences them.

For example, chapter V of *Psychology of the Unconscious* (Jung 1912) explores what happens immediately after the birth of Chi-wan-to-pel, the 'hero' of Miss Miller's fantasies. She records the brief vision of a 'throng of people', followed by an image of 'Horses, a battle, the view of a "City of Dreams" [*cité de rêves*]'. Somewhat surprisingly, Jung barely comments on the first two. He focuses his attention on the single phrase 'city of dreams'. First, he regrets that Miss Miller did not tell her reader precisely of which magazine pictures the city reminded her. He then concedes that the dream-city might be a wish-fulfilment, as in Freudian theory. Then he proceeds to amplify the image with *his own associations to the phrase*. He begins by describing the city as 'a sort of heavenly Jerusalem, as the poet of the Apocalypse has imagined it' (ibid.: 129). Next he identifies it as 'a maternal symbol', and elaborates this claim by referring first to Thea and Cybele, who 'both wear the wall crown', then to passages from Isaiah and Jeremiah, then to Egyptian mythology, then to Chinese mythology, then to Shiva's 'continual companionship with the woman [Parwati]' which lies behind the image of a lingam in a feminine receptacle in Hindu mythology. This latter idea is then amplified by reference to the chest containing a precious content in Greek mythology, which is thrown into the sea. This leads to a discussion of 'the night sea-journey' (Frobenius), which he likens to Noah's experience, a Melapolynesian legend, and then a story from the Ramayana. And we're still *only half way through* his amplification of the single phrase *cité de rêves* (ibid.: 129).

This is argument by very loose analogy. Some might be willing to concede that a city can be regarded as a maternal symbol, but others might have difficulty moving so easily from city-as-container to continual intercourse, and then from the image of a lingam in a feminine container to a floating chest. Indeed, a sceptic might think that the analogy springing most readily to mind is the party game

(Chinese whispers in the UK, telephone in the US) of passing a short narrative from person to person until it no longer bears any resemblance to the initial story. How can we rescue Jung from this charge?

The final chapter, 'The Sacrifice', begins with a paradoxical explanation of the subject of the last part of the previous chapter, Siegfried's longing for Brünnhilde:

> It is the striving of the libido away from the mother towards the mother. This paradoxical sentence may be translated as follows: as long as the libido is satisfied merely with phantasies, it moves in itself, in its own depths, in the mother.
>
> (Jung 1912: 237)

This is a clear challenge to two aspects of Freud's libido theory, which claimed that libido is essentially sexual and that the cause of all kinds of trauma lies in unresolved infantile longings (i.e. longings pertinent to a state that originates in and is ascribed to the past). Jung was now convinced that Freud's insistence on the censor and infantile sexuality could not explain all forms of psychosis. He concluded that if libido is not permitted to follow a path of natural maturation, it will turn in on itself, often expressed by a yearning for an imaginary past, until such time as it can find a way to follow its natural path. Jung suggests that fixing one's attention on a hypothetical infantile sexuality might even aggravate the patient's problem. Instead, patients should be gently induced to assume responsibility for the nature and implications of their difficulties in the present.

There is nothing intrinsically mystical, farfetched, or improbable about such a claim, nor in the later theory, anticipated in the 1912 monograph, that the psyche is 'a self-regulating system' (ibid.: par. 93). To corroborate this view, Jung refers to the 'deathless germs' that become 'new blooms' in '*An eine Rose*' (To a Rose), a well-known poem by Friedrich Hölderlin. This reminds him first of a passage in the *Iliad*, then of a reference that Plutarch made to the Osiris myth, and next to a description of 'heavenly bliss' in '*Hyperions Schiksaalslied*' (Hyperion's Song of Fate). This reminds him of the legend of a great serpent told by Frobenius, then to an African legend told by the same author (ibid.: 241–2). He adds that the motif of the bud appears in a passage by Plutarch, and that Brahma is born of a bud. He then quotes several lines from '*Der Mensch*' (Humanity or Man), another poem by Hölderlin, to illustrate 'the beginning of the discord between the poet and nature' (ibid.: 243). This reminds him of '*An die Natur*' (To Nature), another of Hölderlin's poems, which reminds him of a passage from the Bible, which reminds him of a passage of Gnostic writing, which reminds him of '*Palinodie*' (Palinode), another poem by Hölderlin, and then of '*Empedokles*' (Empedocles), yet another poem, which he sums up in words by Horace. And although this stage in the journey is not over, it is sufficient to illustrate his core concern.

Jung (1922) outlines his methodology as follows. The first step is 'to think of the creative process as . . . an *autonomous complex* . . . a split-off portion of the psyche' (ibid.: par. 115). The next, to ask: 'What primordial image [i.e. archetype] lies behind the imagery of art?' (ibid.: par. 124). For only by discovering this will we understand the meaning of the work of art, which conjures up 'the forms in which the age is most lacking' (ibid.: par. 130). Jung assumes that the creative process emerges from a complex, that a primordial image identifies the nature of the complex, and that the nature of the complex provides the psychological meaning of the work. In short, he assumes the validity of what he should be trying to demonstrate. The 'hard' scientist might have difficulty with the circularity of such a strategy, especially as all his evidence comes from analogy. Nevertheless, Jung follows a recognized method of academic enquiry. He offers a hypothesis and then corroborates it. For example, Leavis (1972 [1948]: 9) begins his classic study with the claim that 'The great English novelists are Jane Austen, George Eliot, Henry James, and Joseph Conrad.' Given that neither James nor Conrad were English born, and that neither Austen nor Eliot were held in high esteem in 1948, this was a provocative, controversial claim. The remainder of his study is concerned with substantiating it. The problem with Jung's strategy is that his evidence rests solely on analogy.

In Jung's defence, however, it must be asked: How else could he have explored his claim that images have far more – and more wide-ranging – implications for the person experiencing them than is usually assumed? As we have seen, Jung was not the first to claim that dream images have an affinity to those encountered in myth. He was the first to approach such images not as signs, but as symbols, i.e. as images that could best be interpreted by comparison with a variety of earlier expressions of a comparable motif. Instead of holding a single, categorical meaning, they harboured multiple implications. He referred to such images as archetypal images.

For Jung, what was vividly imagined was as *real* as the outer world. He knew that Hölderlin had suffered from mental problems: he took the poet's inner anxieties as seriously as he would a dream by one of his patients. He used Hölderlin's case to help him demonstrate the 'reality' of the danger that he thought might be facing Miss Miller – a danger of which she seemed unaware. Jung's purpose was to demonstrate that the images encountered in such products as Miss Miller's fantasies harbour a genuine clue to the possible nature of a conflict, or an implicit challenge, facing the person at the time of the dream or fantasy. Bair (2003: 214) asserts that Miss Miller's fantasies were created from 'within a normal, novelistic imagination'. Although Jung hadn't devised the term at the time, he clearly regarded them as 'active imagination', and probably rightly so (cf. Chodorow 1997). By the time of revising his 1912 text in the 1950s, he had learned that Miss Miller had been committed to a state hospital in Massachusetts and her condition was diagnosed as psychopathy. In his revised text, he emphasized the imminent danger of psychosis that he considered to be implicit in Miss Miller's text and announces proudly that she succumbed to it (1952c: par. 616). He did not know that Miss Miller was probably discharged only a week after being committed. Although nothing certain is known about the remainder of her life, it seems unlikely that she would have been discharged if she had a serious or incurable psychotic condition. Nevertheless, it might well be that she retained a tendency to 'psychopathy'. In all likelihood, Jung's diagnosis was close to the mark.

His readiness to quote Hölderlin places Jung's work in an interesting relation to Plato, the so-called 'father' of Western idealism. On the surface, the fact that he tries to substantiate his claim by reference to a poet might seem at odds with Plato, i.e. with Socrates' view that poets should be kept out of an ideal state because poetry is based on 'imitation' (394e-395b/2000: 83). Closer consideration suggests otherwise. What Plato/Socrates goes on to assert is more complex. He argues that poetry stirs up emotions that do not belong to the viewer or reader, emotions which the viewer/reader does not, is unable, or unwilling to submit to assessment by reason and to bring under control (605b/2000: 326ff.; cf. Lear 1998: 240). Plato's hostility to poetry is based on his view that most people are unable either to assess their emotions objectively or to overcome those that need to be overcome. He refers to emotions aroused by reading or attending a play. Jung extends his concern to include dreams and waking fantasies.

Jung's objective is to demonstrate that the dreams and fantasies of a borderline schizophrenic always harbour a clue as to how the person can reconnect with reality. Hölderlin was overwhelmed by mental illness. In Jung's view, however, the images to which he refers in his poems suggest that – without realizing it – he was trying to find a way out of his predicament. The images in Miss Miller's fantasies harbour the same suggestion. *Psychology of the Unconscious* challenges the claims of psychoanalysis. It argues that focusing on past events (as psychoanalysis invites patients to do) may lead to a worsening of the condition. This can be overcome only by accepting the faint but life-giving challenge at the centre of the trauma – and this always concerns some present difficulty. Jung's study makes a good case for the possibility of treating psychosis by means of psychoanalytic methodology.

The problem is that his methodology has nothing in common with those recognized by the discipline within which he wanted to make his mark. His 1912 study rests entirely on the interpretation of texts through analogy. His claim could not be independently verified. Some of the time, he reflects on Miss Miller's associations to her dreams' material; but most of the time he explores his own associations. And he recognized this.

Typology

Jung was one of the first not only to realize, but also to insist that psychology is an inherently plural discipline (Shamdasani 2003: 77), and that his approach was only one of many possible approaches. He was also the first to insist that every psychological theory necessarily reflects its author's subjective concerns: 'The psychologist should constantly bear in mind that his hypothesis is no more at first than the expression of his own subjective premise and can therefore never lay immediate claim to general validity' (Jung 1930: 85). As Jung later wrote, summing up the differences between himself and Freud: 'philosophical criticism has helped me to see that every psychology – my own included – has the character of a subjective *confession*' (1929: par. 774; my italics). No sooner was *Psychology of the Unconscious* completed than Jung began to wonder why it was that when confronted with the same clinical material, Freud, Adler, and he would view it so differently. The result was *Psychological Types* (Jung 1921).

Psychological Types is a study of the various ways in which individuals have differentiated between tendencies which they believe determine our responses to the world. In the final section, Jung identifies two 'attitudes' (extraversion and introversion) and four functions, two 'rational' (thinking and feeling), and two 'irrational' (sensation and intuition). His claim is that while in theory individuals can draw at will on each of those, in practice they are conditioned by habitual tendencies to privilege a specific combination. Our psychological type determines not only what we perceive but also how we process and respond to it. Jung accompanies every description with an account of the type's unconscious tendencies.

A great deal of misunderstanding continues to surround Jung's theory of psychological types, not least because it appears to describe a psychology of *consciousness*. Sharp (1987) entitles his introduction to the subject *Personality Types*. Beebe (2006: 130) corrects this: 'The commonest assumption has been that [Jung's types] refer to types of *people*. But for Jung they were types of *consciousness*.' This too, however, needs to be clarified. Jung's theory is as much about certain kinds of dreams reflecting typical kinds of consciousness as it is about how certain kinds of consciousness tend to be confronted by certain kinds of unconscious challenges. Jung's study is not about types of consciousness: it is about *typical dialogues* between consciousness and unconscious products.

Jung thought of himself as a thinking type (Shamdasani 2003: 76). Von Franz (1975: 36), who knew him well, agrees. So does Sharp (1987), who defines his auxiliary functions as sensation and intuition. By the time of writing *Psychology of the Unconscious*, it is unlikely that thinking could be defined as Jung's dominant function. The argument presented in this and all his later works is often blurred by an accumulation of ideas that are only loosely, even if interestingly, associated. The suggestion that he was an intuition type is more persuasive (McLynn 1996; Tacey 2006). According to Jung (1921: par. 658), introverted intuition types always move 'from image to image, chasing after every possibility in the teeming womb of the unconscious' – that is, they are always in search of a numinous possibility. So arresting are these possibilities that they tend to assume they are always on the brink of discovering some hitherto unrecognized truth (ibid.: par. 658–9). In other words, they are always looking for an elusive but ultimate 'meaning'. These are precisely the characteristics of Jung's writing.

In 'Psychology and Literature' Jung (1930) expands on his earlier distinction between two modes of artistic creation. He now gives them names. The first he calls the 'psychological' mode. In this category, he places literary works whose psychological implications have been fully explored by the author. Hence, a psychologist could add nothing of value to the understanding of the work. The second he defines as the 'visionary' mode. Works belonging in this category arise from the 'timeless depths' of the psyche and '[burst] asunder our human standards of value and aesthetic form' (ibid.: par. 141). They read as if they had been dictated by an '"alien" will' (Jung 1922: par. 113). In short, they 'demand' a psychological commentary (Jung 1930: par. 143). Jung is solely concerned with what he calls 'visionary' literature. Examples provided by him include Dante's *Divine Comedy*, Colonna's *Hypnerotomachia*, Blake's poetry and paintings, Hoffmann's 'Golden Pot/Bowl', Melville's *Moby Dick*, Wagner's great operas, and Nietzsche's *Zarathustra* (ibid.: par. 142). But when he adds Conan Doyle's Sherlock Holmes stories (ibid.: par. 137), one begins to feel that the category is somewhat arbitrary and depends only on whether a work intrigues him.

His ostensible criterion is whether a work harbours a 'primordial image'; whether it 'demands' a psychological commentary. In other words, whether he could find in it a numinous possibility that would allow him to speculate on some unrecognized truth and ultimate meaning. Jung's interest only in 'visionary' literature illustrates the concerns of his psychological type. Indeed, not only all Jung's major studies, but also analytical psychology generally emerged from, and best represents, the instinctive concerns of introverted intuition.

Kirsch (2000: 236, 245) suggests that the profession has never really taken on board the full implications of this. Very little attention has been paid to the broader issue of why a psychology that is so obviously rooted in the natural tendencies of one psychological type should be seen as a key to all psychological processes. Jung does not appear to have recognized that he embodied his definition of an introverted intuition type. Nonetheless, he offered a persuasive explanation of why some people – including him – are more strongly drawn to religion and religious writings than others.

Psychology and religion

By the time he published *Psychological Types*, Jung had the foundations of his own distinct theories in place. Over the next forty years, he adjusted his formulations, fine-tuned, developed and expanded them, and illustrated their application in a variety of ways. He shifted their emphasis, however, each time he explored a new concern: e.g. religion, alchemy, and synchronicity. Above all, he argued that dreams and fantasies often compensate conscious orientation. Meanwhile, as his private practice grew, he found himself treating more and more people who were not clinically sick; their biggest problem, in his view, was that they had lost a sense of meaning in their lives (Jung 1945: par. 464). He soon made the recovery of a sense of meaning the central issue of his work.

Soon after publishing *Psychology of the Unconscious*, Jung began to describe unconscious experience in terms more commonly associated with religion; for example, his use of the terms 'transcendent function' (Jung 1958) or 'soul' and 'soul-image' (Jung 1921: par. 797–811). Elsewhere, he defines religion as 'a careful and scrupulous observation of what Rudolf Otto aptly termed the *numinosum*, that is, a dynamic agency or effect not caused by an arbitrary act of will' (Jung 1937: par. 6). He might just as well have written that 'religion' describes the instinctive *behaviour* of the introverted intuition type. He became convinced that a 'careful and scrupulous observation of . . . the *numinosum*' is not only fundamental to our psychic health, but is also written into our human genes. For example,

> *I* did not attribute a religious function to the soul, I merely produced the facts which prove that the soul is *naturaliter religiosa*, i.e. possesses a religious function. . . . With a truly tragic delusion these theologians fail to see that it is not a matter of proving the existence of the light, but of blind people who do not know that their eyes could see. It is high time we realized that it is pointless to praise the light and preach it if nobody can see it. It is much more needful to teach people the art of seeing.
> (Jung 1944: par. 14)

There are good reasons why many Jungians might consider this view a core issue in his thinking. It is, however, a claim most likely to be made by an introverted-intuitive type as defined by Jung. Many might find it impossible to accept its premise, not because they are 'blind', but because their own psychological types make it difficult for them to understand, let alone agree with it. Jung often seems to forget his own insistence that the way psychologists 'see' is primarily an expression of their own psychological type.

Jung's language, as well as his insistence on the value of experiences akin to those discussed in religious writings, have led him to being incorrectly labelled a mystic or, worse, being accused of trying to found some kind of sect (e.g. Noll 1994). There is a paradox behind everything Jung wrote about religion. Although he was not at ease with patients committed to their religious beliefs, he increasingly gave the impression that his form of psychotherapy was akin to a religious cure. Institutional religion expects believers to adhere to a system of beliefs. Jung had no wish to undermine a believer's faith. He wanted to avoid disturbing the believer's faith by his own insistence that patients have to learn to 'trust' *the reality of their own unconscious experiences*. A mystic seeks an experience for the sake of the experience; Jung sought inner experience in order to understand better its possible implications. And he sought it for others to help them understand its possible implications for them as individuals. A mystic so values a transcendental reality that he belittles social reality. Jung may have been unusually insistent about the ever-present reality of the psyche, but his reasons were to help alienated individuals to reconnect with the world. He was vividly aware of the dangers of pseudo-mysticism for a susceptible mind. He wrote: '*The possession of the mystery cuts one off from intercourse with the rest of mankind*' (1912: 129). He never deviated from this view.

Jungian psychology provides a useful approach to understanding religious experience. It is not intended as an alternative to this. Jung wrote about religion as a psychologist: 'I am an empiricist and adhere as such to the phenomenological standpoint' (Jung 1937: par. 2). He insists, 'Our science is phenomenology' (Jung 1939: par. 694; cf. Brooke 1991). In all his works, his objective is to understand the nature of individual experience, including experience which has an affinity with religious experience. In a footnote, Jung (1952c: par. 45 n.45) quotes an 1855 letter by Jacob Burckhardt: '*Faust* is a genuine myth, i.e. a great primordial image, in which every man has to discover *his* own being and destiny in his own way.' Jung regarded not only the outer world, but also the world of his own reflections and interests – and especially those of his dreams and fantasies that were unusually numinous – in much the same way. For Jung, both the outer and the inner worlds are mirrors in which we can, if we make ourselves sufficiently self-aware, see both our being and destiny.

The objectives of analytical psychology are twofold: (1) to help individuals who have lost a sense of meaning in their lives to discover and connect with their 'personal myth' (Jung 1963: 3, 171), which Jung believed is indicated by the nature of their dreams and fantasies; and (2) to help individuals better understand the nature of their inner world so that they can reconnect meaningfully with the rest of mankind.

Conclusions

Jung had a very successful private practice. The first, and many of the second generation of Jungian analysts did most of their training with him, and all remembered this experience as one of the most meaningful of their lives. They rightly insist that the clinical encounter and the patients' *Auseinandersetzung* with their own unconscious products are the heart of Jung's ideas. Indeed, Jung was first and foremost a doctor committed to helping his patients. But Jung's mature ideas were not formulated from a close or statistical analysis of his case material. They were elaborated in response to his reading of wide-ranging texts. Jung's training was in psychiatry. He read as a psychiatrist. He thought as a psychiatrist. He considered his objectives to be those of a psychiatrist. And for this reason, he was never able to recognize the extent to which his therapeutic theory is a narrative theory which he then applied in his private practice.

Jung added an Author's Note to *Psychology of the Unconscious*: 'I do not consider scientific work as a dogmatic contest, but rather as work done for the increase and deepening of knowledge. This contribution is addressed to those having similar ideas concerning science' (1912: xxix). This became the conclusion to the revised edition (Jung 1952c: par. 685). Although devised as a petulant swipe at Freud, it nonetheless testifies to Jung's conviction that his lengthy study represented a breakthrough in science.

The word 'science', of course, comes from Latin *scire* (to know). Today we most often use the word to describe a kind of knowledge that can be independently verified. In other words, it is not the question one wishes to explore that defines a work as 'scientific', but the methodology one employs to address the question. In this chapter, I have tried to show that Jung's methodology has both scholarly and academic credentials, and that his intention was to increase and deepen existent understanding of psychosis.

Many Jungians feel that analytical psychology does not belong in academic debate. It is worth insisting that Jung thought otherwise. In 1933, in his late fifties, Jung once again became a university lecturer, this time at ETH (the Swiss Federal Institute of Technology) in Zurich, where he taught for nine years and ceased only because of ill health. He was proud to be elected an honorary member of the Swiss Academy of Science. He was equally proud when the University of Basel created a Chair in Medical Psychology for him. In 1945, in honour of his seventieth birthday, he received an honorary doctorate from the University of Geneva. Jung seems to have welcomed these honours. It may be that his doubts about the suitability of his ideas being taught in universities may reflect the difficulties he experienced with individuals rather than with academia as a place for the exchange of ideas.

This chapter highlights a number of paradoxes. Jung was amongst the first to grasp the importance of the subjective factor in both textual analysis and psychology. And yet, having established this, he never made any concessions to readers who belonged to different psychological types. Nor have his followers. The result is that a great many misunderstandings continue to surround analytical psychology.

Because its objectives are clinical, it has been assumed that analytical psychology is primarily a clinical psychology. Rather, it is a narrative and cultural theory with a marked interest in the nature of images and their relation to consciousness. Its objectives might accord with those of medical science; its methodology rests on academic practice in the humanities and social sciences.

Whilst it is true that analytical psychology has evolved enormously since 1961, this has been almost always through cross-fertilization with other approaches (e.g. with the ideas of Winnicott, Klein, Bion, and others). It has evolved very little from within its own tradition of academic scholarship (cf. Kirsch 2000: 246, 254). Many Jungians today continue to privilege the same texts and the same subjects that interested Jung: hermetic philosophy, alchemy, the nature of religious experience, the anima, the trickster, the *puer*, etc. Archetypal psychology places a useful emphasis on the 'image' experienced by the patient, but the texts to which it refers are almost identical to those that interested Jung. If analytical psychology is a narrative theory, it can only develop itself further by seeking out and engaging with *new texts* in a *new way*.

The choice of cultural traditions that interested Jung, and the way in which he envisaged them, correspond to what one might expect of an introverted intuition type. If analytical psychology aspires to being a significant cultural theory, as Jung thought it was, it must acknowledge not only a far broader history of culture than that in which Jung took an interest, but also a far richer understanding of how recent culture has affected the contemporary psyche.

References

Bair, D. (2003). *Jung: A Biography*. Boston: Little, Brown and Company.
Beebe, J. (2006). Psychological types. In Papadopoulos, R. K. (Ed.) *The Handbook of Jungian Psychology*. London: Routledge.
Bishop, P. (1995). *The Dionysian Self: C. G. Jung's Reception of Friedrich Nietzsche*. Berlin: Walter de Gruyter.
——. (2000). *Synchronicity and Intellectual Intuition in Kant, Swedenborg, and Jung*. Lewiston, NY: Edwin Mellen.
Brooke, R. (1991). *Jung and Phenomenology*. London: Routledge.
Chodorow, J. (1997). *Jung on Active Imagination*. London: Routledge.
Cornford, F. M. (1912). *From Religion to Philosophy*. London: Edward Arnold.
——. (1914). *The Origin of Attic Comedy*. London: Edward Arnold.
Eliot, G. (1871). *Middlemarch*, ed. D. Carroll. Oxford: Oxford University Press, 1997.
Frazer, J. G. (1890). *The Golden Bough* (1st edition). London: Macmillan.
——. (1906–15). *The Golden Bough* (3rd edition). London: Macmillan.
Freud, S. & Jung, C. G. (1974). *The Freud/Jung Letters*. London: Routledge and Kegan Paul.
Frey-Rohn, L. (1984). *Friedrich Nietzsche*. Zurich: Daimon.
Guerin, W. L., Labor, E., Morgan, L., Reesman, J. & Willingham, J. (Eds.) (1992). *A Handbook of Critical Approaches to Literature* (3rd edition). New York: Oxford University Press.
Harrison, J. (1912). *Themis: A Study of the Social Origins of Greek Religion*. Cambridge: Cambridge University Press.
Huskinson, L. (2004). *Nietzsche and Jung*. Hove, E. Sussex: Brunner-Routledge.
Janaway, C. (2002). *Schopenhauer*. Oxford: Oxford University Press.
Jung, C. G. Unless otherwise stated, the following are from *The Collected Works of C. G. Jung* (CW) London: Routledge and Kegan Paul:
——. (1896). *The Zofingia Lectures*. (CW Supplementary A)
——. (1906). Psychoanalysis and association experiments. (CW3)
——. (1907). The psychology of dementia praecox. (CW3)
——. (1908). The content of the psychoses. (CW3)
——. (1912). *Psychology of the Unconscious*. London: Routledge and Kegan Paul, 1951.
——. (1921). *Psychological Types*. (CW6)
——. (1922). On the relation of analytical psychology to poetry. (CW15)
——. (1926). Spirit and life. (CW8)
——. (1927). Analytical psychology and *Weltanschauung*. (CW8)
——. (1929). Freud and Jung: Contrasts. (CW4)
——. (1930). Psychology and literature. (CW15)
——. (1934). A study in the process of individuation. (CW9i)
——. (1935). The Tavistock lectures. (CW18)
——. (1937). Psychology and religion. (CW11)
——. (1939). Psychological commentary on *The Tibetan book of the great liberation*. (CW11)
——. (1943). On the psychology of the unconscious. (CW7)
——. (1944). Introduction to the religious and psychological problems of alchemy. (CW12)
——. (1945). The philosophical tree. (CW13)

——. (1952a). Reply to Martin Buber. (CW18)
——. (1952b). Answer to Job. (CW11)
——. (1952c). *Symbols of Transformation.* (CW5)
——. (1958). The transcendent function. (CW8)
——. (1963). *Memories, Dreams, Reflections.* (Revised edition). New York: Random House.
——. (1973). *Letters* (vol. 1). London: Routledge and Kegan Paul.
——. (1984). *Dream Analysis: Notes of the Seminar Given in 1928–30.* London: Karnac.
——. (1989a). *Analytical Psychology: Notes of the Seminar Given in 1925.* Princeton, NJ: Princeton University Press.
——. (1989b). *Nietzsche's 'Zarathustra': Notes of the Seminar Given in 1934–1939.* Princeton, NJ: Princeton University Press.
——. (1997). *Visions: Notes of the Seminar Given in 1930–34.* London: Routledge.
——. (2008). *Children's Dreams: Notes from the Seminar Given in 1936–194.* Princeton, NJ: Princeton University Press.
Jung, C. G. & Riklin, F. (1904). The associations of normal subjects. (CW2)
Kirsch, T. (2000). *The Jungians.* London: Routledge.
Knox, J. (2003). *Archetype, Attachment, Analysis.* Hove, E. Sussex: Brunner-Routledge.
Lear, J. (1998). Inside and outside the *Republic,* in *Open Minded.* Cambridge, MA: Harvard University Press.
Leavis, F. R. (1972). *The Great Tradition.* Harmondsworth: Pelican. (Original work published in 1948)
Lowes, J. L. (1927). *The Road to Xanadu.* London: Constable.
MacGregor, N. (2010). *A History of the World in 100 Objects.* London: Penguin.
McGrath, S. J. (2012). *The Dark Ground of Spirit: Schelling and the Unconscious.* London: Routledge.
McLynn, F. (1996). *Jung: A Biography.* London: Bantam.
Murray, G. (1913). *Euripides and His Age.* London: Williams & Norgate.
Noll, R. (1994). *The Jung Cult.* Princeton, NJ: Princeton University Press.
Papadopoulos, R. (Ed.) (2006). *The Handbook of Jungian Psychology.* London: Routledge.
Plato (2000). *The Republic.* Cambridge: Cambridge University Press.
Rank, O. (1989). *The Artist.* New York: Norton. (Original work published in 1907)
Shamdasani, S. (2003). *Jung and the Making of Modern Psychology.* Cambridge: Cambridge University Press.
Sharp, D. (1987). *Personality Types: Jung's Model of Typology.* Toronto: Inner City.
Tacey, D. (2006). *How to Read Jung.* New York: Norton.
Tylor, E. B. (1871). *Primitive Culture: Researches into the Development of Mythology, Philosophy, Religion, Art, and Custom.* London: John Murray.
Von Franz, M.-L. (1975). *C. G. Jung: His Myth in Our Time.* New York: Putnam.
Wilkinson, M. (2006). *Coming into Mind.* Hove, E. Sussex: Routledge.

7

KNOWLEDGE, WISDOM, AND THE SCIENCE-COMPLEX IN ORTHODOX CHRISTIANITY AND JUNGIAN PSYCHOLOGY

Byron J. Gaist

Given the prevalence of science and technology in the age of global information, the scientific approach to understanding reality and truth is an integral part of contemporary life. It is a characteristic of modernity which postmodern uncertainties have rightly called into question, yet this questioning does not appear to have drastically changed our lifestyle. Science is so pervasive in our lives, that alternative avenues to knowledge are often viewed as erroneous or outdated. Apologists for science in the humanities and social sciences, even in disciplines such as theology and religious studies, still feel compelled to present their methodologies and research as either rigorously scientific in a positivistic sense or at least compatible with scientific findings. Such is the power of science today.

The Orthodox Christian religion makes an extraordinary claim: there is an invisible world, the noetic realm, which is distinct from the visible, material world we can see and touch. This world is populated by personal beings, intelligent spirits known as angels, some of whom worship and serve God in purity, while others have chosen to pursue self-will instead. Within this noetic realm, Christians who have loved God during their earthly life, the saints, also reside. The invisible world of Orthodox Christianity is different from the visible creation studied by modern science, and different again from the realm of the unconscious, the *mundus imaginalis*, studied by Jung and analytical psychologists. But these three worlds touch, and the boundaries separating them are also their loci of connection. This chapter explores these boundaries by identifying commonalities and contrasts in some of the methods used by natural science, analytical psychology and Orthodox Christianity.

Addiction, experience and science: 'How can I, unless someone guides me?' (Acts 8:31)

Working in a monitoring centre for drugs and drug addiction, I am regularly confronted with the problem of measuring a distressing social phenomenon. Sure enough, there are both quantitative and qualitative criteria for assessing the severity of drug use nationally, and its social and health consequences. One may count the annual number of deaths due to heroin overdose, or study former drug users' attempts at social reintegration for example. Such data collection aims to meet scientific criteria, which are considered crucial for informing social policies which, in turn, will reduce the trade in illicit drugs.

Yet, for all the good intentions of policymakers and researchers, public money and political rhetoric poured into fighting addiction, success is partial. Indeed, politics and statistics are probably the last concern of an actual person *living* the nightmarish experience of drugs. People – often young and gifted – still drag themselves 'through the negro streets at dawn looking for an angry fix', as Allen Ginsberg (1956: 9) eloquently put it. The 'angry fix' may come through drugs, but also alcohol, gambling, sex, online gaming, even food, exercise, and work. Almost anything can become addictive, obsessive, locking the person into an existence under the constant threat of unhappy consequences.

Jungian-oriented psychologists know that targeting drug use as such is never enough. Indeed, fighting any psychopathology in a merely external manner, aiming at symptom removal, is but a temporary analgesic. The root causes of the disorder must ultimately be dealt with. Zoja (2000: 94) attributes drug use to the modern loss of ritual and the cult of manic consumerism, driving some people towards expressing their longing for the sacred through an initiation into drugs, only to discover to their dismay, that 'Repetition supercedes [*sic*] initiation: religious expectation gives way to destructive obsession.' In pointing to the spiritual thirst behind drug addiction, Zoja may be drawing on a considerably older hermeneutic, namely theology. Jung drew on the theological tradition of addressing the deeper causes when providing Bill Wilson, the founder of Alcoholics Anonymous, the helpful formula '*spiritus contra spiritum*' (a letter dated January 30, 1961).[1] Jung suggests that the appropriate response to addiction to alcohol (spirit) must ultimately address our fundamental spiritual thirst. To Jung, it is a thirst for wholeness; to medieval theology the thirst for union with God.

Theologians have known that fighting the symptoms alone is not enough far longer than the relatively young science of psychology has. When opening the Leipzig laboratory in 1879, Wundt used the method of introspection to analyse the contents of a person's consciousness; but Christianity had already drawn the attention of European thought to the significance of inner mental processes in previous centuries. In the eleventh century, Nikitas Stithatos wrote:

> God looks not at the outward form of what we may say or do, but at the disposition of our soul and the purpose for which we perform a visible action or express a thought. In the same way, those of greater understanding than others look rather to the inward meaning of words and the intentions of actions, and unfalteringly assess them accordingly.
>
> (Stithatos 1995: 115–16)

Stithatos might appear to be writing as a depth psychologist drawing on the religious anthropology of Christian tradition, based on older Judaeo-Christian teaching about the condition of the human heart (cf. Gen. 8:21; Jer. 17:9–10; Matt. 5:27–28; Matt. 15:18; Mark 7:21). Theologians may suggest that according to Tradition,[2] Holy Scripture and the witness of the saints, drug addiction is not only harmful (1 Cor. 6:19) but is also based on a profound thirst for spiritual experience (Ps. 42:1) and therefore can be cured only by paying attention to matters which are not immediately concerned with substance use (Matt. 6:31–33). Clearly a genuine theological response to drugs will involve more than Nancy Reagan's simplistic 'just say no' approach.

The discrepancy between scientific research, statistics, and social policy on the one hand, and the *actual lived experience*, the addict's inner condition, on the other, should give pause for thought. While scientific psychology and social policy permit only robust evidence-based approaches, both Jungian psychology and Orthodox Christianity – while not opposed to scientific evidence *per se* – arguably speak more directly to the addict's inner condition. Even though hundreds of addicts recover through spiritual experiences and resources, theologians are consulted regarding drug treatment and policy less frequently than are psychologists and other scientists. The reasons are partly historical and cultural: the history of psychology itself is a case in point. Shamdasani (2003: 4) comments on how, at the end of the nineteenth century, many sought to 'establish a scientific psychology that would be independent of philosophy, theology, biology, anthropology, literature, medicine and neurology, whilst taking over their traditional subject matters'. The suspicion of religion and theology commonly encountered in psychological circles is partly a result of psychology being 'designed' as a scientific substitute for theology; inter alia. Shamdasani argues that in terms of social acceptance, the psychological project has been a resounding success despite the fact that as a 'soft' science its status has not matched that of sciences such as physics or chemistry. Today, progressive citizens might be scandalized if it was revealed that a government primarily sought advice from priests and theologians towards (e.g.) its drug policy – but a historically conscious person must pause to ask, why? How did the 'queen of sciences', theology, the Object of which was once considered the source of all truth, come to be isolated and even proscribed from serious engagement as a source of knowledge?

The scientific revolution and the ascendancy of reason

Surely part of the reason for the general attitude towards knowledge from theology is that in our post-Enlightenment world, *science* reigns supreme as the purveyor of truth in the public imagination – ironically serving a similar function for the person-in-the-street as religion did in the Middle Ages. In my work with addiction statistics, it has often become apparent to me that the public relies on our monitoring centre for its 'scientific' information, but much of what actually reaches the public is strongly influenced by political considerations, management styles, even office dynamics! While this is a separate issue from the contrast between scientific knowledge and lived experience, it further highlights some of the characteristics of the science-complex discussed below, and is perhaps not much different to the medieval use of religion for social control; yet today it is to the scientist we all turn to be accurately informed about the universe. Hart comments,

> The great danger that bedevils any powerful heuristic or interpretive discipline is the tendency to mistake method for ontology, and so to mistake a partial perspective on particular truths for a comprehensive vision of truth as such. In the modern world, this is an especially pronounced danger in the sciences, largely because of the exaggerated reverence scientists enjoy in the popular imagination, and also largely because of the incapacity of many in the scientific establishment to distinguish between scientific rigor and materialist ideology (or, better, materialist metaphysics).
>
> (Hart 2011: 1)

Most of us still live in a Newtonian universe, imagining atoms to be moving in space according to mechanical laws, like billiard balls. Mistaking method for ontology, we take the material world for granted, overlooking the fact that since Einstein and quantum mechanics, matter itself has been equated with energy (a mysterious 'potential for work' the nature of which we don't really understand) and probability has taken over determinism in the scientific worldview. Likewise, there might be disclosed, to receptive minds, a reality that is other than the perceivable material one and yet fully present and real. Such receptive minds do not need to be enlightened saints, but even the 'ordinary' scientist should be able, at least poetically speaking, to see that 'the Divine is inalienably present in natural forms' as Orthodox philosopher Sherrard (2003: 147) suggests. If we acknowledge the spiritual realm at all, we tend to see it as being so totally different that the existence of this world in which we live becomes spiritually 'negative' and 'of no consequence' (ibid.: 147).

Yet still, 'Nothing appears to be more certain', writes Smith (1984: 13), 'than our scientific knowledge of the physical universe.' Smith tries to show how, ever since Descartes' *cogito* placed doubt at the centre of existence and formally consolidated the dichotomy between mind and body, modernity has established the bifurcation of the world (a term Smith borrows from Whitehead) into an orderly realm described by mathematics and physical laws on the one side, and sensory lived experience, on the other. The former, Smith argues, is known by scientists, and the latter by the ordinary man. Essentially the bifurcation postulate states that all qualities (colour, smell, etc.) are subjective, hence the external object is not actually perceived. This creates a split between experience and reality – a split beginning with Descartes and finalized by Kant. Science continues to assume no possible access to *Ding an sich* methodologically, yet imagining that its findings are true pictures of the objective universe. Science thus reduces reality to mathematics, to be interpreted by experts who have access to specialized knowledge: 'This leaves an inherently mathematical universe . . . what we have called the physical universe, not as a mere abstraction or a useful model, but as the objective reality itself' (ibid.: 14). Here Smith, himself a mathematician, makes a significant observation concurring with Hart (op. cit.): 'this reduction of the world to the categories of physics is not a scientific discovery (as many believe), but a *metaphysical assumption* that has been built into the theory from the outset' (ibid.: 14–15; italics mine). In other words, it is not possible to step out into the world trying to make sense of it without taking something for granted, without any *a priori* metaphysics. Similarly, we may add, it is not possible to arrive at any *a posteriori* picture of the world which does not contain metaphysical assumptions resulting from our methodology, the tools we used to paint the portrait, as it were. Whereas for Descartes, metaphysics still lay at the root of the tree of knowledge, the scientific revolution of the sixteenth and seventeenth centuries – to which he lent his genius by advocating methodological scepticism and the use of reason in the natural sciences – culminated in positivism, for which metaphysical statements are nonsensical *by definition*. For Enlightenment positivist philosophers, such as Pierre-Simon Laplace, Saint-Simon, and Auguste Comte, the only permissible knowledge is that which is produced through combining sensory experience with logico-mathematical analysis. For these thinkers, the scientific method essentially dispensed with the old 'superstitions' of metaphysics; and thus, as Smith argues, scientism was born, bringing new superstitions in its wake.

Unsurprisingly, an esoteric culture of experience has emerged at the same time, setting personal and collective subjective 'experience' over and against any 'metaphysical assumptions' that are perceived as enshrined in theological or other dogmas, yet falling prey to these same assumptions within science, as Smith suggests – echoing Jung's (1958: 65) statement, 'you can take away a man's gods, but only to give him others in return'. Historians of science have linked the decline of magic to the rise of science; magic may belong to the superstitious mind of the Middle Ages, but the idea of bending the supernatural to human purposes has found renewed expressions in science and technology (e.g. Webster 1982; Thomas 1971).

Other philosophers of science have come to dominate the epistemological landscape since Comte and the French Enlightenment. Karl Popper and Willard Van Orman Quine held that science is the only legitimate path to knowledge, and questions which cannot be answered scientifically are not 'proper' questions. As Okasha (2002) suggests, their view is based on the doctrine of naturalism, namely that since humans are part of the natural world, and science studies the whole of the natural world, then science should be capable of revealing the whole truth about the human condition. How do we know that what we understand about the natural world is a true reflection of things? Mathematics is a case in point. Its astonishing power to model the world we live in has led, for example, to the discovery of Neptune by Urbain Le Verrier, having predicted the planet's position by measuring discrepancies between the known orbit of Uranus and the orbit as predicted by

Newtonian mechanics. More recently, a Stanford University experiment carried out in space confirmed parts of Einstein's theory of relativity, which he derived mathematically half a century ago (Kruesi 2012). Yet, for all its power and Platonic charm, mathematics may be hardwired into our brain; hence, is its apparent success a reflection of the *real* world or a creation of our brains? A constructivist approach to knowledge, such as Jean Piaget's genetic epistemology, may offer a more dialectical response to how we know that what we understand about the natural world is a true reflection of things in themselves: but even here, does the cognitive stage of 'formal operations' achieved by the adolescent give us *the* final picture of reality or could there be stages of cognition above and beyond it, past humans' cognitive capacity, which would give a truer picture? After all, we know that conditioning principles, such as salience and contingency of stimuli, offer a rat a 'true' model of causal relations in the world; but is the rat's mental schema the final word on reality or just an efficient aid towards survival, a picture of its organismic *Umwelt* as described by Von Uexküll? How is it different for us?

It is perhaps more realistic to humbly accept change in our worldviews and self-images as inevitable. Thomas Kuhn introduced the concept of the 'paradigm shift' to account for the way in which dominant frameworks in the sciences give way to new paradigms. Kuhn introduced a historical perspective into the ahistorical ambitions of the positivists, showing that knowledge grows with time, and not always in a logical or cumulative manner. Likewise to Bachelard (2005), science does not develop in a continuous manner, but through 'epistemological breaks' which introduce abrupt changes in perspective. Bachelard, who was influenced by Jung and critical of Comte's positivism, also wrote of the 'epistemological obstacle' by which mental patterns in science prevent the growth of knowledge, which he perceived as the result of an interaction between reason and experience. The role of the epistemologist, according to Bachelard, is like a psychoanalyst of science, helping science to overcome obstacles to knowledge as patients in analysis might work with their complexes.

Nevertheless, science, and the dualistic rational thought via which it operates, has come to be seen as the official codifier of something we call 'experience', which is itself perceived as the measure of all things. Metallinos (2010) suggests that the philosophical process which led to this emphasis on reason at the expense of metaphysics – or more precisely the exclusion of 'true theology' (referring to the Orthodox hesychast tradition) – can be traced within the history of post-Schism Western Christianity itself, beginning with the rise of scholasticism (thirteenth century) on to nominalism (fourteenth century), humanism/renaissance (fifteenth century), the Reformation (sixteenth century) and the Enlightenment (seventeenth century). By considering the world as an image of transcendent Platonic universalia – a Neoplatonic inheritance from St Augustine which the Seventh Ecumenical Council had condemned in AD 787 – scholasticism paved the way to make the rational mind-intellect (*dianoia*) the instrument of knowledge, logic becoming the tool by which the essence of beings is apprehended. God, moreover, began to be perceived as similar to His creatures via the *analogia entis*, an analogy between created and uncreated which Metallinos, following the teaching of J. S. Romanides, rejects. From then on, it remained for the nominalism of William of Ockham – which Metallinos calls 'the DNA ... of European civilization' (ibid.: 2) – to assert that the universalia are simply names, not real beings. Thus, the seventeenth-century scientific revolution led to the separation of faith and knowledge, resulting in the following 'axiomatic principle':

> New (positive) philosophy only accepts truths which are verified through rational thought. It is the absolute authority of Western thinking. The truths of this new philosophy are the existence of God, soul, virtue, immortality, and judgment. Their acceptance ... can only take place in a theistic enlightenment, since we also find atheism as a structural element of modern thought. The ecclesiastical doctrines that are rejected by rationality are the Triune nature of God, the Incarnation, glorification, salvation, etc. This natural and logical religion, from the Orthodox viewpoint, not only differs from atheism but is much worse. Atheism is less dangerous than its distortion!
> (Metallinos 2010: 3)

It is worth noting that the scientific revolution did not immediately jettison all theological concepts. As Metallinos suggests, certain concepts, such as proofs for God's existence, the soul, virtue, immortality and judgment, retained their hold even on the religious imagination of scientific thinkers. Descartes believed in the soul and located it in the pineal gland, offering the latter as a possible physiological mechanism by which the dichotomy between *res extensa* and *res cogitans* may be breached.

The essential difference between the eras before and after the scientific revolution lies in the introduction of a new methodology for apprehending reality. Indeed, as the Jungian thinker Christou (1976) explains, modern science can be seen as invested in a whole 'knowledge myth'. Separating itself from theology has resulted in an inevitable overestimation of the capacities and limits of human reason, as well as an artificial dichotomy between nature and spirit. As mentioned, psychological science in particular has experienced this split intensely, eager as it has been to set itself up according to the natural-sciences model. Christou makes an impassioned case for the difference between a 'psychology of the soul' and one based either on physical observation or mentalistic accounts. He argues that the 'medium of expression of the meanings of the soul is the symbol' (ibid.: 79). 'Symbol' is an equivalent to 'concept' in non-Jungian psychology, but the ontological reality expressed by the symbol, according to Christou, is that of the soul. Sherrard resonates with Christou:

> The fall may best be understood not as a moral deviation ... but as a drama of knowledge, as a dislocation and degradation of our consciousness, a lapse of our perceptive and cognitive powers ... It is to forget the symbolic function of every form and to see in things not their dual, symbiotic

reality, but simply their non-spiritual dimension, their psycho-physical or material appearance. . . . our crime, like that of Adam, is equivalent to losing this sense of symbols; for to lose the sense of symbols is to be put in the presence of our own darkness, of our own ignorance.

(Sherrard 2003: 146)

It seems apt that Jung (1939) called for modern man to live 'the symbolic life', either by remaining with traditional ritual such as Christian liturgy or by listening to the messages of the unconscious through dreams and other symbolic communications. Jungian psychology focuses not on the *dianoia*, but on the soul, its images and symbols; 'soul' is of course understood differently from the use of the term in theology, but the call to a more complete understanding of the person remains – *ars requirit totum hominem*.

Despite ultimately sending theology, metaphysics, and the soul into epistemological exile, contemporary science has its roots in natural philosophy. Physics, by investigating the fundamental building blocks of physical reality, can still put us in touch with some of the deepest philosophical questions: what is the nature of space and time? What is matter and energy? How are all these fundamental categories related? If we investigate time, for example, we need to look at what happens to matter and energy in liminal contexts such as the event horizons of black holes, and the singularity at the big bang (cf. Coles 2001). News of discoveries, such as the (probable) Higgs boson recently, remind us that current models of physical reality are likely to be revised tomorrow. Science is not exempt from metaphysical assumptions and speculation. When physicist Greene was asked if there is a question that keeps him up at night, he replied with welcome honesty,

I wish it was just one. There are two that, if I allow myself to think about them, make my heart sink. Why is there something rather than nothing? . . . Why *isn't* there nothing? The other question is the nature of time. Time is with us, every moment. . . . But what is time? When we look at the mathematics of our current understanding of physics, time is there, but there's no deep explanation of what it is or where it came from.

(Interview with Gefter, 2011: 31)

While it may be legitimate and even desirable for scientists to ponder questions that are clearly philosophical, reason, mathematics, and the scientific method alone might never entirely answer the mystery of existence. As Metallinos (2010: 3) writes, 'faith is knowledge of the Uncreated, and science is knowledge of the created. Therefore, they are two different types of knowledge, each having its own method and tools of inquiry.' This view could be misinterpreted to suggest Draper's 'conflict thesis' of religion and science, or Gould's 'non-overlapping magisteria', but it serves here to underline that since there are different kinds of knowledge worth pursuing, the *whole* scientist as body, mind, and spirit may benefit from engaging with reality.

The science-complex

We grasp, apparently with tenacious faith, at the fantasy of scientific objectivity, consistently excluding theological insights and overlooking the metaphysical assumptions underlying both the methods and findings of science. What makes modern people react so strongly to the idea of receiving knowledge from anywhere but those sources which are socially and culturally accepted as 'scientific'?

Science undoubtedly rewards humanity with technological advances and insights into the workings of nature, extending our lives and giving us control over many hazards; but this very powerful quality of science might be causing its own 'blind spots', so that modern civilization could be described as being caught in the sway of a powerful science-complex – 'an emotionally charged group of ideas or images' (Sharp 1991: 37) centred around the notion of 'science'. Moreover, this science-complex may be the source of major distortions in our contemporary self-understanding, leading us to a scientistic (as opposed to scientific) view of reality, in which our minds and bodies become machines, the cosmos becomes mere matter and space, time itself becomes the clock by which our inevitable march into nothingness is measured.

Complexes for Jung were the *via regia* to the unconscious, although he pointed out that far from being a carpet-strewn royal road, it 'is more like a rough and uncommonly devious footpath' (1934: par. 210). Identification with a complex clouds our consciousness, causing us to lose touch with ourselves, turning us away from affirming the whole of our nature, but equally distorting our picture of external reality. In other words, complexes make us neurotic. It is the psychoanalyst's job to help us render these complexes conscious – not to get rid of them, which is itself impossible, but to minimize their negative effects, so that we can free up our habitual dysfunctional behaviour patterns and negative emotional reactions. Perhaps too, complexes can affect society just as they affect the individual. As Singer and Kaplinsky (2010) put it, the goal in Jungian psychoanalysis is to make personal complexes more conscious, freeing up the energy contained within them and making it available for psychological development. Their basic premise is that there is another level of complexes within a group's psyche, namely 'cultural complexes', definable as emotionally charged aggregates of ideas and images clustering around an archetypal core which are shared by individuals within an identified collective. Examples of cultural complexes in action include the way social phenomena such as apartheid influenced a white South African's dreams; the countertransference reactions of a white therapist to a black patient (and vice versa); the mirroring of the rise of Islamic fundamentalism in Asia and Christian fundamentalism in the US; or the reaction of Cuban-Americans to the return of Elian Gonzales to Cuba (ibid.; see also Singer 2002; Singer & Kimbles 2004). Looking at the *cultural* layer of the unconscious in this way introduces a much-needed social and historical component to the abstractions of Jungian analysis, thereby also helping analysts avoid the important temptation pointed out by Tacey (2005: 2), for Jungians to 'carry on "as if" direct knowledge of the archetypes is possible'.

If modern society is in the sway of a science-complex, we would need to ask: which archetype might this complex be based on, and what are the social and historical processes that influenced this particular view of science today? Before doing so however, it should be borne in mind too, that from a Jungian perspective complexes are a normal part of any functional individual psyche. For instance, the conscious ego is a complex. 'A complex becomes pathological only when we think we have not got it' (Jung 1943: par. 179). Similarly, functional cultures probably require the energy stored in their particular cultural complexes in order to act out their unique visions and dreams within history – else they would perhaps languish in a sort of collective identity moratorium. If a cultural complex – of which the science-complex may be one variety – is to operate in a culture's favour however, it should be consciously acknowledged and lived through. Singer and Kaplinsky (2010: 8) regard cultural complexes as based on 'frequently repeated historical experiences that have taken root in the collective psyche of a group, and they express archetypal values for the group'. Furthermore, in the consulting room cultural complexes are made conscious as most unconscious conflicts become known, 'through paying close attention to personal, family and cultural history; through analysing dream material that emerges from the unconscious' and so forth (ibid.: 15). Making cultural complexes conscious and getting objectivity about them is, as with personal complexes, 'a long, arduous process of disidentification from contents that emerge from the cultural unconscious as well as the more familiar personal and collective unconscious' (ibid.: 18).

Can the 'arduous process of disidentification' through what Jung called the 'rough and uncommonly devious footpath' take place without standing back from our current ways of regarding reality? When exploring a possible science-complex, can the analytical glance be effective, since it occurs within the same methodological discourse as the science on which it tries to reflect? We have discussed how the historical development of Western theology led to the scientific revolution, and hinted at the possibility that, ironically, this has narrowed down our perspective by excluding different modes of knowledge, such as those found in Orthodox theology and Jungian psychology. It may therefore be argued that in psychology a science-complex will cease to colour our view of the human being only when we become aware of its influences on our scientific imaginations and the social-historical causes of those influences. Moreover, this science-complex may also colour modern theologians' perspectives, since they are products of their culture and time as much as psychologists are.

Jungian complexes are not to be defined precisely, but to be experienced in action. For present purposes, a science-complex could be assumed to be in operation when:

(a) Alongside genuine scientific knowledge, certain essentially unobservable and unverifiable convictions (such as the non-existence of God or the identity of brain and psyche) are maintained as scientistic beliefs.

(b) Forms of knowledge which are perceived as not conforming to strict scientific criteria, such as metaphysical, theological, or other experiential knowledge, are dismissed without serious consideration.
(c) There is an overall eagerness to present work as being 'scientific' when not necessary.
(d) There is resistance to analysing or exposing the unscientific or non-scientific assumptions and origins of particular work.

The above is not exhaustive, nor is it necessary to identify all of these characteristics in order to talk of a science-complex being at work. In sociology, prejudice such as racism and sexism can be divided into 'traditional' and 'symbolic' forms (Hughes & Kroehler 2008). Similarly, in the science-complex there are both the obvious 'traditional' bias of positive-scientific discourse against alternative explanatory discourses, and the 'symbolic' epistemic bias, whereby alternative discourses are accepted as long as they don't encroach on the territory of 'proper' science. A reflective, free-floating analytical gaze will pick up these cultural dynamics without requiring prior rigid definitions.

The science-complex in Orthodox Christianity

A few instances from Jungian analytical psychology and Orthodox Christian theology may suffice to illustrate the point. It should be emphasized that the following is not meant to denigrate or diminish the work of named authors and scientists, which is often of seminal importance in their respective fields. On the contrary, the present attempt is to indicate certain fields of investigation within Orthodox Christianity and Jungian Psychology which are topical and important enough to touch upon living cultural attitudes. After all, if these works did not address the needs of our scientific culture, they would not be relevant or useful to modern aims and pursuits.

In Orthodox Christianity, the science-complex may be seen to be evident in debates such as the one around creation and biological evolution. Rose (2000), for example, adopts a similar stance to fundamentalist Evangelical 'creation science' with respect to evolution, arguing from patristic sources that the account of creation *ex nihilo* in Genesis (in six days, each species being a unique and eternal kind) is incompatible with an evolutionary perspective, which is essentially a scientific regurgitation of pagan myth. Hart (2011), by no means an advocate of 'creation science', points to the extinct thylacine of Tasmania and New Guinea, which was a marsupial resembling a wolf, and the still extant fossa, a distant cousin of the mongoose which looks remarkably like a cat, and comments that although as a theologian he is not qualified to comment on biology, he is pleased to imagine that there is such a thing as the *form* of a wolf or a cat. The point is amusing, but does raise questions about genetics, epigenetics, and those issues falling under the 'intelligent design' debate. To Rose, science and religion are incompatible, religion being superior as a source of knowledge. Although this is presented as *the* only possible Orthodox view, Rose's approach is just *one* acceptable Orthodox view. In contrast, Orthodox theologian Bouteneff (2008) suggests that the Genesis narrative is neither a myth nor an outdated scientific account, but a poem of creation which yields deeper meanings upon closer ponderings. Woloschak (1996) on the other hand, a biologist and an Orthodox Christian drawing on the ideas of Theodosius Dobzhansky, considers evolutionary theory as compatible with Christianity, and maintains *pace* Sergius Bulgakov that a scientific exploration of the world can teach us something about God's own revelation to humanity.

The wealth of perspectives within Orthodoxy shows that Orthodox theology is by no means monolithic. The contrast between compatibilist and incompatibilist accounts of creation and evolution in Orthodox theology is an example of a 'hot' and sensitive issue for many Christians. While having its historical roots already in the Church Fathers (such as St Basil and St Gregory of Nyssa) and in theological debates such as the alternative theological schools of Antioch and Alexandria, it is probably fair to say that reactions to the theory of evolution touch the contemporary nerve of the science-complex in Orthodoxy. As Theokritoff and Theokritoff comment regarding the attempt by fundamentalist evangelical Christians in the USA to introduce 'creation science' into schools as an alternative to 'evolution science',

> Despite an appeal to fairness ... creationists adopt an either/or position, that it is either special creation or evolution, no other view being possible. Some Orthodox even think that the Orthodox Church should join creationists in their efforts, oblivious of the fact that the Church does not endorse or condemn scientific theories and that the fundamentalist evangelical understanding of the Bible is quite different from that of the Orthodox Church.
> (Theokritoff & Theokritoff 2002: 388)

Contrary to fundamentalist thought (religious or scientific), Orthodox Christianity is not antiscientific. Already in the fourth century, theology was using the findings of its contemporary science without experiencing its own eternal truths as being under threat. For example, in St Basil's Hexameron (written circa AD 370), the six 'days' of creation are perceived as representing long periods of time (Basil 1895: Homily 2), and Holy Scripture is acknowledged as giving only slight scientific information, leaving a great deal for man to discover for himself (ibid.: Homily 1). Moreover, St Basil importantly acknowledges that we do not lose our wonder towards creation when we discover the means by which a certain creation took place (ibid.: Homily 1). How astonishing it is that in modern cosmology, 'singularity makes it impossible to know from first principles what the Universe should look like in the beginning' (Coles 2001: 9). For St Basil, 'It appears, indeed, that even before this world an order of things existed of which our mind can form an idea, but of which we can say nothing' (1895: Homily 1). Given the sixteen centuries between Coles and St Basil, there is for both, and for the fields they represent, a remarkable recognition of the limits of human knowledge – and it also appears that there is nothing new under the sun (Eccles. 1:9). It is tempting to find in St Basil's thinking, reading him anachronistically, the seeds of other modern cosmological notions, such as atomic theory, the many-worlds hypothesis, even dark matter, which itself may have historical origins in the former ether hypothesis (1895: Homily 1).

Another area which seems to evoke the science-complex in Orthodoxy is the interface between psychology and Orthodox spirituality. As I have written extensively on the subject elsewhere (Gaist 2010), it suffices here to suggest that the format in which Orthodox spirituality is presented by certain contemporary authors is made to appeal to the expectations of social scientists and to conform to the rigours of a scientific psychotherapy, often with considerable success (e.g. Vlachos 1994; Chirban 2001; Larchet 2005; Chrysostomos 2007). As these authors themselves are likely to attest, the information they offer is not new. It is the 2,000-year-old teaching of the Church. What is perhaps novel – perhaps resulting from needs intrinsic to our era's science-complex which the authors try to address – is that this information is being re-presented as *science*. This is a genuine attempt by theology to address modern scientific knowledge and methodology, sharing its ancient wisdom in fields that do not acknowledge it, arguably to their own loss.

When both theology and science operate consciously, being aware of the possible distortions the cultural science-complex may evoke, a deeper knowledge of ontological truth can be experienced and acquired. In an excellent text on the relationship between Orthodox theology and science, Nesteruk (2003) contends that in both, the fundamental question is that of truth. The Greek Patristic synthesis linked the problem of truth with 'the idea of liturgical experience in order to proclaim that truth, as ontological truth, is only accessible through and within communion with God in ecclesial community' (ibid.: 2). He adds,

> The traditional split in religion and science into truth in theology and truth in science is rooted in most cases in the disconnection of each one's truth from the idea that both science and theology have the common ground of truth, the common source of their ontological otherness: God, whose being – as well as ours in God – is revealed through communion.
> (Nesteruk 2003: 2)

As expanded below, this link between scientific truth and communal liturgical experience renders the relation between Orthodox Christianity and science not only ever-productive and creative, but also an epistemologically viable enterprise.

The science-complex in Jungian psychology

Jung viewed psychology as straddling the divide between the natural sciences and the humanities (Shamdasani 2003). Psychology for Jung was empirical in its object (the psyche is a natural phenomenon), but belonged to the human sciences in terms of its method of explanation. For Jung, the difference between psychology and other sciences was that instead of observing external processes, such as chemical or physical processes, in psychology the psyche is trying to observe itself. Thus in Jung's thought there existed the divide between the subjective and the objective, the individual and the universal – a divide which he hoped to bridge through analytical psychology.

The debate around Jung's own scientific status and the academic or clinical reception of analytical psychology may illustrate some aspects of the science-complex. Shelburne (1988) attempts to offer scientific evidence for Jung's concept of the collective unconscious – a concept which Shamdasani (2003: 88) recognizes as 'generally dismissed as being non-scientific', even though it was Jung's proposal to the scientific community for resolving the universal-individual divide. Shelburne suggests that evidence leading to the theory's falsification may come from cross-cultural occurrences of archetypal motifs in mythologies and religions. If it were possible to locate a human tribe which had no contact with any other humans, and had no religion or mythology of its own, that would count as evidence against the notion of archetypes. Also, evidence may come from ethology: since archetype and instinct are linked, evidence against the existence of innate behaviour patterns in animals would vicariously offer evidence against the existence of archetypes in humans. Finally, evidence may come from research into altered states of consciousness: if experiments designed to produce such states do not yield subjects' reports which describe phenomena similar to Jungian archetypes, this too may count as a refutation of Jung's theory.

Efficacy studies in psychotherapy may indicate a comprehensive need to prove the scientific status of Jungian psychology. Keller et al. (1997) present an efficacy and cost-effectiveness study for outpatient Jungian psychotherapy in Germany, finding improvement following long-term analysis more than six years later. There is nothing wrong with presenting Jungian work in this quantitative manner; but when making analytical psychology conform to clinical or other scientific standards, it should be borne in mind that for Jung every psychology was a subjective confession. In von Franz's words,

> Theories based on statistics formulate an ideal average, in which exceptions at either end are abolished and replaced by an abstract mean. . . . This method leads to scientific knowledge but not to understanding of the actual human being. The result is an increasingly unrealistic, rational picture of the world, in which the individual figures only as a sort of marginal phenomenon.
>
> (Von Franz 1993: 253–4)

Hauke (1998) suggests that Jung's archetypal theory is fundamentally postmodern. It does not only heal the split between the individual and the collective, but also that between matter and mind, the Cartesian *res extensa* and *res cogitans*. Hauke views the archetype as 'a structuring principle that at one end of its continuum manifests as matter, and at the other end, as mind', thereby linking archetype with quantum physics (ibid.: 295). Since Marx, Freud and Nietzsche, followed by Derrida's postmodern deconstruction, Western thought has focused on the fragmentation of experience and meaning. Jung, as Hauke explains, offers a genuinely postmodern alternative to this fragmentation through the process of individuation.

The culture of experience

Collective and personal experience ultimately became a dominant voice in twentieth-century culture and psychology, prompting us today, even as psychotherapists, to put our trust in the contents of immediate awareness as if nothing exists behind or outside these. To cite but one example, Carl Rogers stated that for him, experience is 'the highest authority':

> The touchstone of validity is my own experience. No other person's ideas, and none of my own ideas, are as authoritative as my experience. It is to experience that I must return, again and again, to discover a closer approximation to truth as it is in the process of becoming in me. Neither the Bible nor the prophets – neither Freud nor research – neither the revelations of God nor man – can take precedence over my own direct experience.
> (Rogers 1961: 24–5)

He elucidates, 'My experience is not authoritative because it is infallible. It is the basis of authority because it can be checked in new primary ways. In this way its frequent error or fallibility is always open to correction' (ibid.). Rogers is offering a phenomenological-existential 'twist' to the positivistic tale of scientific discovery by rational analysis of empirical experience by placing his own lived *personal* experience over collective scientific research. Rogers may fall on the side of 'lived experience' as opposed to the 'mathematical description' required by the natural sciences, but his basic polarities may nonetheless originate from, and fit into, the same historical line of thinking which has led from Cartesian methodological scepticism and the mind-body dichotomy in the early modern era to the eventual bifurcation of the world into science and non-science (non-sense?), perceived phenomenon and unknowable *Ding an sich*. He protects himself from being accused of dogmatism by basing the authority of his own experience, not on itself, but on its capacity to be checked and thus to remain open to correction. Rogers was perhaps revolutionary for his time, but his individualism eventually became a norm. It may be said that experience checked against experience has become almost the modern criterion of all truth.

This plea from personal experience may be one ramification of the 'personal equation' which has preoccupied and fertilized the sciences from astronomy to psychology (Shamdasani 2003: 30). Is there a place for the subjectivity of the observer within science? Alternatively, if science addresses universals, is a science of individual experience possible? Rogers seems to have thought so, with his person-centred philosophy addressing everything from subjectivity to the formative tendency of the universe itself. And so did Jung, who offered his 'complex psychology' as 'a superordinate science, the only discipline capable of encompassing the subjective factor held to underlie all the sciences' (ibid.: 30–1). It is worth noting, however, that it may be ultimately impossible to refute another's subjective experience: if one claims *pace* Jung (in his famous BBC interview) to 'know' God, how can anyone disagree? All one can do is to pitch one's own subjectivity against another's.

How is personal experience different from what we normally mean by the word 'dogma'? Hillman (1992: 35) refers to the religious impulse provoked but not satisfied in psychotherapy – since it invites confession but omits prayer – which endows experience with religious values, and makes it sacred and inaccessible to examination; he calls it the 'Dogma of Experience'. Conventionally the word 'dogma' is used to imply that someone's mind is closed, and thus his experience is foreclosed. In lectures given in the 1980s, Zizioulas explains: 'The term is derived from the (Greek) verb "dokein" (= seeming, believing) and originally, its literal meaning was **"that which seems good or proper to someone"**; it also pertains to **belief, ideology, principle, opinion, faith,** and other related meanings' (2005: Ch. 2, online; bold in the original). The term acquired philosophical, political and religious meaning, but in Christianity it remained linked to its initial meaning – e.g., 'as they passed through the cities, they delivered unto them the decrees [*dogmas* in the Greek text] that were validated by the apostles and the elders' (Acts 16:4). Importantly, Zizioulas points out the difference between *dogma* and *kerygma*, with an emphasis on where personal experience comes in:

> 'Dogma' is that which an ecclesiastic community embraces as an (existentially) salvatory truth that applies to every man, and requires its **members** to accept it (through personal experience) as authoritative, because of the specialized relations that it ordains between members, as well as towards the world and God. The kerygma (sermon) on the other hand is whatever is addressed to all persons, publicly, in order that they may become members of the Church, and **only then** (as members of the Church) confess it as a dogma, **having experienced it personally**.
>
> (Ibid.; bold in the original)

This brings us to 'the **dogmas of the Church, as being the authentic decisions pertaining to faith** that are delivered for compulsory acceptance, and are linked to the presence and the inspiration of the Holy Spirit' (ibid.; bold in the original). For a truth to become a dogma rather than a personal opinion, 'it must necessarily go through the community of the Church in its totality, and not only through a few people – be they theologians in the current (academic) sense, or saints' (ibid.).

What we initially hear as kerygma, we eventually confirm as dogma, *but only* after testing it in personal and communal experience. Dogma in Orthodoxy is therefore based on the collective experience of a worshipping community, whose members are each invited to experience the truth personally. Elsewhere Zizioulas (1985: 119) suggests that this truth does not only concern humanity, but also 'has profound cosmic dimensions', so that man becomes responsible for making a 'eucharistic reality' out of nature, making nature, too, capable of communion. Zizioulas reasonably comments that this has implications beyond theological truth, extending to the realm of natural science. Since for post-Einsteinian natural sciences, existence has again become relational, it is possible to speak of a unique truth in the world which may be approached either scientifically or theologically. Nesteruk closely follows Zizioulas in arguing that the scientist's work is para-eucharistic:

> The split between theology and science can be overcome if both are reinstated to their proper relationship to the eucharist, understood in cosmic terms as the offering of creation back to God through art, science and technology. Scientific activity can be treated as a cosmic Eucharistic work (a 'cosmic liturgy'). Science thus can be seen as a mode of religious experience, a view obvious to those scientists who participate in ecclesial communities, but as yet undemonstrated to those outside such communities.
> (Nesteruk 2003: 2)

Of course, not everyone accepts the Church's authority; and many other religions, philosophical systems, political ideologies, psychological schools, and so forth, offer different experiences. Is all experience of equal value? This would seem to be the case if the Orthodox experience of God is jettisoned from the modern vocabulary; but at what expense? Albert Camus (1965: 10), an atheist, interestingly comments that once a man 'has reached the absurd and tries to live accordingly', he 'always perceives that consciousness is the hardest thing in the world to maintain. Circumstances are almost always against it. He must live his lucidity in a world where dispersion is the rule.' Camus continues,

> So . . . the real problem, *even without God*, is the problem of psychological unity . . . and inner peace. He also perceives that such peace is not possible without a discipline difficult to reconcile with the world. *That's where the problem lies.* . . . It is a matter of achieving *a rule of conduct in secular life*.
> (Camus 1965: 10)

Camus recognizes that without metaphysical unity, personal experience is in danger of breaking down. Elsewhere (Gaist 2010) I have elaborated a comparison between Orthodox Christianity and the secular disciplines of Jungian psychology and modern science along precisely those lines. Each has a different methodology, uses a different organ of knowledge, implies a different way of life with different socio-political implications, public commitments, core beliefs and goals; yet, all are capable of communicating, communing, and informing each other.

We may view science, analytical psychology, and Orthodox Christianity as three different paths to knowledge: science as the path of rationality (*dianoia*), Jungian psychology as the path of imagination (*fantasia*), and Orthodox Christianity as the path of the heart (*noesis, theoria*). Each leads persons towards greater wholeness. Yet science offers no secular rule of conduct *pace* Camus, while Jungian psychology does suggest the leading of the symbolic life, listening to dreams, observing synchronicities, and attending therapy.

However, leading analysts after Jung have diverted from his concepts. Hillman (1992: 34) rejects our 'cherished Western dogma' of a unified experiencing subject, placing his trust in the images themselves to 'unify experience by the style in which it is enacted'. Like Orthodox Christianity, Hillman's Archetypal Psychology recognizes the heart as the source of healing, but only Orthodoxy knows it as the seat of the soul, the true self. Melissaris (1997), comparing Zizioulas and Hillman, finds that while both authors agree that human beings are unique, unrepeatable and inexhaustible, Hillman rejects ontology, fearing that it will reduce the person to a fixed point, whereas Zizioulas grounds the person in ontology, for only then will otherness be relational and unshakable (here again we view the essential importance of communion for Orthodox theology, which does not view salvation as an individual affair). Giegerich (2003) calls for a shift of focus away from the individual towards the cultural mind, or 'soul' in his use of the word. Drawing on Heidegger's phenomenology and Hegel's dialectical movement of consciousness, Giegerich develops his psychology in contrast to the 'personalistic' approaches of Jung and Hillman. He embraces the 'end of meaning', viewing meaning as a 'metaphysical womb' from which man has been born first into myths and metaphysics as a '*contra naturam* womb' and, following nineteenth-century modernity and the death of God, into a 'sign-using, linguistic being' conscious of having logically transcended meaning (ibid.: 5, 8, 9). We cannot do justice to the full scope of Giegerich's thought here. However, Melissaris' points regarding Hillman may apply also to Giegerich. Since the loss of meaning has been a cultural phenomenon of the twentieth century, it is not surprising to find post-Jungians taking this intellectual direction. But the idea of a non-personalistic psychology based on soul as cultural zeitgeist reminds us of Gnostic notions of the soul trapped in the prison of the human body (in this case, trapped in the individual psyche). The Orthodox response would be to point out that Christ really took on a human body and a human psyche.

Conclusion: paths to wisdom

Postmodern persons find themselves in a predicament where the loss of meaning and the fragmentation of experience pose serious challenges to personal integrity. Healing narratives, such as those provided by Orthodox Christianity and Jungian Psychology, have been challenged by the ascendancy of modern science, itself growing out of historical developments in theology and philosophy.

However, postmodernism opens up a space whereby it is possible to discern the utility of bringing together concepts and techniques from different realms of thought in the service of experience. We may benefit from modern science, Jungian psychology or Orthodox Christianity, whether our personal path is religious or secular. Indeed, the three realms may be viewed as three paths to knowledge: the path of reason, the path of imagination, and the path of the heart.

Here it may be possible at last to address the question of which archetype the science-complex might be based on. We may reply that it is none other than the archetype of Wisdom, Holy Sophia, in whom the Russian philosophers like Vladimir Solovyov, Sergius Bulgakov, and Pavel Florensky perceived a Chokmah, a divine feminine aspect of God. Christ in Orthodox theology is known as both the Sophia (Wisdom) and Logos (Word) of God, and all who thirst for knowledge are thus drawn into meeting Him. As Bamford (1993: xvi) writes in his introduction to Bulgakov's book on Sophia: 'Theology, philosophy, science, art are not separate disciplines, but parts of one and the same wisdom, of the same apprehension of Sophia, manifested to us in creation and in the Scriptures, in nature and in the Church.' Both the psycho-spiritual disciplines of Jungian psychology and Orthodox Christianity, when considered in tandem, potentially offer an opportunity for personal growth (individuation, theosis) through incarnating in some way the archetype of Sophia, or wisdom. Yet, this profound opportunity may be subverted by the grip of the science-complex, which left unchecked can result in the introduction of closed, Gnostic epistemologies (Papadopoulos 2006) with resulting tendencies towards fundamentalist interpretations of traditional dogmatic religion on the one hand, or scientistic pretensions to natural-scientific status on the other. It is suggested that this risk of epistemological imbalance occurs when the legitimate desire for gnosis is unaccompanied by an equally important apophatic, ascetic and phenomenological attitude of epistemological openness and an appreciation of the limits of human reason, which both disciplines in fact already contain, and from which they may mutually benefit through a sharing dialogue. This however, needs to be accompanied by openness to ontology and to the correct understanding of 'dogma', if it is to be a product of genuine community and communion.

Complexes make us lose sight of the forest for the trees. The science-complex has often restricted our sight to a positivistic caricature of the world and ourselves. Using proper discernment, theology and Jungian psychology and other experiential paths to Wisdom, if no longer claiming the crown from each other as 'queens of the sciences', at least can be reinstated as helpful handmaidens, wise virgins to those who want to see the Word in the World, to experience the Logos in the *logoi* of creation.

Notes

1 The letter is available on: www.barefootsworld.net/jungletter.html (accessed August 30, 2012).
2 Tradition (capital 'T') in Orthodox theology has Holy Scripture at its core as the writings of the community of faith in the Old and New Testaments, interpreted through the later writings of the Church Fathers, the Ecumenical Councils and Church worship

(hymnography, etc.). As Lossky (1974: 147) explains, Tradition is nothing less than 'the communication of the Holy Spirit', the life of the Church in the Holy Spirit which leads the Church 'into all truth' (John 16:13), enabling her to preserve the truth taught by Christ to His Apostles. Importantly, Lossky distinguishes Tradition from 'traditions' (plural, lower-case t) which change across places and eras according to local needs. Thus Orthodox Tradition is truly universal, not bound to cultural expression.

References

Bachelard, G. (2005). *On Poetic Imagination and Reverie*. Putnam, Connecticut: Spring.
Bamford, C. (1993). Foreword. In Bulgakov, S., *Sophia: The Wisdom of God*. Hudson, NY: Lindisfarne Press.
Basil the Great (1895). Hexaemeron. In Schaff, P. (Ed.) *Nicene and Post-Nicene Fathers* (Series II, Vol. 8). Edinburgh: T&T Clark.
Bouteneff, P. C. (2008). *Beginnings: Ancient Christian Readings of the Biblical Creation Narratives*. Grand Rapids, Michigan: Baker Academic.
Camus, A. (1965). *Notebooks 1942–1951*. New York: Harvest.
Chirban, J. T. (2001). *Sickness or Sin: Spiritual Discernment and Differential Diagnosis*. Brookline, MA: Holy Cross Orthodox Press.
Christou, E. (1976). *The Logos of the Soul*. Dallas, Texas: Spring.
Chrysostomos, Archbishop (2007). *A Guide to Orthodox Psychotherapy: The Science, Theology and Spiritual Practice Behind it and its Application*. Lanham, Boulder: University Press of America.
Coles, P. (2001). *Cosmology: A Very Short Introduction*. Oxford: Oxford University Press.
Gaist, B. (2010). *Creative Suffering and the Wounded Healer: Analytical Psychology and Orthodox Christian Theology*. Rollinsford, New Hampshire: Orthodox Research Institute.
Gefter, A. (2011). Thoughts racing along parallel lines. *New Scientist*, 209 (2798): 30–1.
Giegerich, W. (2003). The end of meaning and the birth of man. *Guild Lecture No. 284*, London: Guild of Pastoral Psychology.
Ginsberg, A. (1956). *Howl and Other Poems*. San Francisco: City Lights Books.
Hart, D. B. (2011). Lupinity, felinity and the limits of method. Available: www.firstthings.com/onthesquare/2011/10/lupinity-felinity-and-the-limits-of-method/david-b-hart (accessed August 28, 2012).
Hauke, C. (1998). Jung, modernity and postmodern psychology. In Alister, I. & Hauke, C. (Eds.) *Contemporary Jungian Analysis*. London: Routledge.
Hillman, J. (1992). *The Thought of the Heart and the Soul of the World*. Putnam, Connecticut: Spring.
Hughes, M. & Kroehler, C. J. (2008). *Sociology: The Core* (8th ed.) London: McGraw-Hill.
Jung, C. G. Unless otherwise stated, the following are from *The Collected Works of C. G. Jung* (CW) London: Routledge and Kegan Paul:
——. (1934). A review of the complex theory. (CW8)
——. (1939). *The Symbolic Life*. Guild Lecture No. 80. London: Guild of Pastoral Psychology.
——. (1943). Psychotherapy as a philosophy of life. (CW16)
——. (1958). *The Undiscovered Self*. London: Routledge.

Keller, W., Westhoff, G., Dilg, R., Rohner, R. & Studt, H. H. (1997). Efficacy and cost effectiveness aspects of outpatient Jungian psychoanalysis and psychotherapy: A catamnestic study. Available: http://web.utanet.at/salzjung/dgap-eng.htm (accessed August 29, 2012).

Kruesi, L. (2012). Probing Einstein's relativity. *Astronomy*, March 2012: 24–9.

Larchet, J. C. (2005). *Mental Disorders and Spiritual Healing: Teachings from the Christian East*. Hillsdale, NY: Sophia Perennis.

Melissaris, A. G. (1997). *Personhood Re-Examined: Current Perspectives from Orthodox Anthropology and Archetypal Psychology, a Comparison of John Zizioulas and James Hillman*. Katerini, Greece: Epektasis Publications.

Metallinos, G. (2010). Faith and science in Orthodox gnosiology and methodology. Available: www.oodegr.com/english/epistimi/faith_n_science.htm (accessed August 21, 2012).

Nesteruk, A. (2003). *Light from the East: Theology, Science, and the Eastern Orthodox Tradition*. Minneapolis: Fortress Press.

Okasha, S. (2002). *Philosophy of Science: A Very Short Introduction*. Oxford: Oxford University Press.

Papadopoulos, R. K. (2006). Jung's epistemology and methodology. In Papadopoulos, R. K. (Ed.) *Handbook of Jungian Psychology*. London: Routledge.

Rogers, C. (1961). *On Becoming a Person*. London: Constable.

Rose, Fr. S. (2000). *Genesis, Creation and Early Man: The Orthodox Christian Vision*. Platina, California: St Herman of Alaska Brotherhood.

Shamdasani, S. (2003). *Jung and the Making of Modern Psychology*. Cambridge: Cambridge University Press.

Sharp, D. (1991). *C. G. Jung Lexicon*. Toronto: Inner City Books.

Shelburne, W. A. (1988). *Mythos and Logos in the Thought of Carl Jung*. Albany: State University of New York Press.

Sherrard, P. (2003). A single unified science. In Cutsinger, J. S. (Ed.) *Not of this World: A Treasury of Christian Mysticism*. Bloomington, Indiana: World Wisdom.

Singer, T. (2002). The cultural complex and archetypal defences of the collective spirit. *San Francisco Jung Institute Library Journal*, 20 (4): 5–28.

Singer, T. & Kaplinsky, C. (2010). Cultural complexes in analysis. In Stein, M. (Ed.) *Jungian Psychoanalysis: Working in the Spirit of C.G. Jung*. Chicago: Open Court.

Singer, T. & Kimbles, S. L. (2004). *The Cultural Complex*. New York: Brunner-Routledge.

Smith, W. (1984). *Cosmos & Transcendence: Breaking Through the Barriers of Scientistic Belief*. La Salle, Illinois: Sherwood Sugden.

Stithatos, N. (1995). On the inner nature of things and on purification of the intellect: One hundred texts. In Palmer, G. E. H., Sherrard, P. & Ware, K. (Eds.) *The Philokalia*, (Vol. 4). London: Faber and Faber.

Tacey, D. (2005). The cultural complex. *Spring: A Journal of Archetype and Culture*, 73: 248–52.

Theokritoff, G. & Theokritoff, E. (2002). Review article: Seraphim Rose, *Genesis, Creation and Early Man: The Orthodox Christian Vision*. *St Vladimir's Theological Quarterly*, 46: 365–90.

Thomas, K. (1971). *Religion and the Decline of Magic*. Harmondsworth: Penguin.

Vlachos, H. (1994). *Orthodox Psychotherapy: The Science of the Fathers*. Levadia, Greece: Birth of the Theotokos Monastery.

Von Franz, M.-L. (1993). *Psychotherapy*. Boston: Shambhala.

Webster, C. (1982). *From Paracelsus to Newton: Magic and the Making of Modern Science*. Mineola, NY: Dover.
Woloschak, G. E. (1996). *Beauty and Unity in Creation*. Minneapolis: Light & Life Publishing.
Zizioulas, J. D. (1985). *Being as Communion*. London: Darton, Longman, Todd.
——. (2005). On dogmatics and dogmas. Available: www.oodegr.com/english/dogmatiki1/A2.htm (accessed August 28, 2012).
Zoja, L. (2000). *Drugs, Addiction and Initiation: The Modern Search for Ritual*. Einsiedeln, Switzerland: Daimon Verlag.

8

JUNG'S RELATIONSHIP TO SCIENCE AND HIS CONCEPT OF PSYCHOCULTURAL DEVELOPMENT

Peter T. Dunlap

One approach to the question whether Jung's work is scientific is to survey various definitions of 'science' and attempt to fit Jung's psychological theory within one or another of those definitions. Since Jung is accused of introducing metaphysical or mystical categories into his conceptual framework, particularly in the case of the concepts of 'archetype' and 'collective unconscious', clearly there cannot be a comfortable fit without considerable twisting and turning.

Another approach, the one taken here, focuses on Jung's vision of the reciprocity between processes of individual development and cultural transformation. When considered in the light of recent interest in the psychosocial, historical, and political function of our emotional experience, as well as existing theory and research regarding adult, group, and leadership development, Jung's speculations about transformative archetypal images emanating from a collective unconscious can be seen as articulating a theory of *psychocultural* development that reaches across both scientific and humanistic disciplines (Dunlap 2012).

The concept of psychocultural development

I define psychocultural development as a *complex transactional field* (an idea I owe to Stanley McDaniel) containing the domains of individual development and cultural transformation, which in the modern era have been problematically perceived as separate.

Towards describing individual development in adulthood, I take from Kegan (1982: 19) the premise that 'the evolution of the activity of meaning making' may be viewed as the primary frame for understanding human development. It is beyond the scope of this chapter to discuss Kegan's model in any detail, but it is relevant here that it identifies specific behaviours at each developmental level – presented as five orders of consciousness spanning from childhood to adulthood – in a way that enables his model to be tested empirically. Both Kegan and Jung are interested in the reconciliation of the subject/object divide in human experience through individuals' subjectivity. In sequential stages of development, individuals become increasingly able to reflect on their world as well as their own responses to it as objects of awareness.

A primary feature of Kegan's 'fifth order' entails awareness of the multiplicity of the psyche; that is, the way in which one's identity can be expanded to include a heightened awareness of other's identities, and how the 'other' can reside within an intrapsychic dimension of complex identity. The contemporary Jungian community is highly attuned to this dimension of adult experience. However, a recognition and exploration of multiplicity does not necessarily constitute this advanced order of consciousness. Moreover, Kegan describes the need to establish a consensual process for determining what is 'true' as well as a hierarchy of values and priorities; that is, the propriety of what needs attention. This requirement makes it difficult to implement Jung's desire to be scientific, for the Jungian community is characterized by plurality and divergence in its thinking and institutions – which appears, and may in fact be, pre-paradigmatic.

The cultural domain of psychocultural development concerns the ways that individuals or groups collaborate about, struggle over, and negotiate for, resources and power. This intrinsically implies a political dimension. In political science, 'development' is conceived of as *political development*, referring to the origins of social organization and the historical movement toward democratic institutions. Fukuyama (2011) identifies what social structures are necessary for political development, and how they have played out across the histories of civilizations. However, Fukuyama does not sufficiently account for the experience of the individual in the process of political development. Political psychologist Pye (1966) at least acknowledges *citizenship development* as a relevant factor in larger political developments. The failure to account for the individual in such theorizing underestimates the impact of individual agency. Chilton (1991: 26) addresses the divide between individual and collective experience by defining political development as having both individual and cultural dimensions, challenging us to look more closely at the interaction between the micro and macro levels of political development (see also Dunlap 2011). Bringing a post-Jungian perspective to political science, Andrew Samuels (1993) applies the term 'political development' to individuals, averring that people develop 'politically' in addition to developing psychosexually, psychosocially, etc. Yet, his insight has not led to any concerted effort within analytical psychology to build a research agenda exploring this dimension of individual development.

Because the idea of being 'political' has specific connotations (e.g. engaging in the electoral process), and because Jung's own vision is far more expansive than that, I prefer the term *psychocultural*. I use it to refer to Jung's vision of development through a reciprocal relationship between the individual and culture. A full-blown theory of psychocultural development would integrate research and theories concerning biological, group-oriented, moral, historical, and religious domains, as sketched below.

The *biological domain* refers primarily to the affect system, i.e. the emotions, and concerns how individuals, groups, and communities form their identities in relation to affect. Groups socialize their members into feeling and acting in particular ways. Familial and community norms are communicated to children and adults in ways that lead to either affect repression or affect freedom. By *affect freedom*, I simply mean the capacity to use the full range of our emotional experience for assessing circumstances, motivating and directing action, and connecting with others (Dunlap 2008). Affect freedom enables individuals to draw from their bodily, subjective responses to situations and to connect to collective dimensions of experience. This enables them to have a vital sense of the future, within a broader experience of human development, as it can be reached through the unique leadership capacities nascent in each affect (Omer 2005). If our identities are to some extent affect driven, sensitive individuals encounter whatever it is their culture denies as a psychological state of repressed identity. While Jung's discussions of affect tend to emphasize its negative impact, he also identifies the positive role of differentiated feeling in moral development. For Jung (1946: par. 451), this requires the integration of 'unconscious contents' by means of a 'moral evaluation' that enables individuals to become 'the moral leaders of mankind'.

The *group-oriented domain* places individual development in the context of opportunities for community. For instance, drawing from Lewin's field theory and other sources, Agazarian (1997) identifies stages through which groups develop, and cultivates methods that aid that development by removing barriers to the natural movement of groups toward differentiation and integration of differences. Jung's writings about the life of the group and the influence of emotional and imaginal patterns on that life can be relevant here. Jungian insights inform group-oriented work to do with group shadow dynamics, such as scapegoating (Perera 1986; Coleman 1995).

The *moral domain* identifies developmental stages of moral reasoning. Directly relevant work applies Kohlberg's stages of moral development in childhood and adolescence in work with groups (e.g. Chilton 1991). Jung may have had little faith in a group's ability to embody moral experience, insofar as moral experience requires an individual's active realization, and 'relatively few individuals can be expected to be capable of such an achievement' (1946: par. 451). This has been challenged within the Jungian community by Samuels (1993: 57), who argues that every individual has some level of 'political energy' that can be tapped into through attending to our emotional experience.

The *historical domain* concerns influences in the course of centuries or millennia that have given rise to the conditions that support psychocultural development.

Finally, the *religious domain* refers to the implications of religious experiences and religious institutions for psychocultural development. Processes in this domain can be difficult to investigate scientifically, but this is where Jung and his followers have a great deal to offer.

The question of science

A theory of psychocultural development is only implicit in Jung's work in some respects, but quite explicit in some other important respects. Yet, its premises have been expressed in ways unacceptable to the dominating scientific paradigm. It is my belief that a more detailed explication of how Jung's theory may correlate with recent advances in affect science, political psychology, and more, will establish his work more firmly as a scientific endeavour.

Jung writes:

> When a problem which is at bottom personal, and therefore apparently subjective, coincides with external events that contain the same psychological elements as the personal conflict, it is suddenly *transformed into a general question embracing the whole of society*. In this way a personal problem acquires a dignity it lacked hitherto, since the inner discord always has something humiliating and degrading about it.
>
> (Jung 1921: par. 119; my emphasis)

Here Jung posits a dynamic interchange between personal development and cultural transformation. Jung attempted to articulate this insight in scientific language. Unfortunately, what passed for the 'scientific language' of his time was hardly capable of supporting the conceptual framework which had developed out of his intuition and which guided his empirical research. In looking for a proper means of expression, Jung coined the terms 'collective unconscious' and 'archetypal image' for concepts that have largely been dismissed as idiosyncratic, metaphysical, or mystical. Because his analyses focused on images derived from the collective inheritance of humankind, such as those persistent over history in mythological and religious motifs, and because his technical terms were not understood as *functional* terms, what he put forward as an empirical study of the dynamic interplay between the personal and the collective was not construed as scientific.

This bias persists today. It accounts for the tension within the Jungian community regarding the scientific status of Jung's work, and the tension between Jungian psychology and general expectations regarding what is scientific. The paradigm of science was derived from the effort to *eliminate* subjective factors in favour of a methodology guaranteeing 'objectivity'. Thus Jung's broad category of the 'objective psyche' with its associated concepts of the collective unconscious and archetypal images, appeared simply as a contradiction in terms; and in particular, 'archetype' conjures up the metaphysical bogeyman of Plato's Forms. In his London lectures of 1935, Jung expressed his frustration with this misinterpretation, saying, 'it is very difficult to let psychology be a living thing and *not to dissolve it into static entities*' (1968 [1935]: 65; my emphasis).

Whether or not Jungian concepts ever gain recognition within the scientific community, they are nevertheless central to his understanding of psychocultural development. This suggests at least three tasks. First, we can continue to use these concepts in our own esoteric manner to guide our own inquiry. Second, we can continue the debate about the scientific standing of these concepts, looking for ways to test for their validity based in our own language and practices but sensitive to the need for connecting with other disciplines. Third, we can identify what *specific functions* these concepts play in Jung's theorizing and explore alternative theoretical frameworks incorporating *those same functions*, which would likely enable us to communicate Jung's meaning in the language of other disciplines without evoking the critique of stasis or mysticism. The present discussion is limited to the third task.

I suspect that, in Jungian theory, the *function* performed by the cluster of key concepts (such as the objective psyche, collective unconscious, and archetypal images) is to provide a source of knowledge about the human species: its history, present compromises or repressions, and its future opportunity. In combination with his analytic practices, they provide Jung a way of helping individuals connect to that knowledge for the sake of identifying and mitigating their unique problems. In a recent paper concerning the capacity of the imagination for the objective discernment of the human condition, Nicolaus (2012) neatly summarizes Jung's theorizing about the individual's capacity to tap into a source of collective knowledge. Nicolaus speculates that the imagination might be considered 'a capacity to understand the pre-predictive dimension of our experience' that occurs to us as 'symbolic images, which cohere in a "world-image" that provides the initial background and context for which any subsequent discursive understanding can unfold' (ibid.: 106). Basically, Nicolaus claims that the imagination opens new realities *as images*, enabling us to talk about and act on such an experience even as the images profoundly impact us. Following both Jung and Nicolaus, I ask: can we really have a pre-predictive experience that leads us not only toward resolution of our own personal conflicts but also of cultural ones as well? And, if so, are there contemporary sources of knowledge, both scientific and humanistic, that could support and help us broaden the impact of Jung's thinking?

For many, accepting the legitimacy of Jung's concept of archetypal imagery is commonsense. There is no doubt that our dreams, cultural stories, and artwork are made up of patterns that we can recognize. Also, for many, it may seem obvious that, for all of our individual and cultural diversity, we are of a single species and that this commonness would appear in our dreams, stories, art, behaviour, and possible futures. As Jung notes,

> In the end we have to admit that mankind is not just an accumulation of individuals utterly different from one another, but possesses such a high degree of psychological collectivity that in comparison the individual appears merely as a slight variant.
> (Jung 1910: par. 927)

However, we live in a time when it has been necessary to challenge this collectivity due to fears that such a perspective would be, and has been, used to privilege a few. No sooner than evolutionary theory was proposed, it was used to support cultural prejudice. The resulting backlash makes it difficult to find value in shared experience.

It is against this background that Jung's theory of archetypal images should be considered. Because such images are said to connect us to something shared, common, and morally necessary they are suspect. Jung's awareness of the totality of human experience was based, in part, on these images, but he could not identify a 'scientific' explanation for their source. Despite the cultural milieu that leads us to doubt the extent of our shared humanity, there is other, contemporary, research that supports the notion that human beings have a great deal in common with one another. One important example of this is the resurgent interest in emotion that crosses several disciplines.

On affect science and Jung's understanding of the role of emotion

In contemporary psychology, the affect system is believed to have evolved so as to prepare an organism physiologically and behaviourally to respond to its environment, making it 'adaptive phylogenetically' (Frijda 1994: 116). As many researchers aver, affects occur as fixed behavioural patterns, having identical features in old and young alike, and are shared within the human species as well as with other mammals due to common limbic brain structures, resulting in considerable universality. Paul Ekman puts it this way:

> The evidence on universals in the emotional signals . . . suggests that although the affect programs are open to new information learned through experience, the programs do not start out as empty shells, devoid of information. Circuits are already there, unfolding over development, influenced but not totally constructed by experience.
>
> (Ekman 2003: 66–7)

While there are different views regarding the extent of the universality of emotions, there seems to be sufficient agreement to support the notion that our emotional experience may be a source of collective knowledge that could help us account for Jung's intuition about our psychocultural development. While affect science is primarily focused on the role of emotion in our intra- and interpersonal experience, numerous other disciplines have pursued an understanding of emotion as one determinant of individual *and* group identity.

Relatively little attention has been paid to Jung's efforts to identify the role of emotion in psychocultural development, although it parallels his discussion of the imagination in this context. For Jung, archetypes have both creative and destructive functions for individuals and groups. He speaks of the way in which archetypal images influence behaviour at both levels, emphasizing the destructive role they play when they are not part of a culture's thought or guiding practices. But also, he makes clear they can be integrated either through the traditions that hold groups together or through an individual act of conscious awareness. For Jung, emotions too have this twofold possibility.

Jung notes the potential of emotions for activating a destructive mass mindedness. This is especially the case when groups are cut off from traditions. Without tradition, we become susceptible to the worst forms of group contagion, which swell up through our emotional experience, overwhelming our identity:

> Emotion, incidentally, is not an activity of the individual but something that happens to him. Affects occur usually where adaptation is weakest, and at the same time they revealed the reason for its weakness, namely a certain degree of inferiority in the existence of a lower level of personality. On this lower level with its uncontrolled or scarcely controlled emotions one behaves more or less like a . . . passive victim of his affects . . . singularly incapable of moral judgment.
>
> (Jung 1959: par. 8–9)

His identification of emotional contagion in groups is not his last word on the subject. He also thought that it is possible to resist such mass mindedness by working with the emotions involved. He wrote: 'In the face of this danger the only thing that helps is for the individual to be seized by a powerful emotion which, instead of suppressing or destroying him, makes him whole' (1958: par. 722). While, for Jung, emotions may be a somewhat neglected younger sibling when compared to the imagination, clearly Jung is working with both in a similar manner. Whether working with archetypal imagery or with evoked emotion, he asserts that these can provide the individual with wisdom about the limitations of collective culture.

To exemplify the positive role of the archetypal image and, indirectly, point toward a role for emotion in psychocultural development, Jung (1934) tells the story of the life of Nicholas of Flue (1417–1487). In his telling, Jung emphasizes the role of the image of the holy Trinity in transforming Nicholas, a farmer and military man, into 'brother Klaus', a hermit and man of wisdom. While Jung's primary focus is on Klaus's encounter with the Trinity image, he seems also to pay attention to the role of emotion. Jung cites Woelflin, a contemporary of Klaus, who noted that Klaus terrified many with his countenance. Woelflin accounted for that by reporting another image, in which Klaus saw

> [A] piercing light resembling a human face. At the sight of it he feared that his heart would burst into little pieces. Therefore, overcome with terror, he instantly turned his face away and fell to the ground. And that was the reason why his face was now terrible to others.
>
> (Woelflin, quoted ibid.: par. 13)

In the affect literature, the face is considered the primary site of emotion expressions (e.g. Ekman 2003). What does this suggest about the role of emotion in Klaus's development, his emergent leadership and thus cultural transformation? Did the terrible image open him to necessary layers of fear and other painful emotions that were not only his but were also those of conventional culture that had been neglected and repressed? Was this awakened fear in any way part of a realization of his wisdom? These are questions worth considering.

Jung recognized how emotions functioned, like archetypal images, independently of individuals' conscious awareness. It *happened* to them. Despite viewing emotion as destructive, he also acknowledged its potential to lead us to our 'future development' as it reveals a dimension of unconsciousness needing to be made conscious (Jung 1939: par. 498). Jung does connect emotion and individual development, and while he doesn't specifically link these to cultural transformation, he imagines the integration of both image *and* emotion as leading to the emergence of moral leadership (Jung 1946: par. 451), upon which in turn cultural transformation certainly depends. But, like the problem that many have with the notion that symbolic images are universal and thus their meanings are applicable to the whole species, who is to say that the emotions have such a reach? Is there a way in which our emotional experience contains some group level content? We can turn to contemporary research in affect science, history, and cultural anthropology to begin ferreting this out.

While it is beyond the scope of this chapter to discuss contemporary research regarding emotions and their group level content, it is important to at least show that Jung's intuition about how emotion might connect individual development and cultural transformation may be substantiated.

Historian Rosenwein (2006: 2) describes how social norms shaped the individual's experience of emotion, controlling what types of emotional displays are considered appropriate or taboo, thus constituting what she calls 'emotional communities' that define the humanity of a group by their attitudes toward their own and each other's emotions. Similarly, cultural anthropologist Reddy (2001: 129) shows how a people could consciously develop their emotional community seeking 'emotional refuge' with one another in a way that supports psychocultural development. Applying this idea to the decades leading up to and including the French Revolution Reddy writes: 'For a few decades, emotions were deemed to be as important as reasoning in the foundation of states and the conduct of politics' (ibid.: 143).

Also, Omer (2005) identifies what could be the mechanism for this reciprocity between individual development and cultural transformation. He views each emotion as the raw foundation out of which specific human leadership capacities emerge. For example, Omer thinks that through a cultural practice of mourning grief is transmuted into the capacity for compassion; similarly, fear transmutes into courage through encouragement and intimacy practices as shame can be transmuted into the capacity for having a conscience and humility through a practice of accountability.

The following historical events exemplify Omer's insight: during the salt march from Sabarmati to Dandi Mahatma Gandhi exposed himself to physical violence and incarceration in order to draw the attention of the world to the British repression of shame for their treatment of his people (Omer 2005). Gandhi's acts of cultural leadership transmuted his own and his followers' fear into courage and the British people's shame into a rudimentary conscience, one capable of recognizing the social trauma of prejudice and their own active and passive perpetuation of this horror. Martin Luther King's own path followed Gandhi's as he helped the American people face their shame for the treatment of African-Americans. King recognized the role of affect in leadership development when he extoled his followers 'if he puts you in jail, you go into that jail and transform it from a dungeon of shame to haven of freedom and dignity' (speaking in 1962 [King 1988]).

Concluding reflections

I believe that the possibility of psychocultural development rests on affect freedom. Creating humane democratic institutions is in part defined by fostering attitudes and practices that enable citizens to use the full range of their emotional experiences to support themselves, their families, and their community. This was intuited by Jung:

> It is obvious that a social group consisting of stunted individuals cannot be a healthy and viable institution; only a society that can preserve its internal cohesion and collective values, while at the same time granting the individual the greatest possible freedom, has any prospect of enduring vitality. As the individual is not just a single, separate being, but by his very existence presupposes a collective relationship, it follows that the process of individuation must lead to more intense and broader collective relationships and not to isolation.
> (Jung 1921: par. 758)

This clearly expresses Jung's vision of reciprocity. With each consolidation of humane institutional forms, there would be a concomitant transformation of the emotional community of a people.

Confirming this thesis would require some shared research agenda between several disciplines. Jung seems to have attempted it without significant interdisciplinary support. While we have not yet placed such intuitions on a solid scientific footing, we are beginning to ground them in a range of scientific and humanistic research projects that can be understood as corroborating his pursuit of knowledge.

The practices developed by Jung focus almost exclusively on the personal. Fortunately, there has been substantial work within the Jungian community to move his vision of psychocultural development out of the clinic and into the commons. Introducing their edited volume, Singer and Kimbles (2004) attribute emotions that overwhelm individuals and groups to *cultural complexes*, which in turn can be addressed and transformed. Samuels (1993) identifies how painful emotional connections to politics can be paralyzing, causing us to internalize fear, shame, or anger as self-disgust. Samuels encourages us to pursue new forms of psychological citizenship by turning emotion toward political action. Kimbles, Singer, and Samuels are part of a post-Jungian generation that has come to recognize the transformative value of emotion.

It has been more than fifty years since Jung's death, and we are finally establishing enough distinct views of the *collective human being* to more generously understand the role played by some of his seemingly obscure concepts in his theorizing. The private language of 'archetype' and 'collective unconscious' has supported the creation of a thriving Jungian community capable of contributing to the social welfare, in part, by identifying the way in which individual experience or subjectivity could become a primary vehicle for the realization of objective knowing.

However, claims of the objective nature of the imagination – i.e. that the imagination connects us to experiences at the species level – has created tensions with other intellectual communities. In order to pursue collaboration, it is necessary to learn to speak in other people's languages. As Jung (1956: par. 585) said, we may be living in the 'Kairos', a time of widespread transformation. During this time, the objectivity of the imagination, in its esotericism, can be connected to a necessary public language. This language will have many dialects one of which is emerging within a nexus of active research into the psychosocial, political, and historical function of human emotions.

Acknowledgement

It is with gratitude that I dedicate this chapter to professor Stanley V. McDaniel. Not only did Professor McDaniel help me view C. G. Jung in an expanded light when I was first reading the Collected Works in 1979, but he also assisted by providing helpful feedback on this chapter.

References

Agazarian, Y. (1997). *Systems-Centered Therapy for Groups*. London: Karnac.
Chilton, S. (1991). *Grounding Political Development*. London: Lynne Rienner Publishers.
Coleman, A. (1995). *Up from Scapegoating: Awakening Consciousness in Groups*. Wilmette, Illinois: Chiron.
Dunlap, P. T. (2008). *Awakening Our Faith in the Future: The Advent of Psychological Liberalism*. London: Routledge.
——. (2011). A Transformative political psychology begins with Jung. *Jung Journal: Culture and Psyche*, 5: 47–64.
——. (2012). The unifying function of affect: Founding a theory of psychocultural development in the epistemology of John Dewey and Carl Jung. In I. Semetsky (Ed.) *Jung and Educational Theory*. Oxford: Wiley-Blackwell.
Ekman, P. (2003). *Emotions Revealed*. New York: Henry Holt and Company.
Frijda, N. (1994). Emotions are functional, most of the time. In P. Ekman & R. Davidson (Eds.) *The Nature of Emotion* (pp. 112–22). New York: Oxford University Press.
Fukuyama, F. (2011). *The Origins of Political Order*. New York: Farrar, Straus and Giroux.
Jung, C. G. Unless otherwise stated, the following are from *The Collected Works of C. G. Jung* (CW) London: Routledge and Kegan Paul:
——. (1910). Marginal notes on Wittels: "Die Sexuelle Not." (CW18)
——. (1921). Psychological types. (CW6)

———. (1934). Archetypes of the collective unconscious. (CW9i)
———. (1939). Conscious, unconscious, and individuation. *The Collected Works of C. G. Jung* (CW9i) London: Routledge and Kegan Paul:
———. (1946). The fight with the shadow. (CW10)
———. (1956). The undiscovered self. (CW10)
———. (1958). Flying saucers: A modern myth. (CW10)
———. (1959). Aion. (CW9ii)
———. (1968). *Analytical Psychology: Its Theory and Practice*. New York: Random House. (Originally published in 1935)
Kegan, R. (1982). *The Evolving Self*. Cambridge, Massachusetts: Harvard University Press.
King, M. L., Jr. (1988). *The Speeches Collection of Martin Luther King, Jr*. MPI Home Video.
Nicolaus, G. (2012). Schelling, Jung and the imaginatio vera. *International Journal of Jungian Studies*, 4: 104–20.
Omer, A. (2005). The spacious center: Leadership and the creative transformation of culture. *Shift: At the Frontiers of Consciousness*, 6: 30–3.
Perera, S. (1986). *The Scapegoat Complex*. Toronto: Inner City Books.
Pye, L. (1966). *Aspects of Political Development*. Boston: Little, Brown & Co.
Reddy, W. (2001). *The Navigation of Feeling*. Cambridge: Cambridge University Press.
Rosenwein, B. (2006). *Emotional Communities in the Early Middle Ages*. Ithaca, NY: Cornell University Press.
Samuels, A. (1993). *The Political Psyche*. London: Routledge.
Singer, T. & Kimbles, S. (Eds.) (2004). *The Cultural Complex*. New York: Brunner-Routledge.

Part II

DIALOGUES

9

DIALOGUE 1

Placing Jung

Mark Saban and Raya A. Jones

MARK SABAN: In the introduction to this volume, Raya Jones focuses on the question of dialogue. This seems important to me too. I see Jung as in dialogue with science in a particularly interesting way. On the one hand he is not contained within, identified with science, but nor is he cut off from, rejecting, outside of science. I have found Raya's historical survey of the shifting and uncertain relationship of psychology to science, in Chapter 3, most helpful in highlighting the profound differences that exist between Jung and mainstream academic psychology with regard to this question, but also in throwing light upon the various positions post-Jungians have taken with regard to it. It seems to me particularly important to separate these two questions out from each other. They are distinct, though related, topics.

In Chapter 2, I have focused upon the context behind Jung's understanding of certain scientific ideas. What I have contributed seems more or less in tune with Joe Cambray's Chapter 1, which offers a broader portrait of that context. Both of us point out that it is not helpful to look at Jung and science within too narrow a conception of what science is. I would take this further and suggest that it would be contrary to the spirit of Jung's psychology *as a whole* to extract a single component (e.g. the archetype) and then to subject that particular 'claim' (i.e. that the human psyche contains archetypes) to the kinds of 'scientific' procedure (e.g. falsification) which Raya has described as part of the methodology of modern science. This is the case because Jung's psychology is not intended to be a collection of discrete scientific claims which are Jungian merely in the sense that they all happen to have been made by Jung. One important aspect of Jung's repeated emphasis upon wholeness is his claim that for psychotherapy to be effective it needs to treat the whole psyche, or to encourage wholeness in the psyche. Raya's mention of Dilthey is helpful here. As she points out,

> Dilthey contended that for psychology to imitate a method that was successful in the natural sciences would involve treating an interconnected whole as if it were merely an assemblage of discrete entities, and, moreover, 'neglecting the lived sense of dynamic striving for intrinsically posited goals in favour of a non-teleological, hypothetico-deductive system'.
>
> (This volume: 54)

Jung should perhaps be seen in the context of those German-speaking biologists, neurologists and psychologists of the first half of the twentieth century who embraced the idea of 'holism'. As Harrington (1999: xvi) points out, they 'argued that a continuing commitment to responsible science *was* compatible with an ethically and existentially meaningful picture of human existence; but only *if* one were prepared to rethink prejudices about what constituted appropriate epistemological and methodological standards for science.'

Moreover, for Jung the psychology itself functions as a whole; and, by holding together the difficult tensions or opposites which may be identified in both individual and collective, it offers a model of dynamic wholeness *in itself*. It does so, not by, in some mysterious way, fusing the opposites into one, but by allowing them to be in productive though difficult dialogue with each other. The obvious example for this is his encouragement of dialogue between conscious and unconscious aspects of the psyche. In short, Jung is putting science into dialogue with non-science, within the whole that is his psychology. Such an ambitious attempt will inevitably put that psychology into critical tension with the conventional scientific position.

RAYA JONES: Mark makes an important point about transcending the science/non-science binary. I can see its merit as a pragmatic standpoint in clinical practice as well as towards personal growth generally. But if we want to bring Jung into some academic context, we might want to ascertain the credibility of specific concepts of his; and for that, we need some criteria for making our judgement. Those criteria are likely to reflect one's disciplinary context. As scholars, we are accountable to our peers: we need to justify bringing 'Jung' as authority on something in our context. Hence, because my primary context is psychology, I try to identify in what ways 'Jung' is/isn't congruent with what is perceived as scientific in psychology. The binary is an element not only of academic life but also of social reality in general, as I tried to illustrate in my chapter's discussion of scientism.

MARK SABAN: I can see the problem of 'bringing Jung as authority'. But for me Jung is valuable not because he produces claims that possess that kind of authority within any one discipline, but because he draws attention to, and thus problematizes, the ('archetypal') structures that underlie the disciplines themselves. Jung thus offers an approach, rather than a set of claims. It is true that this leaves open the question, 'why should we accept this approach?', but rather than answer this by attempting to prove the scientific 'existence' of archetypes, I would rather offer a more pragmatist justification, which is I think more in tune with Jung's general approach: If to think in terms of the archetypal throws new light on a question, then that is enough. Jung himself says that concepts such as the archetype are only ever offered as heuristic tools. It may seem a strange comparison, but I don't see Foucault as being brought into academic discussion as an 'authority', but rather as someone who introduces certain problematics into any given topic. That is what Jung too, at his best, can offer.

RAYA JONES: In my monograph (Jones 2007), I tried to bring Jung into line with the concerns of postmodern psychology as someone who opens up questions that contemporary psychologies understate, hence his value. The questions are important even if we don't agree with his answers. Perhaps my use of the word 'authority' needs clarifying. My point is that Jung is well qualified to raise questions in psychology – as opposed to holding that Jung or Freud have no value in psychology because their pursuit of explanation wasn't done scientifically (which has been the prevailing attitude in traditional modern psychology).

References

Harrington, A. (1999) *Reenchanted Science: Holism in German Culture from Wilhelm II to Hitler*. Princeton, NJ: Princeton University Press.

Jones, R. A. (2007) *Jung, Psychology, Postmodernity*. London: Routledge.

10

DIALOGUE 2

Typological determinism and the possibility of transcending subjectivity

Leslie Gardner, Terence Dawson, Peter T. Dunlap, Mark Saban and Robert A. Segal

LESLIE GARDNER: Terence's contention (Chapter 6) is that there is something fatalistic or predetermined about reactions, and that is a feature of Jungian psychology due to its founder's introverted nature. In response, my reaction to Jung from a distance and only through his texts is that he seems a gregarious and outgoing mentor-type – his introversion is mixed with a big dose of the sensational and the extravert. Now I could be wrong, but my deep associations to what must have been a charismatic figure are not those of a reaction to a self-directed fellow.

TERENCE DAWSON: I don't think there is anything fatalistic or predetermined about Jungian psychology. Jung recognized and acknowledged that his 'psychology' reflected his own psychological or typological bias. Jung's current standing in academic debate tells us that very few are persuaded by his ideas. Jungians have responded to this either by ignoring the lack of interest in academia, or by repeating what was misunderstood but (metaphorically) speaking more slowly and loudly as if those who can't understand are hard of hearing. To me, neither of these strategies shows Jungians in the best light.

Another way of coping with our marginalization might be to apply one of Jung's own 'auxiliary tools'. I understand Jungian psychology to be an expression of an introverted intuition-thinking type. I don't think this lessens the value of his ideas. Indeed, I find the admission that his ideas were rooted in his own psychology to be unusually honest, in other words, a very useful lever. My point is that Jungians need to find a way of engaging with the views of other 'types' – types that are not instinctively drawn to Jungian psychology – and a greater recognition of typological tendencies might provide a useful first step toward achieving this.

LESLIE GARDNER: To state it more broadly, since in your estimation Jung was an intuitive-introvert type, you imply that this combination of traits impacted on the nature of the psychology he developed. It is in that way I mean it was 'predetermined' – theoretically, you propose, he'd not have come up with these ideas if he'd been an extravert type.

At this great distance and with evidence of letters, memoirs and comment by others, my assessment is otherwise about him. First of all, I am not certain that despite his own claims, it is what he was. (I am not convinced by his typology ideas anyway.) But if this introversion is to be a comment about the nature of his science, i.e. an attribute of it, then the implication is also that it is hidebound, fatalistic. It is not only that introversion is a confining and constraining sort of attribute, but that the application of a type to a form of psychology is constraining.

I find Jung's focus on paradox, and philology and association renders his analytical psychology an open-ended, dialogical (if you like) endeavour, always aware of audience. He's almost recommending relativism, perspectivism – more focused on receptivity than closed-ness. One aspect, therefore, introversion (if I've got that right) doesn't work for me; it does not seem to apply.

To summarize: your thinking as I take it that any psychology deriving from an introverted type has attributes you ascribe to analytical psychology, and, you recommend we take this on board in critiquing it.

TERENCE DAWSON: Again and again, Jung insisted his ideas on psychological types were not to be used as descriptions of personality types. They were not to be imposed on any product. They were only ways of helping him to explain the patterns and issues he noticed in unconscious products, such as dreams, and their relation to the dreamer.

You say you are 'not convinced by his typology ideas'. I partly agree: I consider *Psychological Types* (Jung 1921) fascinating for the questions it raises. His 'General Description' is often more woolly than precise, he often rambles, and is often infuriatingly vague. But in spite of my frustration with his descriptions, I still find them useful 'shorthand' for thinking about the individual way each of us approaches a topic.

It remains a fact that human beings tend to see things – e.g. a dream, a text – in very different ways. We note different things in what we see or read, we think about what we note in different ways, we express our views very differently. And (I assume we can agree on this) no investigator can note such 'differences' without trying to find some typical characteristics underlying the observation.

Yes, I am of the opinion that Jung was an intuitive-introvert type and that 'this combination of traits impacted on the nature of the psychology he developed'. I do not think he would have 'come up with these ideas if he'd been an extravert type'. But I do *not* think this makes his ideas 'predetermined'. As I see it, the patterns, issues and concerns he wrote about are an expression, a 'confession' if you like, of an introverted intuition-thinking type. I also believe that introverted intuition can manifest itself in almost countless different ways. Introverted intuitives are not all alike.

In your summary, you lose me. I do *not* believe 'that any psychology deriving from an introverted type has attributes you ascribe to analytical psychology'. This is cart before the horse. I think Jungian psychology is derived from one possible kind of introverted intuition type.

You argue that Jung's work is a science (of a kind). If so, then surely contemporary theorists might be expected to show an interest in where their theory comes up against a brick wall (i.e. where others show no interest, and sometimes even manifest hostility toward it). If we can agree on this, then let us not fuss overmuch about my reasons for thinking a little more highly about Jung's psychological types than you do, or why I consider they might help us to find common ground with non-Jungians.

PETER DUNLAP: Examining the regularities of our personalities and imagining how they might impact the object of our attention follows one of Jung's more promising research trajectories. In my own perusing of the type issue, I've come to suspect a few things, several of which already have been commented on here:

1   Our sensitivities are patterned, which influences our interests.
2   These patterns are generalizable, meaning that in a given time and place others will share our inclinations.
3   It is possible to treat these sensitivities as objects of awareness and thus gain a degree of objectivity in relation to them, thus enabling collaboration.
4   However, some of the patterns exist on such a 'generational' (used loosely) scale that the objectivity possible may take quite a while to realize.
5   The implications of this way of thinking for the science of psychology generally and for 'Jungian psychology' specifically are substantial, which I will attempt to briefly articulate, as best that I have them so far.

Even though his primary sensitivity, introverted intuition, provided him with undigestible imagery, Jung hung in there and made meaning of them. He attempted to discern the objectivity of their meaning, that is, their accuracy and generalizability, by grounding these images into existing research in multiple fields, thus using his auxiliary sensitivity, extrovert thinking. The potency of his work led to the formation of the Jungian community, which continues to attempt to work out the objectivity of his meanings. This community has taken on, worked to objectify and thus gain purchase over, both Jung's sensitivities and the way in which they have shaped this community. All of this is taking place within a context of Western culture, which includes its sensitivities and inclinations.

Following my own sensitivities, which is the subjective route to objectivity according to Jung (1921: par. 10), as an introverted thinking type, extroverted feeling is in my shadow. I have spent a few decades *thinking* about *feeling*, and come up with a couple of things, which, to the extent that I've worked my subjectivity successfully, will be generalizable.

Extroverted feeling, as best I can tell, is a type of moral glue that holds people together within a group identity. Its absence provokes dissociation. With the political groups I work with, I try to support the differentiation of this sensitivity, thus turning it into a capacity (as a result of having made it an object of awareness). In the Jungian community, and in many other communities, the relative lack of differentiated feeling may result in an indulgence in our differences.

Jung succeeded at differentiating the objective capacity of the imagination, now we explore how to make this increasingly scientific, and, one of the ways of doing this is to extend his community's consciousness toward shadow of the culture, toward the function of extroverted feeling.

MARK SABAN: I am not sure I buy this theory that analytical psychology, by virtue of being a product of C. G. Jung (introvert), is therefore a) an introverted psychology (whatever that might mean) and b) attracts introverts. The whole point of Jung's *Psychological Types* was to attempt to address, and (as much as is possible) overcome the aspect of the personal equation as perceived in the psychologies of Freud and Adler. It therefore attempts to transcend this problem by allowing for the different possible combinations of typological functions which can occur in individuals. The fact that Jung may or may not have been an introverted thinker (for example) does not definitively doom analytical psychology to being merely a typical product of an introverted thinker. By virtue of making his own typological biases conscious he is freed to create a theory which is not destined merely to play those biases out unconsciously, which is what he accuses Freud and Adler of doing. The theory of typology is therefore supposed to be rising above the problem of a psychology determined by the typology of its creator. Those who claim that analytical psychology is limited by the typological biases of its founder need to do more than state that one thing leads to another – they need to show in what ways this is the case.

As to the undoubted fact that those who are attracted to analytical psychology are predominantly (though not exclusively) introverts, this can surely be explained by the fact that Jungian psychology, like all other depth psychologies, is geared to the exploration of the psychic interior. This is, by definition, what introverts are interested in: the inner world. In other words, introverts are typologically better suited to that kind of work than extraverts are. But it is no more an objection to Jungian psychology that this is the case than it would be an objection to carpentry that people with a highly developed sensation function tend to be better at it.

One of the attractions of the theory of analytical psychology is that it attempts to identify one-sidedness and ultimately to facilitate the compensatory movements which can enable the process of individuation. That compensation may occur in the direction of either extraversion or introversion, depending upon the case of the individual, group, or culture.

It occurs to me that typology offers a helpful perspective on the question of science. Western science has a one-sided bias in the direction of extraversion, to the extent that it finds it difficult to acknowledge anything but the external object as an 'object' of study, and it thus insists upon the epistemological centrality of 'objectivity'. (Remember that Jung defines extraversion as a bias toward the external object.) The compensation required then will tend toward introversion, i.e.

toward the inner object, and this can only be achieved through the recognition of the importance of, and indeed through the exploration of, subjectivity. This compensation is precisely what Goethe was aiming for in his scientific work; and to my mind, Jung takes this theme up and amplifies it.

TERENCE DAWSON: Mark, you write, perfectly reasonably: 'Those who claim that analytical psychology is limited by the typological biases of its founder . . . need to show in what ways this is the case.' You're quite right: but it would require a full-length study to do this. This is why I have contented myself with repeated references to the most obvious evidence of such limitation: the fact that Jung no longer occupies a place at the 'main table' of intellectual debate, as (I think) he probably did between the 1930s and the 1970s. I haven't given statistics, because I don't know them, but it has long been evident that Jungian analysis is not for everyone.

You write: 'One of the attractions of the theory of analytical psychology is that it attempts to identify one-sidedness . . .' I agree, entirely. But there continue to be a great many that are not swayed by this attraction. Is it not possible that this might have something to do with what Jung would have called their psychological type? It is precisely because of what you describe as one of the 'attractions' of his ideas that I think it time we renounced our assumption that Jung has produced a theory that works equally well for everyone.

I prefer to think: how might this limitation best be addressed? I might be wrong about this, but I regard it as quite possible that indifference/hostility to Jungian theory may be rooted in typological tendencies manifest not only in Jung's writings, but also in the views of his critics.

MARK SABAN: All I am looking for is any evidence for systematic typological limitations within the theory of analytical psychology. The status of Jung or analytical psychology in intellectual discourse at any historical moment can't function as evidence one way or the other, because there are numerous different possible reasons for it and not all of them to do with Jung or analytical psychology. At issue here is – not the particular way in which Jung or Jungians put the theory into practice (which is likely to be influenced by typological biases) – but the theory itself. My opinion is that the ways in which that theory has become sedimented institutionally and therapeutically do not do full justice to the potential of the theory.

Some of this can be explained typologically: The combination of the fact that introverts have been generally attracted to Jung and analytical psychology, along with Jung's own personal equation, has meant that the culture around the first and second generation of Jungians has been very inward looking and 'cultic', and there has been a powerful distrust of the outside world, especially the academic world. The theory tells us that this bias toward introversion required compensation in the direction of the inferior, i.e. toward extraversion. But this didn't occur. On the contrary, there was a kind of self-congratulatory wallowing in inwardness which has meant, among other things, a loss of intellectual context for analytical psychology, and a corrosive and self-fulfilling distrust of 'outsiders' and outside ideas.

Thankfully, this is beginning to break up, thanks, among other things, to the IAJS and its academic members like you, Raya and, for example, Paul Bishop, who have done such sterling work opening up the field and letting some fresh air into what has been for too long a stagnant and stifling atmosphere.

By the way, I am not claiming that Jungian therapy, or even Jungian theory, is for everyone. All I am arguing is that its undoubted limitations are not reducible to the typology of its founder in the way you are implying.

TERENCE DAWSON: I am not trying to imply that the 'undoubted limitations [of analytical psychology] are reducible to the typology of its founder'. At least, this is not my major concern.

Jungian dream interpretation has all the characteristics of an introverted intuitive approach. According to Jung, introverted intuition types are always moving 'from image to image, chasing after every possibility in the teeming womb of the unconscious' – they are always in search of a numinous possibility (cf. 1921: par. 658). So arresting are these possibilities that they tend to assume they are always on the brink of discovering some hitherto unrecognized truth (cf. par. 658–9). In other words, they are always looking for an elusive but ultimate 'meaning'. This seems to fit with Jung's characteristic procedure. And yet because Jung also manifests some characteristics of a thinking type, I would regard him as an *introverted intuition-thinking* type.

What I am suggesting is that other types may experience the unconscious rather differently from an introverted intuition type. For example, no other type has quite such a predilection for chasing after images, let alone ascribing 'meaning' to them. It is because Jungian theory has its own special idea of what constitutes meaning that most academics choose to ignore Jung. Jung's definition of meaning simply doesn't 'click' for them. Why should it? Many of them (but not all, you'll be glad to know) are thinking types.

It seems to me that one possible way forward for Jungian psychology would be to investigate how it could better engage with types for whom a Jungian-coloured 'meaning' is not their instinctive dominating concern. For example, thinking types tend to prefer 'explanation' to 'meaning'. But what a Jungian understands by 'explanation' will probably seem circular to a thinking type, and therefore unsatisfactory.

I am not criticizing Jung for chasing 'meaning'; I am not even criticizing his theory for doing so. I am simply noting that Jung privileges one possible typological orientation and that if Jungian theory aspires to be a 'science' it should endeavour to engage with other typical ways of seeing. And typology still seems to me a good starting point.

MARK SABAN: Of course, dream interpretation is only one aspect of the *practice* of Jungian therapy and it can't really stand for the whole of Jungian theory.

But even here, in the *practice* of therapy there are aspects which can seriously benefit from extraverted attitude types and to the functions of, for example, sensation and feeling. A good therapist really needs to be able to utilize three of his/her functions to a reasonable level. (The fourth function is of course doomed to eternal inferiority – though this of course gives it the privileged position of being the doorway to the unconscious.)

My old therapist was highly introverted-intuitive, such that she was disconcertingly able to come up, at one leap, with an astonishingly convincing interpretation of any dream I presented. In my case, though I certainly use my intuition when interpreting dreams, I need to think my way more steadily toward an interpretation, and I need to work towards it in close concert with my client. My therapist's approach was impressive and effective, but there are some advantages to mine, I think. No doubt every Jungian analyst responds to dreams in an individual way, and some of that difference will be to do with typology. On the whole, as I said before, introversion is probably more helpful than extraversion when it comes to plumbing the depths of one's own or others' interiorities.

ROBERT SEGAL: Two quick points:

(a) I do not grasp what is meant by subjectivity other than as bias – that is, as something to be recognized and removed.
(b) Nor I do grasp what makes objectivity directed externally.

Science can and does explain mental states as well as outward behaviour. And to explain is to account for why subjects think, feel, and act as they do.

Jung seems to want to transcend the bias – the subjectivity – of psychology by classifying approaches into types. The typology is what is intended to encompass the bias of any one type. I myself have never fathomed how recognition of bias overcomes it, but so Jung seems to argue.

But even if it turns out that Jung fails to overcome his own type, his psychology can be re-characterized as that which, while limited in its applicability, hones things that are really there, just not all the things that are there. So Jung's psychology thereby becomes narrower in scope but not therefore subjective within its constricted scope. The limitation does not reduce objectivity to subjectivity – which for me is another name for intellectual failure. It merely narrows the range of the discipline.

MARK SABAN: Robert,

(a) Jung believes that there is no psychology without subjectivity. Its object is its subject. No Archimedean point etc. So, for Jung at least, it cannot be removed.
(b) OED seems to recognize an intimate connection between objectivity and the external: 'Objectivity = the quality or character of being objective; external reality; objectiveness.'

In order to explain mental states scientifically the scientist takes up an objective stance: the mental states need to be external to the observer, otherwise objectivity cannot be guaranteed. The mental states are internal to the person who entertains them, but external to the scientific observer. In order to do so, the subjective states of the scientist need to be excluded. He needs to take up the view from nowhere. Jung argues that when this is performed, something important about the psyche gets left out. One only has to read works of academic psychology to see that he is right.

He argues that subjective bias can never be completely overcome, but it can at least become relatively conscious. If on the other hand it remains unconscious, it can distort conscious life far more.

His aim is not to favour subjectivity over objectivity but to establish a creative tension between the two. Both are important, especially in psychology.

ROBERT SEGAL:

(a) Jung seems to commit the commonplace self-contradiction of relativism: claiming to know – objectively – that all things are relative.
(b) It is not the aim of science (quoting Einstein) to duplicate the taste of the soup. Science seeks to account for mental states. Yes, mental states are hard even to capture, much less to explain. But hard does not mean impossible. I don't see how the observer is somehow inherently unable to explain the most subjective of states.

MARK SABAN: I don't think Jung's position can be reduced to commonplace relativism. In my opinion, he retains a scientific desire to explain, and to find the best explanation. But for him the best explanation involves the inclusion of both subjective and objective aspects. This is why, as I try to explain in my chapter, his objectivity is more 'objective' than commonplace objectivity, because it allows for the inclusion of more data. One of his critiques of ordinary science is that it refuses to include this factor, because, due to a systematic blindness, it is unable to see it.

I don't think Jung would disagree with (b). Jung doesn't think that it is utterly impossible to make any explanation of mental states. He writes twenty volumes of collected works trying to do so. But he does think that the best way to do so is to find a way to allow the subjective into the picture. He thinks that it is impossible to fully explain mental states if they are approached only 'objectively' (just as it is impossible to do so by only taking into account conscious activity and ignoring the unconscious).

ROBERT SEGAL: There is no reason that if Jungian psychology is of limited applicability, it cannot be expanded. And yes, Jung is to be touted, not criticized, for trying to overcome subjectivity. My wariness is just that he doesn't seem to show how subjectivity can be overcome once it is recognized.

What makes a discipline scientific is that it is self-correcting: that it subjects its claims to tests, which it can fail. I ask repeatedly: how does Jungian psychology try to correct itself?

TERENCE DAWSON: Far from trying 'to correct itself', it seems to me that Jungian psychology is hell-bent on not doing so. For example, all of us working on this project seem to agree that Jungian psychology is a psychocultural theory of some kind. We may phrase this differently, but more or less we are in accord that Jungian psychology is rooted in culture. What is the evidence for such a claim? That Jungian psychology refers to myths, religious writing, fairytales, a handful of medieval texts, selected mystics, alchemical texts and selected individuals such as Goethe and Nietzsche, and Kant with less certainty. To anyone but a Jungian there might seem to be some glaring and sizeable lacunae in this list. It escapes me how anyone can claim that Jungian psychology is a cultural psychology when its interest in culture is so limited and what it has to say about culture is so predictable.

I happen to think that it is a cultural psychology. Therefore, it should explore this aspect of itself more intelligently than it does at present. Whilst I understand the need for Jungian analysts to learn from useful methods and practices developed by non-Jungian therapies, I believe they could learn far more from a better understanding of culture and cultural history. Jung was slow to realize his theories were rooted in culture, and so it is no surprise that his followers have followed suit – in my view, to the immense impoverishment of his legacy. As I see it, Jungian psychology has a huge untapped potential.

If it is a science at all, Jungian theory is an armchair science. As such, its natural allies are the humanities. But instead of seeking out allies in philosophy, literature, sociology, etc. (religious studies is a rare exception, as there are quite a few Jungians in this field), a great many Jungians are astonishingly resistant to the possibility that such disciplines could have anything to contribute to Jungian wisdom.

PETER DUNLAP: Forgive me for jumping in mid-stream, but, this is interesting. As best that I can tell, Jung uses the word subjectivity to mean the experience of the person. Through 'subjectivity' a person gains an increasing degree of 'objectivity', by plumbing the depths of their subjectivity, that is, the more they know about themselves the more they understand the limits of their type/character/personality/etc. Understanding these limits enables them to see in a way that is generalizable, that is, could be applied to others. However, this 'in-depth' seeing cannot be easily communicated to others unless there were to be a way of helping them go through some comparable process of refining their own 'type'.

Jung, like many others including James and Dewey, is connecting subjectivity and objectivity and opposing both to embedded collectivity. In this opposition both analytical psychology and Jungian psychology (to use Raya's distinction?) are still required to pursue the requirements of generalizability.

Reference

Jung, C. G. (1921). Psychological types. *Collected Works of C. G. Jung* (Vol. 6). London: Routledge.

11

DIALOGUE 3

Truth, facts and interpretation

*Terence Dawson, Mark Saban, Peter T. Dunlap,
Robert A. Segal and Leslie Gardner*

TERENCE DAWSON: Robert Segal (Chapter 5) suggests that while Jung provides a persuasive theory of human nature, Frazer offers a more 'credible' and therefore 'more scientific' theory of myth. This might seem to be a well-balanced conclusion, but it is also misleading. Frazer had a theory about myth; strictly speaking, Jung did not. He had a theory about archetypal images, which is not the same thing. Frazer was interested in the possible significance of Adonis for an ancient society, Jung, only for a modern individual who happened to be fascinated by an image reminiscent of Adonis. (Jung's is not a theory of behaviour, i.e. if a man does x, he must be a puer.) If one wants to compare the status of their claims as 'science', one needs to measure Frazer's theory of myth against Jung's use of myth in understanding a modern problem. It seems to me that Jung's theory might come out better in Robert's comparison if this distinction were allowed.[1]

This raises a more general issue concerning the nature of archetypal images. According to Jung, archetypal images reveal 'the deeper levels of the psyche' (Jung 1931a: par. 105). I would imagine most or all Jungians could agree on this. But what exactly is meant by describing this layer as the collective unconscious? As Raya reminds us regarding the gender of the sun, all archetypal images may be culturally specific (see Chapter 3). The evidence used to corroborate the claim that an image is archetypal is almost always taken from a culturally loaded text, very often a work of literature in which a traditional story has been *adapted* for its author's specific purpose. In my view, there is no such thing as a 'myth' that exists independently of the artistic formulation that allowed it to survive, whether in writing, stone, or other medium.

Jung divided literary works into two categories: the 'psychological' (in which he had no interest) and the 'visionary': the latter includes all myths. I have never been happy with this distinction: it makes analytical psychology seem like a kind of theosophy. If archetypal images were regarded as anchored in culture, a major reason for the marginalization of analytical psychology might evaporate. As I see it, all texts are equal. A text is a fact. Its interpretation is not.

I see 'interpretation' as humankind's most important way to advance understanding (this is, of course, a possible definition of science). But because every *text* (dream or literary) is open to continually evolving interpretation, I do not consider it useful to describe any aspect of an interpretative methodology as science. Science often progresses by making mistakes; but little by little, 'facts' establish themselves. Interpretations of texts change over time; they do not necessarily become better, let alone 'factual'. Jung was right to insist that inner experience is a fact. But he never made this claim about his interpretations or even about his objective:

> I have no theory about dreams . . . On the other hand, I know that if we meditate on a dream sufficiently long and thoroughly, something almost always comes of it. *This something is not of course a scientific result to be boasted about or rationalized* . . . I must content myself wholly with the fact that the result means something to the patient.
> (Jung 1929: par. 86; my italics)

Elsewhere Jung describes his purpose as simply to bring about a way of looking at an issue that will lead to better understanding it. Following Paracelsus, somewhat confusingly, he called this theoria (1941: par. 218). This is what Raya is arguing (if I understand her correctly). Why, then, must we be so 'science complex' driven that we feel compelled to describe interpretation as 'science'? In my view, interpretation touches on humankind's most fundamental ability: our ability to 'read' the world. All creatures, great and small, do the same, but we're rather better at it. It is what makes us human. Why not rejoice in it and underline the difference between interpretation and fact-obsessed science?

MARK SABAN: I find myself unconvinced by Terence Dawson's argument that Jung's psychology is *primarily* a narrative and cultural theory 'applied' *post hoc* in his psychotherapeutic practice. Firstly, it seems to me to make the mistake of falling into an either/or binary: Jung's psychology is either science or narrative, either academic or clinical, either aesthetic or scientific. As I have tried to argue, it is both, or rather it exists in tension between these 'opposites'. Second, to make narrative *primary* in this way flies directly in the face of Jung's insistence on the primary nature of image ('image is psyche'). Dawson relies heavily upon the example of Jung's 1912 transitional work, republished as *Symbols of Transformation* (Jung 1952a) to support his claim. It is, however, hard to find much evidence for this thesis in Jung's mature works. *Psychology and Alchemy* (1944) amplifies dream images through alchemical images. 'Psychology of the Transference' (1946) depends entirely upon alchemical images. Even where Jung works with text (as in 'Answer to Job' [1952b], the Zarathustra seminar [1988], or indeed *Symbols of Transformation* itself) he invariably reads it by moving from image to image, reading the text as an image, as though it were a dream or a myth. In *Memories, Dreams, Reflections*, Jung (1973) reads his own life in this way. My point is that for Jung image is the primary medium of psyche because image is prior to language. In this he differs from Freud (and Lacan) for whom language is primary.

TERENCE DAWSON: Mark, thank you for pointing out some of the things I need to clarify. I do not think we're at odds over anything: we're just giving words a different weight. By narrative, I mean exactly what Jung meant when he wrote (1): 'I never, if I can help it, interpret one dream by itself. As a rule *a dream belongs in a series*' (1937: par. 53; my italics) and (2): with reference to 'sticking to the dream images' in order to establish a context: 'Every interpretation is a hypothesis, an attempt to read an unknown *text*' (1931b: par. 322; my italics). A series of eight cartoon images, without *any* words in them, constitute a 'narrative' in the sense I use the word; ditto for an alchemical text. I am not trying to advance a new 'theory' about Jungian analysis based on semiotic language! The aim of my chapter is simply to *describe* what Jung does in his writing and reflect on it. I am in full agreement with you, Mark, when you say: 'But for me Jung is valuable not because he produces claims that possess that kind of authority within any one discipline, but because he draws attention to, and thus problematizes, the ('archetypal') structures that underlie the disciplines themselves' (this volume: 154). Well said.

MARK SABAN: Terence, I think I understand your remarks about Jung and narrative better now, and as you say, we are not as far apart on this as I had thought.

However, we do still differ on the question of the scientific status of Jung's psychology. You draw a very clear distinction between science ('fact-obsessed') and interpretation (changing over time). But I am not sure this dichotomy is convincing. As you remark, Jung 'describes his purpose as simply to bring about a way of looking at an issue that will lead to better understanding it'. A 'better understanding' of things is surely precisely what science aims at. It seems to me (a) that science (especially social science, but arguably even the hard sciences) is more interpretive (and less 'fact-obsessed') than you give credit for, and (b) that Jung is more attached to the idea of (if not 'factual' then empirical) truth than you are acknowledging. I would say that the undeniable tensions between 'fact-obsession' and 'interpretation' are real, but that they exist within science (and within Jungian psychology).

I strongly agree with your point about archetypal images and the collective unconscious. Some good work needs to be done exploring what it really means to continue to claim that 'archetypal images' reveal the deeper levels of the psyche, if one is not making the further claim that there 'exists' a collective unconscious outside of and beyond culture, i.e. If one has jettisoned the archetype-in-itself. Hillman played with these ideas but, to my mind, he never really thought them through.

TERENCE DAWSON: Mark, you're quite right: Jung very often does come across as 'attached to the idea of (if not "factual" then empirical) truth'. But this is not the whole story. In cautious moods, he would admit:

> The essential character of hermeneutics, a science which was widely practiced in former times, consists in making successive additions of other analogies to the analogy given in the symbol: in the first place of subjective analogies found by the analyst in the course of erudite research. This procedure is an infinitely complex and varied picture, in which certain 'lines' of psychological development stand out as possibilities that are at once individual and collective. There is no science on earth by which these lines could be proved 'right': on the contrary, rationalism could very easily prove that they are not right. Their validity is proved by their intense value for life.
>
> (Jung 1916: par. 495)

Jung was of course using the word science here in two very different ways, but his 'meaning' is categorical: he recognizes that the claims he makes are only 'possibilities'.

I think it preferable to lean on the more cautious Jung. I am not sure whether I believe in any single truth, or even 'partial' truth (whatever this might mean!). As I see it, we interpret; and our objective is to be as coherent as possible. It remains for the reader to decide whether this 'clicks' for him or her.

I am interested in Jung not because I think he had access to truth. I am interested in Jung because his theory provides me with the best 'auxiliary tools' that I know for exploring the issues that capture my imagination. See Jung's reply to Martin Buber: 'I have set up neither a system nor a general theory, but have merely formulated auxiliary concepts to serve me as tools, as is customary in every branch of science' (1952c: par. 1507).

I have a secondary reason for preferring we acknowledge that Jungian psychology is based on interpretation. Insisting that Jungian psychology gives one access to the truth is the surest way to ensure Jung's marginalization from all serious intellectual debate. Like you, I believe that Jung's legacy still has an enormous amount to contribute to the world. Why, then, must we continue pulling the carpet from under our own feet? If we want to persuade others of the value of Jung's ideas, one has to speak the lingua franca of our time.

PETER DUNLAP: Here is a question: what benefit do we gain by separating the pursuit of facts from interpretation? It seems to me they are in a reciprocal relationship. As we glean facts about the world we are drawn to wonder about their applicability, that is, how do they help us? I think of that wondering as interpretive. Such interpretations lead to more questions and fact gathering. And so on. Mark, I agree with and appreciate your response to Terence.

DIALOGUE 3: TRUTH, FACTS AND INTERPRETATION

Terence, your response in turn to Mark was very interesting. But I get concerned when you write: 'I am interested in Jung not because I think he had access to truth. I am interested in Jung because his theory provides me with the best "auxiliary tools" that I know . . .'

I suspect that the word 'truth' is loaded for you in a certain way that is different for me. And, in this difference, I suspect, we have quite different agendas. Now these agendas might never meet or perhaps they could. In the meantime, we certainly can talk. My own has me interested in building consensus within groups and using the social sciences to consolidate a moral and political mandate in relationship to things like global warming, social justice, etc.; and, I think we need something like analytical psychology to do this as well as it needs to be done. If the institutions that are working out analytical psychology don't want it turned in this direction, then there are likely to be other tools to accomplish the task. However, for now, I think that analytical psychology is one of the very best psychologies for working out the political psychology needed by our time.

There is a use of the word 'truth' that does not risk sending us back into an age of faith but does put some pressure on us to see if we can get our hobbyhorses to rock with some degree of commonality. In this context, 'fact', 'truth' or 'objectivity' might be defined the way a new generation of historians are using the term (objectively) to mean, 'a commitment to honest investigation, open process research, and engaged public discussions of the meaning of historical facts' (Appleby et al. 1994: 10).

TERENCE DAWSON: Peter, you ask: 'What benefit do we gain by separating the pursuit of facts from interpretation?' My answer: the necessary *basis* for serious discussion.

In the nineteenth century, a great many Westerners considered the statement 'Jesus is the son of God' to be a fact. Even today, many still believe it to be so. A Buddhist is unlikely to share this view. In similar fashion, not all psychoanalysts accept that the unconscious compensates consciousness. A Jungian might consider 'The witch in Simon's dream is an anima-figure' to be simply descriptive. A Freudian would consider it to be a first step in interpretation. A psychic fact, if I may use such a phrase, exists only for the individual who believes it.

It may be easier for academics in a literature department to recognize that all interpretation of 'texts' is rooted in time, in subjectivity, and in rhetoric. Each generation interprets a text afresh. In the eighteenth century, *King Lear* was performed with a happy ending. German Romantic critics taught us how to think about 'interiority' in Shakespeare's plays; this issue 'clicked' for most late nineteenth- and early twentieth-century audiences. Their insights fuelled readings until the 1960s, when critics began to understand Shakespeare as a 'political' writer; today, this reading 'clicks' with more audiences than 'interiority'. Neither 'clicking' proves that either interpretation is factual. I share Mark's concern that this 'interiority' be not forgotten simply because readers began to 'click' with new issues.

Academic interpretation aspires to uncover a hitherto unnoticed aspect of a work. In this sense, it evolves; it has a 'history'. But it does not necessarily improve. Changing a focus of concern does not necessarily lead to sharper insights about the whole. Even the sharpest interpretative insight is only a critical interpretation or opinion, never a 'fact'.

Science moves *toward* the establishment of an indisputable fact. Good interpretation builds *from* facts. The 'subject' of a text (e.g. a dream) might be described as a fact; all the 'themes' we read into it are arrived at by subjective interpretation. Jung's concept of the self is no more, nor less, factual than Freud's Oedipus complex. Both are the result of interpretation.

ROBERT SEGAL: Science does not 'move toward the establishment of an indisputable fact'. Science does not seek certainty, and most scientific explanations are both statistical and corrigible. Science does not aim to prove that the earth circles the sun. It aims to explain why. It aims at what you call interpretation.

TERENCE DAWSON: Robert, the reason you can give this example is because it is now considered a fact that the earth does circle the sun. This was not always so: Ptolemy thought the sun circled the earth.

If sufficient people test a hypothesis and come to the same result, this result will become a fact (e.g.) about 'why' the earth revolves around the sun. I withdraw the 'indisputable' which I used rather carelessly and to which you rightly object. In my earlier response to Mark I wrote, 'Science often progresses by making mistakes, but little by little "facts" establish themselves.' We cannot today pretend that it is only a possibility that the earth circles the sun.

No comparable facts ever emerge from textual interpretation. When Ernest Jones (1910) applied psychoanalysis to Hamlet, he produced a new and provocative reading of some aspects of the play. But his reading doesn't explain the whole play. Kott's (1964) 'existential-political' reading cast the character of Fortinbras in an equally fresh and exciting light. Each argument represents a possible but partial reading. Neither argument uncovers any 'fact' about Hamlet. Each simply uncovers a different possibility for us to consider. Proving that one can read Hamlet as a political play does not prove that Hamlet is a political play. In similar fashion, proving that a Jungian approach offers a coherent reading of a dream does not prove that the interpretation is correct. A Freudian might be able to offer an equally coherent reading. Coherence suggests only that a reading is worth considering, which is not the same thing. In years to come, the earth will still be circling the sun, water will still be boiling at 100 degrees centigrade at ground level, and academics will still be niggling about wording, but I am fairly sure that my great-great grandchildren will be reading Hamlet in a way that I cannot even begin to imagine.

PETER DUNLAP: I appreciate the idea that textual interpretations change with the times; and, I accept the notion that these are not facts. Perhaps, for this reason

DIALOGUE 3: TRUTH, FACTS AND INTERPRETATION

I don't find myself using the word 'facts'. I do find myself using the phrase 'warranted assertion'. Somewhere here is a distinction between types of inquiry.

I see the *science* of psychology to be about generating interpretations that are then tested for the sake of explanation and prediction. Such a framework is needed for those questions that I have for which I am looking for answers. In this context, interpretation is a phase of scientific inquiry and is in an intimate and reciprocal relationship with the next phase of looking for evidence to substantiate or falsify the interpretations.

It is in this context that I find Jung's work invaluable. While he does not ground his intuitions sufficiently in existing scientific discourse, he does pursue his subject matter empirically. Does he succeed? By some measures yes, much of his research has led to further research that adds to human knowledge. By other measures no, the veracity of his work is not broadly recognized.

The task that I am interested in pursuing is substantiating Jung's scientific standing in the eyes of a significantly broader community. The importance of his research (his data collection and theorizing or interpreting) is beyond doubt to me. However, what I see a little bit in our conversation so far is that your interests are markedly different than mine. I draw attention to this because I think its impact on our conversation and generally that of conversations taking place in the Jungian community are underestimated. I suspect that if we continue this conversation and stay focused, somehow, on each other's different agendas our conversation will lead in a very interesting direction.

ROBERT SEGAL: Jungian interpretations, though also Freudian and many other ones, are unscientific not merely because they fail to predict new facts but because they typically fail even the lesser test of applicability. Ever come upon a Jungian interpretation of anything that was conceded to be a failure by the interpreter? As Popper so acutely pointed out against Freudian and Adlerian interpretations of behaviour, they are compatible with any state of affairs.

LESLIE GARDNER: Jung comments in a late essay, 'Approaching the Unconscious',

> Whoever denies the existence of the unconscious is in fact assuming that our present knowledge of the psyche is total. And this belief is clearly just as false as the assumption that we know all there is to be known about the natural universe. Our psyche is part of nature, and its enigma is as limitless. Thus we cannot define either the psyche or nature. We can merely state what we believe them to be and describe, as best we can, how they function.
>
> (Jung 1978 [1964]: 6)

Jung claims that consciousness is a recent development in human history. His proposals about individuation track development of the human psyche from unconscious murky mix with a personality's immersion in surroundings, to a more sharply defined sense of an ego, further differentiated into an individual. He agreed with Lévy-Bruhl's notion of 'mystical participation' as the primitives' fundamental modal presence in the world. Jung's view was further developed by Erich Neumann into an outline of a historical trajectory from myth to enlightened awareness of the conscious human being across society, where he locates the origins of consciousness.

I would propose that these views are based on an idiosyncratic and paradoxical view of what fact is. The significance of 'fact' is questioned in Jung's theorizing in continuing meta-commentaries. First, he sits 'fact' closely in the context of a causal, determinist dimension. He begins this way to accommodate his audience, and then, by associating it to positivist underpinnings, he shows us that he catches himself (and us) out always in a paradox. He discovers that scientific fact is, in fact, linked closely to contingency, and to subjective analysis – so he is at odds with his assumptions about how to reach scientific, empirical conclusions.

By revealing this to us, he opens our minds to an innovative view of scientific fact which is not so much based on empirical data, but based on data that we understand as suspect, or inflected by the observer's tools, both intellectual and instrumental. His discussions in his early essay 'The Role of the Unconscious' (1918) and in the late essay cited above reiterate this life-long belief.

How the human psyche translates symbolic knowledge into meaning remains a mystery. To address this, Jung proposes we shift our questions.

Note

1 **ROBERT SEGAL**: I find odd the claim that Jung is not offering a theory of myth. He seeks to answer the key questions: what is the origin, what is the function, and what is the subject matter of myth. What more does he need to do? And he is arguing against Frazer even more than against Freud. He discusses 'primitive' and ancient myths as much as modern ones, and he considers more than archetypal images. In my edited *Jung on Mythology* (Jung 1998), I've collated what I deem is Jung's whole theory of myth.

References

Appleby, J. O., Hunt, L. A. & Jacob, M. C. (1994). *Telling the Truth about History*. New York: W. W. Norton.
Jones, E. (1910). The Oedipus-Complex as an explanation of Hamlet's mystery: A study in motive. *American Journal of Psychology*, 21: 72–113.
Jung, C. G. Unless otherwise stated, the following are from *The Collected Works of C. G. Jung* (CW) London: Routledge and Kegan Paul:
——. (1916). The structure of the unconscious. (CW7)
——. (1918). The role of the unconscious. (CW10)
——. (1929). The aims of psychotherapy. (CW16)
——. (1931a). Archaic man. (CW10)
——. (1931b). The practical use of dream-analysis. (CW10)
——. (1937). Psychology and religion. (CW11)

——. (1941). Psychotherapy today. (CW16)
——. (1944). *Psychology and Alchemy*. (CW12)
——. (1946). Psychology of the transference. (CW16)
——. (1952a). *Symbols of Transformation*. (CW5)
——. (1952b). Answer to Job. (CW11)
——. (1973). *Memories, Dreams, Reflections*. New York: Pantheon Books.
——. (1978). Approaching the unconscious. *Man and His Symbols*. Picador. (Original work published in 1964)
——. (1988). Nietzsche's Zarathustra: Notes of the seminar given in 1934–1939. Princeton, NJ: Princeton University Press.
——. (1998). *Jung on Mythology* (Edited: R. Segal). Princeton, NJ: Princeton University Press.
Kott, J. (1964). *Shakespeare, Our Contemporary*. London: Methuen.

12

DIALOGUE 4

Wisdom and archetype

Raya A. Jones and Byron J. Gaist

RAYA JONES: Does the 'science complex' have an archetypal core? In Chapter 7, Byron Gaist answers in the affirmative:

> Here it may be possible... to address the question of which archetype the 'science complex' might be based on. We may reply that it is none other than the archetype of Wisdom, Holy Sophia, in whom the Russian philosophers... perceived a Chokmah, a divine feminine aspect of God.
> (This volume: 136)

I'm not familiar with the sources cited by Byron, but I do know that Chokmah – or to put it more phonetically, *chochmah* – is the ordinary Hebrew word for wisdom. In the Kabbalah, it is one of the ten attributes (*sphirot*; lit., enumerations) whereby the Infinite is revealed. It is paired with *Binah*, which also means wisdom, but with subtly different nuances. *Chochma* (but not *binah*) can overlap the English word sagacity. *Binah* is closer to cleverness or shrewdness. The Kabbalah triangulates both with *Da'at*, which means knowledge. The Modern Hebrew word for science (*mada*) is etymologically related to *da'at*. Hence, at least in Hebrew, science is to do with knowledge but not with wisdom. Linguistics aside, being a scientist doesn't ipso facto make one wise. I would go as far as saying that modern science is anti-wisdom – it idealizes *da'at* without *chochma* or *binah* – insofar as it privileges evidence-based factual knowledge, and is suspicious of claims to an understanding based solely on intuition or personal experience. The tension between factual knowledge and insightful wisdom is a key to Jung's identity crisis as a scientist, it seems to me. Noting that it is an unbreakable rule in scientific research to take something as known only insofar as it can be verified by facts, Jung (1948a: par. 384) identifies the constraints thus imposed on psychology, a discipline that 'does not exclude the existence of faith, conviction, and experienced certainties of whatever description', but 'completely lacks the means to prove their validity in the scientific sense'.

Byron nevertheless has a point in placing Sophia at the core of the science-complex, not science per se. The science-complex is about expectancies regarding science, not what science actually is. But it depends on how we conceptualize 'science complex'. As laboured in my chapter, my concept should be differentiated from the post-Jungian concept of a cultural complex, which assumes *a priori* an archetypal core. I categorically stated (before reading Byron's chapter) that it doesn't make sense to speak of an archetypal core of a science-complex (this volume: 51). Byron has made me rethink. While I do not recant my concept, I now wonder about the extent to which Sophia might be projected onto what I call the science-complex. That is, instead of positing an archetype which generates a science-complex – i.e. functioning as its nucleus – I'm proposing that a naïve perception of what science is about involves a displacement of Sophia. It is a psychological process not unlike projecting archetypal motifs of alien visitations on certain material phenomena of an unknown nature, as Jung interpreted accounts of UFOs (see Chapter 4, this volume).

A further consideration towards asserting Sophia as displaced in the science-complex arises from the classical Jungian construal of archetypes as bipolar. For instance, in Chapter 5, Robert Segal reminds us of the nurturing and smothering mother. What would be the sinister pole of Sophia? Perhaps it is wisdom without compassion, e.g. Machiavellian shrewdness. But is it still really Sophia, 'a divine feminine aspect of God'?

BYRON GAIST: In response to my chapter, Raya Jones takes up discussing my suggestion that the archetypal image of Sophia is at the core of the science complex. It may be productive to entertain this as a possibility, even if we are simultaneously convinced of its ontological verity or its falsity: as Corbin (1953: 9) suggested, statements and images do not question the reality of the transcendent object, but they interpret them. What then, would Sophia disclose to us, if she really did reside within our cultural science complex?

Raya amplifies part of the theme with reference to the Kabbalah and Hebrew etymology, by identifying tensions between wisdom/knowledge and sagacity/shrewdness, suggesting that perhaps the sinister pole of the Sophia archetype is to be found in that wisdom which is without compassion – indeed, it may be noticed that whereas *Chokhmah* (wisdom, corresponding to the brain) lies on the *kav yamin*, the right pillar of mercy, *Binah* (understanding, corresponding to the heart) is found on the *kav smol*, the left pillar of severity – and both are necessary to produce *Da'at* (conscious knowledge).

Evdokimov (1994: 49) suggests that man expresses his freedom by incarnating values, and his relationship with values is always creative: it is a relationship which has never existed until we bring it into existence, and in this sense we are what we do. Most importantly, the reason for this creativity is because the Wisdom of God precedes our existence, and in Evdokimov's own words 'everyone carries within himself "a directing image", his own wisdom (*Sophia*)' (ibid.: 49). In other words, human wisdom is an innate archetype which is a created Sophia, distinct from but created in the image of divine wisdom, or the heavenly Sophia – hence we may naturally thirst to read the book of nature, as our creaturely Sophia directs us. Looked at from a Platonic perspective, Sophia is the locus of all the Ideas of God on the world and on beings (what I referred to as the *logoi* in my chapter). An integral view of knowledge, one which is truly sophianic, thus provides a link between the ideal and the empirical, making God known in the world and in the human realm. The created Sophia must attain to likeness of her heavenly counterpart, but human freedom has overthrown the sacred order and perverted the sophianic way of relating to the world, rendering cultural knowledge into a parody (a 'demonic mask'; ibid.: 66) darkening the face of Sophia. Equally, the sinister aspect of the Sophia archetype may also be represented in the tension between Eve and the Virgin Mary as New Eve, the woman robed with the sun (Rev. 12:1) and the whore of Babylon (Rev. 17:5). The fruit of the Tree of Knowledge which Eve picked in curiosity and disobedience, can be viewed as the positivistic caricature of scientific knowledge which lacks the chaste and integrated interiority of the feminine 'fiat' spoken by the New Eve; the fruit of the Tree of Life symbolized by the cross, may be viewed as the combination of scientific knowledge and compassion.

Evdokimov (1994: 66) reminds us that sophianic knowledge is 'opposed to any agnostic or idealistic acosmism, to any evolutionistic naturalism, and it views the cosmos liturgically'. This does not imply that a sophianic view rejects science or scientific theories: what is rejected is precisely that knowledge which is devoid of compassion, knowledge which is not lived and experienced in an active participation, for which perhaps, no price is paid – since the beauty of the world, the conformity between the empirical elements and their ideal norm, can only be established in this way. One example of knowledge lacking compassion may be found in today's ecological crisis, brought about through adverse human influences in emissions and the irresponsible use of technology.

The Jungian conception of science beyond the science complex is very similar in this respect. Jung chose psychiatry as a profession because he felt it was 'the empirical field common to biological and spiritual facts . . . the place where the collision of nature and spirit became a reality' (Jung 1989 [1961]: 109). Indeed, the collision of nature and spirit may have found its apotheosis in 'Answer to Job', where Jung (1952) suggests that Yahweh grows in His own self-reflection, remembering His own absolute knowledge via an anamnesis of His partner, Sophia. The stimulus for this event is in fact, the failure of the attempt to corrupt Job; man thus stimulates the growth of God.

Thus, perhaps the spirit within nature leads to the transformation of the nature of Spirit. It will not be possible to offer anything but a general flavour of sophiological thought here, but the mythological imagery in the above paragraph could be seen as rendering the work of scientific discovery even more important than has so far been discussed. Sophiology is an entire stream of modern Orthodox Christian theology, particularly in its post WWII development – and, it needs to be said, this way of thinking has caused its own share of controversy within theology, a controversy which owed possibly more to the historical context of its evolution, than to the actual content of the speculative teachings. As Corbin (1985 [1953]:

19) points out, Orthodox sophiology poses the problem of the relation between God, the world and man; 'of all the Christian theological schools today . . . it is the one most likely to understand Jung's sophiological message'. If in Orthodox Christianity scientific research and discovery is a cosmic eucharistic work which causes man to offer creation back to God and render glory unto Him; and if for Jung the suffering experiential consciousness of Job contributes to the growth of divine consciousness in Yahweh, bringing about a transformation of the God-image for both God and man, then we may conclude that by learning more about the world and ourselves using inductive reasoning and the scientific method – and then integrating this knowledge into our lives – we can incarnate the Self into the world, becoming more authentic and whole in the process: but only if we can look through the veil of the science complex, into the beautiful face of Sophia.

RAYA JONES: In my reading, Jung distanced his own concept from Plato, although he duly acknowledges the history of the idea: 'In Plato . . . an extraordinarily high value is set on the archetypes as metaphysical ideas, as "paradigms" or models, while real things are held to be only the copies of these model ideas' (Jung 1948b: par. 275). Like Spinoza or Kant, Jungian archetypes imply knowledge structures intrinsic to mental operations; but to Jung, the existence of the mind and its dynamical configuration requires a natural-scientific explanation – and here he turns to evolution theory. He does liken his idea to Plato's – e.g. saying they are 'living dispositions, ideas in the Platonic sense, that perform and continually influence our thoughts and actions' (1954: par. 154) – but they are similar to Platonic Ideas only insofar as archetypes exist in a realm that is not directly knowable to us. In Jung, contra Plato, this realm is envisaged as originating in Nature. I discuss all this and more in Jones (2003).

If you mean 'creaturely Sophia' and 'created Sophia' as discrete concepts, these may correspond to the distinction between archetypes-as-such (the 'creaturely', the archetype as a content-free living disposition that emerges from our biological constitution) and archetypal manifestations as the concrete imaginal content (the 'created') by which this aspect of our existence is knowable to us. To talk of 'Sophia' seems to me to speak of a 'created' image, for she is of distinctly European origin. Are there parallels indigenous to Far Eastern, African, Native American, or other cultures? This isn't a rhetorical question. It's worth investigating.

Even if we grant the archetypal quality of what Sophia represents to us, it might be a jump to place her at the core of the science complex. I'm not rejecting the idea outright, but I remain unconvinced. It's food for thought, for sure.

BYRON GAIST: If I were to continue the conversation, I would point to transcultural images of Sophia. Jung (1952: par. 610) mentions the Indian Shakti. Additionally, Athene, Saraswati, Neith and others come to mind. The special reception of the Platonic Idea in the Church Fathers and Jung is a broader issue which I briefly touched on in my book on creative suffering (Gaist 2010: 124–6). For the Church Fathers, the polarity between sensible and intelligible realms (which may be said to apply to Platonic Ideas) is of a different order, and less fundamental, than that between created and uncreated – hence there would not in principle be a conflict with Jung's 'naturalistic' understanding of archetypes, since Ideas (and hence archetypes) are not perceived as the ontological foundation of reality. The significance of the created/uncreated polarity in theology may also cast some light on the difference between the 'creaturely' and 'heavenly' Sophia.

References

Corbin, H. (1985). The eternal Sophia. *Harvest*, 31: 7–23. (Original work published in 1953)

Evdokimov, P. (1994). *Woman and the Salvation of the World*. Crestwood, NY: SVS Press.

Gaist, B. (2010). *Creative Suffering and the Wounded Healer: Analytical Psychology and Orthodox Christian Theology*. Rollinsford, New Hampshire: Orthodox Research Institute.

Jones, R. A. (2003). Mixed metaphors and narrative shifts: Archetypes. *Theory & Psychology*, 13: 651–72.

Jung, C. G. Unless otherwise stated, the following are from *The Collected Works of C. G. Jung* (CW) London: Routledge and Kegan Paul:

—— (1948a). The phenomenology of the spirits in fairy tales. (CW9i)

—— (1948b). Instinct and the unconscious. (CW8)

—— (1952). Answer to Job. (CW11)

—— (1954). Psychological aspects of the mother archetypes. (CW9i)

—— (1989). *Memories, Dreams, Reflections*. New York: Random House. (Original work published in 1961)

13

DIALOGUE 5

Ways forward

Joe Cambray, Peter T. Dunlap and Raya A. Jones

JOE CAMBRAY: It has been a pleasure to learn from the other authors of this book; much new thought has been provoked by their chapters and the subsequent discussions. I will make a few brief comments based on a view that, as a possible science, analytical psychology is best served by an emergentist stance.

Raya Jones (Chapter 3) helps us look more deeply at the cultural differences in the formulation of how 'science' is conceived, including historical dimensions. By implication, the nuanced differences touched upon by Raya, suggest to me that the positivistic, mechanistic science which so discomforted Jung, was itself based on an implicit archetypal fantasy which he did not analyse: nature as a permanent, unchanging entity with underlying laws that are true everywhere in the universe for all time. What could be more archetypal than ubiquitous principles true outside time and space; a mythic machine. However, the developments in the theories and practice of science in the twentieth century have gradually eroded the legitimacy of this claim. Nevertheless, the tension between the archetypal and the cultural is not something restricted to those who follow the classical scientific method. Analytical psychology itself has not really come to terms with these aspects of the psyche; too often cultural productions are identified as archetypal, as when a Western European root of an image or symbol is the most that should be claimed. A theory with greater differentiation of these aspects together with fuller understanding of how they function and their impact on individuals embedded in them is needed.

The bifurcation of the heart and intellect that Raya points to in Jung's work, with the heart laying claim to the whole, is for me a key element in the dilemma of the role of subjectivity in scientific and analytic thought. Any formulation of theory or detailed observation involves selection processes, which inevitably are influenced by values, with subjective echoes. Similarly, there is growing concern in various fields that the complete splitting of subjectivity from objectivity does not lead to the deepest human understanding of truth but instead may keep us bound to theories and methods that are inherently unsuited to examining the genuine complexity of the world. In addition to my limited discussion of this topic in Chapter 1, I would cite philosopher Thomas Nagel's (2012) explorations of the problems of the origins of life and the place of values in our world. He examines all the options he find reasonable, and lands on an emergentist framework. While not embracing all his arguments, I believe he is asking essential questions, and find many of his reflections compelling. Views of this sort may supply a necessary component in any full description of the world, spanning both nature and culture. I'm postulating the process of emergence as archetypal, though I think we are still quite far from anything like a full description of our world.

Mark Saban's opposition of subjectivity to objectivity (Chapter 2) raises related aspects of this terrain. His use of Goethe, straddling the divide between the scientific/objective and the artistic/subjective, feels a companion piece to my chapter. The German Romantics who engaged in scientific research did so generally through holding this tension, largely because the gap between these perspectives had not yet grown to the proportions it would reach later in the nineteenth century. Some of the ideas of the 'teleo-mechanists' Mark mentions deserve a fresh look as precursors to some contemporary views, again echoed in Nagel's study.

In response to Leslie's request for more information: In the scientific community, complexity theory arose as a response to the study of systems with multiple interacting components that display a capacity for spontaneous self-organization and the emergence of new properties of a higher order than the components and not reducible to an understanding of those components. Such systems therefore have holistic features that cannot be explained by analytic reduction; they are not just 'complicated' (like a Swiss watch) but the interactions within the system produce new properties that cannot have been predicted from the components. While General Systems Theory, as developed in biology by Ludwig von Bertalanffy (in 1928) was extended to various other fields from the 1930s on, it was the work of Ilya Prigogine on the thermodynamics of non-equilibrium systems that revealed the capacity of such systems to produce dissipative structures through self-organization. Prigogine's work was a catalyst for scientists and scholars who went on to elaborate complexity theory. Stuart Kauffman, a leading theoretical biologist, has concluded on the basis of high-speed computer modelling that life emerges at the edge of order and chaos: too much order (concentration), and molecules are rigidly bound in ways that do not allow separate proto-cells to form (with autocatalytic contents); too much chaos (dilution), and adequate concentrations of the right material cannot be achieved. In this model – a modern creation myth – life is an emergent property of the proto-biochemical soup (the prima materia) under just the right conditions. This line of thinking has been applied to a host of disciplines, from physics (including the origins of the universe) to sociology, psychology, philosophy, literature, business (organizational life) and more. I believe it represents the first flowering of a paradigm shift in the sciences that is returning the holistic features of many aspects of the world to scientific discussion and reflection.

For the Jungian community, the applications of this approach to the study of mind and the questions of consciousness are most relevant (see Cambray 2002, 2005). As an analyst, I find it is quite useful to apply complexity theory to therapeutic action. This is not unique to Jungian analysis; in fact, therapists from many camps are interested in the application of these ideas. In short, therapeutic change is most likely to occur at the edge of order and chaos as studies of enactments, reverie and other manifestations of the interactive field, including transference/counter-transference dynamics have demonstrated. How interactions at this edge are handled seems to be one of the crucial features for potential change of the system (which includes the therapeutic dyad and hence Jung's idea that a deep change requires transformations in both partners).

PETER DUNLAP: Describing the Romantic roots of Jung's approach to science, Joe Cambray (Chapter 1) emphasizes that the current scientific milieu was forged between the socio-political needs of the early modern period and the early successes of a 'reductive, mechanistic worldview' that came to dominate science during that time (this volume: 10). Much of the goal of this science was to minimize the impact of individual subjectivity on scientific investigation while maximizing commercial and sociopolitical power. Joe suggests that other currents of scientific thought, historical and contemporary, are more capable of accounting for the complexities of human experience.

In addition to the Romantic sources of Jung's relationship to science, we can look at what the Romantic spirit neglected – its insufficient attention to human suffering – and how that became institutionalized within Jung's psychology in its problematic introversion, carried forward to this day in the ambivalence toward science within the Jungian community. By taking Joe's lead and reconnecting to the holistic roots of Jung's vision, it is possible to address this limitation. It is possible to imagine a Jungian psychology that embraces not only the holism of the senses and intuition regarding the natural world and the human psyche, but also the social world – a task that requires the differentiation of an extroverted feeling function towards activating empathy, a moral necessity.

Building on the tradition of Romanticism, Jung began to differentiate an understanding of the imagination as a capacity for discerning emergent, objective human experience, which challenged the positivist paradigm within which objectivity and subjectivity were opposed by claiming that subjectivity was the route through which the human being became capable of objective discernment. I have come to think of the Jungian community as an example of what Martin (1955: 14) characterized as a 'creative minority which, if it is successful in transmitting its vision to the great mass of the people, leads the civilization through the time of troubles to a new creative achievement'. However, for that to take place, this community should confront its own one-sidedness.

In the eighteenth and nineteenth centuries, the transformations of the modern age led not only to a radical new understanding of nature but also to a new awareness of human suffering. During the French Revolution, the plight of the underclass was recognized and translated into an egalitarian worldview that set out to remediate that suffering at increasingly sophisticated social and political levels. During the nineteenth century, this egalitarian philosophy was expounded by those supporting women's suffrage, the abolition of slavery, and farmers' and workers' rights. While significant progress has been made over the past hundred years, it has not led to a worldview sufficiently developed to meet current challenges of social injustice, environmental degradation, institutional abuse of power, and lack of belonging experienced under the alienating conditions of modern individualism.

Despite our best efforts to distinguish between individualism and individuation, the Jungian community may be caught in a historical milieu that we perpetuate by failing to differentiate the experience of extroverted feeling. In this context, I identify the function of extroverted feeling to be to connect people to one another with an increasing empathic awareness of each other's needs, suffering, and the unique contribution to our communities that we could each make. This recognition would support our returning to one another from those paths of extreme individualism.

Joe's chapter has identified several directions of research through which the Jungian community could use its exceptionally well-developed understanding of the imagination to connect to other research communities. He draws attention to the value of subjectivity and affect, particularly in the work of Damasio, which connects well to my foray into emotion-focused research, touched upon in my chapter. He also turns attention beyond the individual to the way that traumatic memory can be transmitted epigenetically. While he uses this as tentative evidence for the collective unconscious, it can also be seen as a turn outward toward the recognition of socio-political implications of such phenomena.

JOE CAMBRAY: I find myself largely in agreement with Peter's points about the larger socio-political realities in the world during the time of the Romantics. However, from my reading of Alexander von Humboldt, he at least was sensitive to this. Humboldt was one of the first scientific voices to challenge the views then prevalent in Europe about the supposed inferiority of non-white, non-western Europeans. He was an early champion of the value and importance of cultural differences, which he attempted to link to differing physical and biological environments, also making him one of the first environmentalists. It is certainly true that Jung might well have picked up more fully on this strand of Humboldt's thinking (Jung's comments on the dreams of African Americans he saw at St Elizabeth's hospital in Washington, DC, are distressing even if superficially making a point about the archetypal quality of dreams).[1] We are left to speculate about the significance of Jung's omission of these scientific sources that clearly influenced his work but without attribution.

Similarly, the social action and social justice potential of analytical psychology is still limited but has been growing, especially since 2001. I won't detail this here due to limited space, but the work of our colleagues in China in response to the Sichuan earthquake in May 2008 is one important case in point. While there are numerous other examples I could mention, from analysts involved in various responses to 9/11 in New York City, to work with mothers and infants in South Africa, to programmes helping with orphans in China and street children in Colombia. I am still in accord with Peter about the need for this side of analytical psychology to be developed much more fully.

RAYA JONES: Thank you both for rounding up our project with a reminder that analytical psychology is 'an eminently practical science', as Jung (1946: par. 172) characterized it, adding that 'learning is its by-product . . . not its principal aim', which is 'a great difference from what one understands by "academic" science'. Joe implicitly extends Jung's claim that this 'practical science . . . does not investigate for investigation's sake, but for the immediate purpose of giving help' (ibid.) by pointing to expanding the potential of analytical psychology as a helping profession. Peter centres on the potential contribution towards formulating a conceptual model which could be applied for raising political consciousness, incorporating a Jungian perspective with emotion science (see Chapter 8).

There is a tendency in the Jungian community to privilege feeling over thinking. Yet, curiosity is a basic human motivation. Developmental psychologist Lewis (2010) places *interest* between contentment and distress as the most rudimentary emotions present in the first months of life. Similarly, leading emotion scientist Izard includes 'interest', and likewise Panskepp and Watt include 'seeking', in their classifications of basic emotions (Tracy & Randles 2011). Why dismiss learning as a principal aim also for analytical psychology?

You've indicated two ways forward for analytical psychology. I'd like to consider also a third, which echoes Joe's project in promoting the emergentist stance. Namely, to reconsider Jungian premises in an investigation for investigation's sake, seeking to ascertain their tenability (and risking their disconfirmation) in calibration with 'academic' science.

Note

1 In a letter to Freud, dated November 11, 1912, Jung reported on his travels in the USA and mentioned that in St Elizabeth's hospital he 'analysed 15 Negroes, with demonstrations' (Freud & Jung 1977: 516). The *Collected Works* editors cite that letter in a footnote to Jung's (1921: par. 747) claim that he was 'able to demonstrate a whole series of motifs from Greek mythology in the dreams and fantasies of pure-bred Negroes suffering from mental disorders'. For a detailed case analysis, see Jung (1935: par. 81ff.). The abstract of a lecture given in November 22, 1912, based on his study in St Elizabeth's hospital, starts:

> The psychoses of Negroes are the same as those of white men. In milder cases the diagnosis is difficult because one is not sure whether one is dealing with superstition. Investigation is complicated by the fact that the Negro does not understand what one wants of him, and besides that is ignorant [does not know his age, has no idea of time].
>
> (1912: par. 1285; square brackets in the original)

References

Cambray, J. (2002). Synchronicity and emergence. *American Imago*, 59: 409–34.
—— (2005). The place of the 17th century in Jung's encounter with China. *Journal of Analytical Psychology*, 50: 195–207.

Freud, S. & Jung, C. G. (1977). *The Freud/Jung Letters*. London: Routledge and Kegan Paul.
Jung, C. G. The following are from the *Collected Works of C. G. Jung* (CW) London: Routledge and Kegan Paul:
—— (1912). On the psychology of the Negro. (CW18)
—— (1921). *Psychological Types*. (CW6)
—— (1935). The Tavistock Lectures. (CW18)
—— (1946). Analytical psychology and education. (CW17)
Lewis, M. (2010). The emergence of human emotions. In Lewis, M., Haviland-Jones, J. M., & Barrett, L. F. (Eds.) *Handbook of Emotions* (3rd edition). New York: Guilford Press.
Martin, P. W. (1955) *Experiment in Depth*. New York: Pantheon Books.
Nagel, T. (2012). *Mind and Cosmos*. Oxford: Oxford University Press.
Tracy, J. L. & Randles, D. (2011). Four models of basic emotions: A review of Ekman and Cordaro, Izard, Levenson, and Panksepp and Watt. *Emotion Review*, 3: 397–405.

NAME INDEX

Adams, D. 1, 5
Adler, Alfred 41, 54, 84, 111, 159, 171
Agazarian, Y. 142, 149
Allen, C. 57, 67
Amrine, F. 39, 43–4, 48
Appleby, J. O. 169, 172
Aquinas, Thomas 101
Aristotle 23, 30, 48, 71

Bachelard, G. 123, 137
Bair, D. 14, 27, 99, 100, 102, 107, 109, 116
Baker, L. R. 58, 67
Bakhtin, M. M. 5
Bamford, C. 136, 137
Banks, Joseph Sir 11–12, 14
Baraitser, L. 57, 67
Barthes, R. 60, 67
Basil, Saint 129–30, 137
Beebe, J. 111, 116
Berlin, I. 12, 13, 26, 27
Bishop, P. 39–40, 48, 105, 116, 161
Blanchard, P. 55, 67
Bleuler, E. 98, 99, 104, 107
Boas, F. 18, 26
Boedeker, D. D. 96, 97
Bortoft, H. 45–6, 48
Bouteneff, P. C. 129, 137
Bowen, M. 15, 27
Boyle, Robert 11
Brahe, Tycho 10
Brain, R. M. 20, 27
Brooke, R. 114, 116
Bruner, J. S. 66, 67
Burkert, W. 96, 97

Camus, A. 134–5, 137
Carey, N. 25, 27

Carter, D. 50, 64, 67
Chilton, S. 141–2, 149
Chirban, J. T. 130, 137
Chodorow, J. 109, 116
Christou, E. 124, 137
Chrysostomos, Archbishop 130, 137
Cole, S. 52, 67
Coleman, A. 142, 149
Coles, P. 125, 129, 137
Comte, A. 51–2, 55, 58, 67, 85, 122, 123
Connolly, A. 25, 27
Cook, Captain James 11–12, 14
Coon, D. J. 52, 53, 67
Corbin, H. 175, 176–7, 178
Cornford, F. M. 102, 116
Costall, A. 53, 67
Cotrell, A. P. 45, 48
Cunningham, A. 12, 26, 28

Damasio, A. 23, 28, 60, 182
Darwin, Charles 16, 17, 20–1, 26, 28
Daston, L. 37, 47, 48
Derrida, J. 132
Descartes 121–2, 124
Detienne, M. 84, 89, 97
Dilthey, W. 54, 57, 153
Dobbs, B. J. T. 11, 28
Dreyer, E. L. 26, 28

Einstein, Albert 20, 21, 71–5, 81, 121, 163
Ekman, P. 145, 146, 149
Eliade, Mircea 82
Eliot, G. 102, 109, 146
Ellenberger, H. F. 47, 48
Epel D. 24, 28
Evdokimov, P. 175–6, 178
Eysenck, H. J. 56, 67

NAME INDEX

Farah, R. M. 65, 67
Feyerabend, P. 36, 48, 54, 67
Forster, Georg 11, 14
Foucault, Michel 58, 63, 67, 154
Franz, M.-L. von 26, 86, 97
Frazer, J. G. 84, 85–6, 89, 90–1, 92, 96, 97, 102, 116, 165, 172
Fredericksen, D. 59, 67
Freud, Sigmund 3, 6, 20, 35, 40–1, 42, 54, 57, 59, 83–4, 87, 99, 100–4, 106–8, 111, 114, 116, 132, 155, 159, 167, 170, 172, 183, 184
Frey-Rohn, L. 105, 116
Frijda, N. 145, 149
Frosh, S. 57, 67
Fuchs, A. H. 53, 67
Fukuyama, F. 141, 149
Fulford, T. 11, 12, 28

Galileo 10
Galison, P. 47, 48
Gefter, A. 125, 137
Giegerich, W. 135, 137
Gilbert, S. F. 24, 28
Ginsberg, A. 119, 137
Goethe, J. W. von 13, 20, 26, 30–1, 35–45, 47, 48, 88, 160, 164, 180
Grant, D. C. 54, 67
Guerin, W. L. 102, 116

Hacking, I. 48
Haeckel, E. H. P. A. 10, 14, 20–1, 22, 26, 28
Harari, E. 54, 67
Harrington, A. 154, 155
Harrison, J. 192, 116
Hart, D. B. 121, 122, 128, 137
Haslam, N. 65, 69
Hatfield, G. 53, 67
Hauke, C. 131–2, 137
Healy, P. 57, 67
Heijmans, B. T. 25, 28
Helferich, G. 14, 16, 28
Hillman, James 18, 28, 64, 96, 97, 133, 135, 137, 167
Hogenson, G. B. 15, 26, 28, 60
Holdrege, C. 47, 49
Homans, P. 47, 48, 65, 67
Hughes, M. 128, 137
Humboldt, Alexander von 13–19, 20–1, 26, 28, 182
Hunt, H. T. 61, 65, 68
Huskinson, L. 105, 116

James, William 20, 48, 53, 68, 77, 164
Janaway, C. 105, 116
Jardine, N. 12, 26, 28
Jones, E. 170, 172
Jung, Andreas 14, 28

Kant, Immanuel 20, 101, 121, 164, 177
Kaplinsky, C. 126, 127, 138
Kegan, R. 140–1, 150
Keller W. 131, 138
Kepler, J. 10
Kimbles, S. L. 126, 138, 148, 150
King, M. L., Jr. 147–8, 150
Kirsch, T. 112, 115, 117
Kline, P. 55, 68
Knox, J. 60, 105, 117
Kott, J. 170, 173
Kroehler, C. J. 128, 137
Kruesi, L. 123, 138
Kuhn, B. H. 39, 49
Kuhn, Thomas 36, 57, 123
Kumar, K. N. P. 61, 68
Kusch, M. 53, 66, 68

Lacan, J. 81, 167
Lakatos, Imre 55, 57, 68
Lamarck, J-B. 20, 24
Lanius, R. A. 23, 28
Lannamann, J. W. 60, 69
Larchet, J. C. 130, 138
Latour, B. 48, 49
Lear, J. 13, 28
Leavis, F. R. 109, 117
Leibniz, G. W. von 11, 12
Lévy-Bruhl, L. 89, 102
Lewin, K. 53, 68, 142
Lewis, M. 183, 184
Lilienfeld, S. O. 52, 68
Lowes, J. L. 102, 117
Lyell, Charles 16
Lyotard, J.-F. 66, 68

MacGregor, N. 105, 117
Maehle, A-H. 21, 28
Mainzer, K. 18, 28
Mair, M. 54, 68
Martin, F. 61, 68
Martin, P. W. 181, 184
Marx, Karl 54, 59, 132
Maxwell, J. C. 20
McGrath, S. J. 105, 117
McLeod, J. 65, 68
McLynn, F. 111, 117

NAME INDEX

Mead, G. H. 64, 68
Megill, A. 48, 49
Melissaris, A. G. 135, 138
Metallinos, G. 123–4, 125, 138
Milar, K. S. 53, 67
Moss, S. A. 62, 68
Mülberger, A. 57, 59
Müller, G. H. 16, 28
Murray, G. 102, 117

Nagel, T. 179, 180, 184
Neisser, U. 56, 68
Nesteruk, A. 130, 134, 138
Neumann, E. 96, 97, 172
Newton, Isaac 10–11, 38–9, 41
Nicolaus, G. 144, 150
Nietzsche, F. W. 59, 102, 112, 132, 164
Noll, R. 113, 117

O'Sullivan, S. 63, 68
Okasha, S. 122, 138
Omer, A. 142, 147, 150
Ørsted, H. C. 19–20, 29
Overington, M. A. 73, 81

Papadopoulos, R. K. 100, 117, 136, 138
Parker, I. 50, 58, 68
Perera, S. 142, 150
Phelan, J. 60, 68
Pickering, A. 48, 49
Plato 101, 110, 117, 143, 177
Popper, Karl 4, 36, 54, 57, 68, 122, 171
Porter, T. 35, 49
Principe, L. M. 11, 29
Pye, L. 141, 150

Ramachandran, V. S. 23, 29
Randles, D. 183, 184
Rank, Otto 100, 101, 117
Rapaport, D. 57, 69
Reddy, W. 147, 150
Richards, R. J. 17, 21, 26, 29
Ricoeur, P. 59, 69
Riklin, F. 98, 117
Ritter, J. W. 19
Robbins, B. D. 47, 49
Roesler, C. 65, 69
Rogers, Carl 132–3, 138
Rose, Fr. S. 128–9, 138
Rosen, D. H. 62, 69
Rosenwein, B. 147, 150
Rowland, H. 47, 49

Rupke, N. 26, 29
Ryle, Gilbert 93

Sabini, M. 20, 29
Said, E. 78–9, 81
Samuels, A. 3, 64, 141, 142, 148, 150
Scanlon, J. 54, 57, 69
Schelling, F. W. J. 19–20
Schrag, C. O. 64, 65, 69
Seamon, D. 47, 49
Seidman, S. 64, 69
Sepper, D. L. 13, 26, 29
Shamdasani, S. 30, 33, 34, 41, 49, 57, 69, 110, 111, 117, 120, 130, 131, 132, 138
Sharp, D. 111, 117, 126, 138
Shelburne, W. A. 131, 138
Sherrard, P. 121, 124–5, 138
Sherry, J. 35, 49
Shotter, J. 60, 69
Simonton, D. K. 52, 69
Singer, T. 51, 69, 126–7, 138, 148, 150
Skar, P. 27, 29
Smith, W. 121–2, 138
Snelders, H. A. M. 19, 20, 29
Snow, C. P. 9
Spinoza, B. 177
Stein, M. 65, 69
Stephenson, R. 38, 49
Stevens, A. 59, 69
Stithatos, N. 119–20, 138
Sturm, T. 57, 69

Tacey, D. 3, 6, 111, 117, 126, 138
Theokritoff, E. 129, 138
Theokritoff, G. 129, 138
Thomas, K. 122, 138
Toulmin, S. 71–2, 73, 78–9, 81
Tracy, J. L. 183, 184
Tylor, E. B. 102, 117

Vico, G. 71, 78, 79
Vlachos, H. 130, 138

Waddington, C. H. 24, 27, 29
Walls, L. D. 16, 17, 18, 29
Weber, Max 58, 63, 64, 69
Webster, C. 122, 139
Wetzel, W. D. 19, 29
Whitmont, E. 96, 97
Wierzbicka, A. 50, 69
Wilkinson, M. 105, 117
Willer, S. 23–4, 29
Wilson, B. 119

NAME INDEX

Wilson, S. 62, 65, 68, 69
Winch, P. 93
Wittgenstein, L. 58–9, 69
Woloschak, G. E. 129, 139
Wundt, W. 34, 42, 53, 101, 119

Yates, F. A. 11, 29

Zajonc, A. 47, 49
Zizioulas, J. D. 133–5, 139
Zoja, L. 119, 139

SUBJECT INDEX

abductive reasoning 92, 95–6
addiction 118–20
Adonis 82–97, 165
affect science 143, 145, 147
alchemy 11, 26, 37, 44, 102, 112, 115, 164, 166–7
anima 64, 73–4, 79, 115, 169
anima mundi 18
animus 64
anthropology 9, 33, 36, 102, 120, 138, 147
Archaic Man 65
archetypal psychology (Hillman) 115, 135
Archetypal Symbol Inventory 62
archetype theory 51, 52, 59, 60, 126–7, 136, 140, 143, 144, 146, 149, 153; cultural specificity of 62–3, 165; history of the idea 15, 20, 24, 26, 131–2, 177–8; innate 60, 62, 92, 175; and mythology 82–3, 127, 131, 145, 165, 180, 182; psychological function of 45–6, 63, 73, 76, 109, 115, 167; and science 2, 30, 65, 71, 105, 154, 179
archetypes: father 89; hero 88; mother 86, 89; numbers 72; puer 84, 86–8, 91, 94, 115 *see also* Adonis; Sophia (wisdom) 136, 174–8; trickster 115
astrology 36, 37
astronomy 10, 41, 132
authority 44, 72, 75–6, 77–9, 124, 132, 134, 154–5; experiment 62

biology 9, 21, 24, 33, 53, 120, 128, 180
brain 2, 27, 60, 105, 106, 123, 127, 145, 175; Age of 65; *see also* neuroscience

chemistry 9, 11, 44, 52, 120
collective unconscious 2, 18, 25, 54, 55, 62, 65–6, 76–7, 78, 91, 127, 131, 140, 143–4, 149, 165, 167, 182
complexes 1, 51, 57, 98, 101, 104, 108–9, 123, 127, 133; cultural 51, 126–7, 148; Oedipus 83, 87, 170; science *see* science-complex; *see also* discursive complex, psy-complex
complexity theory 9, 18, 23, 180
creation science 128–9
cultural complexes *see* complexes
cultural forms 15, 25, 50
cultural theory 100, 115, 166
culture 64, 77, 83, 85, 96, 100, 102, 115, 141, 165, 167, 177; ancient 85, 91, 102; diversity 77, 131, 144, 177, 179, 182; 'culture of experience' 122, 132; influence 9, 12, 30, 33, 127, 128, 142, 145–6, 159–60, 164; and nature 15, 180; practices 101; and psychoanalysis 101, 103; transformation 140, 143, 146–7; Western 32, 37, 135, 158

deductive reasoning 73, 92–3, 96; *see also* hypothetico-deductive method
discursive complex 50
disenchantment of the world 58, 59

evolution (biological) 15, 20, 24, 30, 60, 128–9, 144, 176–7
extroversion 56, 158–9, 181–2

flying saucers see UFOs
Flying saucers: A modern myth of things seen in the sky 75–80
French revolution 95–6, 147, 181

Galilean revolution *see* science
geography 15

SUBJECT INDEX

hermeneutics 59–60, 64, 73, 168

idealism 9, 105–6, 110, 176
inductive reasoning 54, 73, 92, 93–4, 96, 177
introversion 56, 101–12, 113, 115; Jung as introvert 156–62, 181

Jung's view of science *see* science, Jung's view of

libido 14, 107–8
logos *see* mythos/logos

materialism 32, 35, 42, 98, 105–6, 121
Memories, Dreams, Reflections 32, 46, 70, 166
metaphysics 20, 34, 35, 42, 52, 53, 71, 91, 98, 121–3, 125, 126, 128, 134, 135, 140, 143, 177
Mysterium Coniunctionis 44
myth criticism 102
mythology 36, 82, 101, 107, 131, 183
mythos/logos 33, 64

narrative theory 102, 104, 114–15, 166
neuroscience 2, 23, 24, 56, 60, 65, 66, 105
numinous 111–13, 114, 161

objectivity 9, 13, 33, 35, 36–42, 46, 48, 55, 74, 84, 126, 127, 143, 159, 162–4, 169, 179–81
Oedipus complex *see* complexes

philosophy 33, 52, 53, 101, 105, 106, 120, 125, 135, 136, 164, 180
physics 9, 10–11, 18, 20, 21, 34, 35, 41, 52–3, 74–5, 120, 122, 125, 180, *see also* quantum physics
political development 141
political science 141, 143, 169
positivism 13, 32, 35, 47, 52, 54, 56, 57, 70, 77, 118, 122, 123, 132, 136, 172, 176, 179, 181
postmodernism 54, 56, 59, 60, 63, 65–6, 118, 131–2, 135–6
psychoanalysis 3, 13, 17, 26, 41–2, 52, 53, 57, 65, 78, 99, 100–1, 102–3, 106–7, 110, 123, 126
psychocultural 140ff., 164
Psychological Types 102, 111, 112, 157, 159
psychology as science 33–5, 42, 47, 51ff., 56, 60, 84, 99, 103–4, 114, 120, 130–1, 132–3, 171
Psychology of the Unconscious 99, 102, 107, 110–11, 112, 114
psy-complex 58

quantum physics 21, 26, 30, 60–1, 74, 121, 132

Red Book, The 10, 16, 20, 22, 26
religion 64, 82, 83, 85, 91, 96, 100, 101, 102, 112–13, 124, 134; contrasted with science 3, 57, 74, 120–1, 125, 128, 130–1, 136; Orthodox Christianity 118, 120, 128–30, 134–6, 177
Romanticism 11, 12ff., 37–8, 169, 180–2

science, concept of 3, 9, 31, 36, 44, 50–1, 52, 75, 84, 91, 114, 135, 143, 153, 163, 166, 167–8, 170, 181; anti-science 51, 64; contrasted with art 22, 31, 37–8, 43, 70–1, 74, 78–80; contrasted with religion *see* religion; as hermeneutical 13; limitations 32–3; method 54–6, 73, 121–2, 153; as myth 124; rhetoric 57–8, 73, 78–80; 'poetical science' 70, 71, 78, 80; pseudo-science 36; social-political implications 11, 118–19, 120, 133; *Wissenschaft* 31, 36, 50–1; *see also* deductive reasoning, science-complex, scientism, worldview
science, history of 10ff., 41, 120–2, 125; Galilean revolution 53, 72; Interpretative Turn 56; 'paradigm shifts' 22, 57, 123, 180; roots in Romanticism 12–14, 19–21, 23; 'science wars' 36; scientific revolution 32, 120, 122, 124, 127
science, Jung's view of 9, 21–2, 30ff., 70, 74, 98–9, 103–4, 114, 130–1, 168
science-complex 50–1, 58, 59, 61, 118, 126–7, 131, 166, 174–7; in Orthodox Christianity 128–30, 136
scientism 51, 122, 126, 127, 136, 154; forms of 59–64
social sciences 36, 56, 60, 65, 115, 118, 130, 167, 169
sociology 9, 52, 128, 164, 180
subjectivity 9, 23, 33, 37–8, 46, 50, 55, 57, 71, 74, 77, 84, 132–3, 140, 149, 158, 160, 162–4, 169, 179–82

symbol (Jungian theory) 2, 11, 62–3, 71–2, 74, 83, 87–8, 90, 101, 103–4, 107, 124–5, 135, 144, 147, 168, 172, 179
Symbols of Transformation 166
synchronicity 11, 18, 26, 60–1, 71, 112

theology 33, 118–20, 123–5, 127–30, 134–6, 176, 178
truth 2, 4, 9, 34, 36, 37, 43, 63, 66, 70, 79, 80, 104, 111–12, 118, 120–2, 124, 129–30, 132–4, 137, 161; Four Noble Truths 57
typology (Jungian) 55–6, 110, 113, 115, 157–9, 161–2

UFOs 71–2, 74, 75–80, 175

Weltanschauung see worldview
Wissenschaft see science
word association studies 9, 26; Word Association Test 21, 61, 78, 98
worldview 1; egalitarian 181; mechanistic 10, 181; scientific 3, 22, 121, 123; *Weltanschauung* 3, 37, 99

Zofingia lectures 21, 98